3

SOCIAL AND MENTAL TRAITS OF THE NEGRO

43283

STUDIES IN HISTORY, ECONOMICS AND PUBLIC LAW

EDITED BY THE FACULTY OF POLITICAL SCIENCE
OF COLUMBIA UNIVERSITY

Volume XXXVII]   [Number 3

Whole Number 99

SOCIAL AND MENTAL TRAITS
OF THE NEGRO

Research into the Conditions of the Negro Race in Southern Towns

A STUDY IN RACE TRAITS, TENDENCIES
AND PROSPECTS

BY

HOWARD W. ODUM

AMS PRESS
NEW YORK

COLUMBIA UNIVERSITY
STUDIES IN THE
SOCIAL SCIENCES

99

The Series was formerly known as *Studies in History,
Economics and Public Law.*

Reprinted with the permission of Columbia University Press
From the edition of 1910, New York
First AMS EDITION published 1968
Manufactured in the United States of America

Library of Congress Catalogue Card Number: 68-56677

AMS PRESS, INC.
New York, N.Y. 10003

PREFACE

THIS work has three purposes. First, it is an effort to contribute something toward a scientific knowledge of the Negro. It aims to describe the conditions of negro life in Southern communities and to analyze the essential qualities of the race. Second, it is presented, not as a final treatment of the entire subject but as a beginning, along with other special studies,[1] for a scientific but practical study of the Negro in the South. Third, it tries to interpret the Negro Problem and to some extent to suggest means by which the heart of the problem may be reached. It seeks to avoid generalities and to present qualitative, specific, concrete results. The suggestions made look toward the improvement and development of the negro race and to the establishment of relations between the races which shall be permanently satisfactory.

In the prosecution of the investigation assistance has been received with varying degrees of co-operation from many persons throughout the South. Much encouragement has been offered by a large number of those interested in the study of the Negro and in the Southern problem. It is hoped that the results of the study will repay to some extent all those who have assisted in various ways.

[1] See " Religious Folk-songs of the Southern Negroes " by the author in *The American Journal of Religious Psychology and Education,* July, 1909, vol. iii, pp. 265-365. It is the purpose of a companion work on *Negro Folk-songs and Folk-thought,* to be published, at an early date by the American Folk-lore Society, to study something of the social psychology and folk-ways of the Southern negroes and to present some aspects of the Negro's mental imagery, style and habits.

Special thanks are due to Professor David H. Bishop of the University of Mississippi and to President W. L. Weber of the Centenary College of Louisiana for valuable suggestions and criticisms, to Professor Albert Bushnell Hart of Harvard University for important critical suggestions and aids, to President G. Stanley Hall of Clark University for his personal interest, encouragement, and assistance, and to Professor Franklin H. Giddings and Professor Edwin R. A. Seligman of Columbia University for invaluable criticisms, suggestions, and co-operation in making it possible for the work to appear in its present form.

Special acknowledgment is also due Dr. Thomas P. Bailey, Superintendent of the Memphis City Schools, formerly Professor of Psychology and Education in the University of Mississippi, under whose direction the special studies were begun. Throughout the work his suggestions and co-operation have been helpful. The best results of the studies herein presented will be only a meagre testimonial to his discriminating study of the Negro and to his scientific interest and enthusiasm in promoting original research into many important problems.

Perhaps the more natural arrangement of chapters would be in the order: Home Life and Morals, The Negro Offender, Social Status, Fraternal Organizations, Churches and Religion, The Emotions, Education, and The Negro Problem, with a summary of discussions. The plan on which the results are presented in this book, however, is to pass from the more external conditions, through the special religious and social activities of the Negro, to his more private life; then, to proceed from the more general social life and traits to the discussion of the total problem and to the conclusions. In this way it is hoped that each chapter will be carefully correlated with all the other chapters.

H. W. O.

COLUMBIA UNIVERSITY, APRIL 1, 1910.

CONTENTS

CHAPTER II

THE NEGRO CHURCH AND RELIGION

CHAPTER III

FRATERNAL ORGANIZATIONS AND BENEVOLENT SOCIETIES

CHAPTER IV

THE HOME LIFE, DISEASES AND MORALS OF THE NEGRO

CHAPTER V

THE NEGRO OFFENDER

CHAPTER VI

THE SOCIAL STATUS OF THE NEGRO

CHAPTER VII

THE EMOTIONS OF THE NEGRO AND THEIR RELATION TO CONDUCT

CHAPTER VIII

THE NEGRO PROBLEM: AN ESTIMATE OF THE NEGRO

APPENDIX

CHILDREN DIFFER IN ENVIRONMENT

By Thomas P. Bailey, Ph. D., Supt. of Schools, Memphis, Tenn. 299

INTRODUCTION

DISCUSSIONS of the Negro in the South have become so frequent and so varied that he may well be called the central figure in Southern problems. But the Negro is too often judged only partially. The North estimates him by a limited number of industrious and competent workmen and by the more intelligent negroes. In the South the Negro is estimated purely from everyday contact under domestic and industrial conditions, and this general estimate of the black man is influenced much by what is heard about him in common talk and political harangue. The fact is neglected that the Negro has a life and environment of his own which the whites do not see, which after all may be at the bottom of his actions. To understand the real Negro, he must be known in his home, in his more private activities, at his church and lodge, where, as a rule, he is not a creature of restraint in his natural actions, as well as in the common appearances of the Negro's everyday life.

The white community sees the destructive factors that are at work among the negroes; it sees little of the constructive factors that make for better conditions. The community is kept informed of negro crime and vice through the press, the courts, and the common trend of events and conversation; of the negro school and church, whether good or crude, it sees little. Likewise, little attention is given to the rich variety of negro life, negro folk-songs and folk-thought, to the inner qualities of the Negro's nature or to the essential causes of his conduct. Observing the loafer on the streets, the crowds of negroes who come to town on Saturday, the jovial good-natured darkies, or the formal appearances of groups of negroes is not knowing the Negro; nor can he be judged alone from the laborer or the criminal at large.

While the white community does not know the Negro at his best, it is also true that it does not know him at his worst. Painful as the fact is, it must nevertheless be recognized. The negro loafer is observed on the street; he is not seen as he obtains his living from some hard-working woman who has toiled for her wages, nor as he corrupts other members of his race. The community sees the criminal in the courts; it does not see the long train of crimes that has brought him there. The thoughtful white man sees the laborer and recognizes such a negro as a worthy and industrious citizen; but the white man does not see him as he struggles—or more exactly does not even struggle— against the onrush of his animal nature which leads him to neglect and abuse himself, his home and his family. It is generally admitted that the Negro does not get justice on many occasions; people do not as well remember that his faults are often overlooked. Many times he is not apprehended for an evil for which the white man is punished. This is not a rare but a common experience. Much is heard of the cases brought to trial; the world hears nothing of the frequent instances in which the weakness of the black race is accorded patience by the stronger race.

The fact that there are individuals among the negroes who are worthy of the highest respect is gladly recognized and gives hope that better possibilities lie within the race. Groups or communities of such negroes would do much toward bettering conditions; but they do not exist in this relation, and here, perhaps, may be found the key to the situation. With the groups of families the community is formed, associations and surroundings are fixed, and a central point from which a greater influence emanates is determined. The group communities form the towns; the conditions of the county are largely influenced by those of the town. And just as the town in the South is a very potent unit in the total social structure, just so the larger communities among the negroes invariably set the standard of relationship, both among the negroes themselves and between the whites and blacks. To know the Negro, then, in this relation of groups or communities, is to know him best; to assist him here is to assist him most effectively. So it is the purpose of this work to study, not specimens or eccentric characters, not picturesque or sensational phases of negro life, but representative life that is common to the great mass of negroes; to find out something of his home life, his labors, his faults and his virtues, his school ideals and work, his social life and standards, his lodge life, his church and his religion. In short, the purpose is to reach some insight into what the Negro appears to be and what he really is, what he may desire to be and what he may possibly become in his future development.

In approaching such a discussion of the Negro, it is necessary to note that particulars vary widely; that the problem is different in every state and county and community according as conditions vary. The negroes in parts of South Carolina, for instance, are different from those in Georgia in certain particulars; those in South Mississippi are quite different from those gathered in larger towns of the South. Again, it is not surprising to find that the negro problem hardly exists where there are only a few negroes. A certain county in Alabama has only one negro to every twenty-five hundred whites, and there are a dozen counties in the Southern States where there is only one negro to every hundred and seventy-five whites. On the other hand, there are fourteen counties in the South where seven-eighths of the people are negroes, and six counties in Mississippi where the whites form less than ten per cent of the population. Similarly the numerical proportions vary in different degrees throughout the South.

Again, the question is less acute and complex in sections where negroes assume a submissive and deferential attitude than it is in those communities where they assume an obstinate or aggressive attitude. The situation is different in a town where the negroes make a special effort to pass on the outside of the sidewalk from that in a town where the opposite is true. The problem, in its immediate and practical aspects is different in the cities from that in the towns; that in the towns differs from that in the country; conditions in the rural districts themselves vary widely. The negro who has been more or less left to himself is quite different from the negro who, by constant observation, has sought to imitate the white man's culture and attainment on the one hand, or who has assimilated the white man's vices on the other. Conclusions may not be stated dogmatically, unless qualified to include numerous exceptions. Indeed, it must be said that exceptions to the general rule of conduct are notable among the negroes. Likewise it would be a serious mistake to assume that all negroes are alike in character and conduct. It is very likely that the great majority of negroes in these communities possess the weaknesses and defects portrayed in the following pages, but there are many exceptions, worthy citizens among them who play an important part in the general life of the community. The other extreme which asserts that these characteristics are not representative because there are many exceptions is as ill-founded. So long as the average of race characteristics and race capacity are of a proved order, exceptional cases of individual development will not suffice to

characterize the race.   For the millions may not be judged
by the " submerged tenth " nor by the " chosen ten."

But it is possible to secure and formulate results obtained
from careful studies of a limited number of communities,
based on co-operation on the part of negroes, on results
obtained by many who have labored among the negroes, on
the testimony of physicians and professional men of repute,
and on careful concrete studies in which no pains has been
spared to make them accurate and exhaustive.   The facts
brought out by these studies ought surely to have some
value.   It is not claimed that the conclusions reached apply
to the negro race as a whole in the South or in any state;
they are intended to be qualitative as they apply to certain
phases and tendencies of life in the communities studied.
But they are applicable to a large number of communities
in the South; and while these towns are not typical in every
respect, comparison of the results with further extensive inquiry seems to establish the fact that the conditions described in this work are similar to those of the majority of
average communities in the South composed of whites and
blacks.

Fifty towns in Mississippi, Alabama, Georgia, Florida
and Tennessee, most of which are county seats, were taken
as the main basis for the investigation herein presented.
Their population varies from fifteen hundred to ten thous-
and inhabitants, the average being about four thousand.
Some twenty other towns representing North Carolina,
South Carolina, Texas and Louisiana were studied to some
extent for purposes of comparison.   In the chapter on the
negro criminal, data from the larger cities are included
also.   For a number of years data have been gathered
from all possible sources in the Southern States.   Continued research and comparisons for verification have been
made for two years since the first work was summarized.

The studies strive to emphasize the most important phases of the problem, which are, for the most part, at the same time those most neglected. The study is one of town life rather than city or rural; it is further a study of community relationship, showing something of negro life as it is related to the whites. The work is qualitative and its purpose is to get at a proper beginning rather than to generalize on ultimate solutions.

The difficulties in the way of making accurate investigations into the conditions of negro life are greater than can be realized by one who has not undertaken the task. Aids in making investigations must be had from both whites and blacks. The whites, for the most part, are lacking in accurate knowledge of specific existing conditions; the blacks are very untrustworthy and secretive. Among the whites there is an abundance of general knowledge and opinions about the Negro; but accurate information which can be put in tangible form is almost entirely wanting. This ignorance of vital particulars is surprising. Again, it is difficult to obtain accurate information from public records, from officers and clerks, since there is little provision made for the separation even of the more significant and important statistics of whites and blacks. The negroes are by nature and cultivation secretive. The average black seldom gives correct information in regard to more important details. Most negroes are skilful in making up plausible stories even as they talk; they often expand on minute details having no foundation in fact. It is only when the more reliable negroes feel confident that the information is sought by a sincere searcher and that the purpose is friendly, that any effort on the Negro's part is made to convey the desired information. Conclusions based upon testimony, whether from whites or blacks, if they are to be reliable, can be reached only through repeated inquiry from various sources, and by carefully checking all results. This method has been followed in these investigations; in this way, too, comparative data have been invaluable.

Other difficulties present themselves. There is a marked tendency on the part of the whites to look with suspicion and ridicule upon all searchers after facts about the Negro. They are, moreover, considered as mere theorists. Such an attitude is not without a good foundation in some respects; but this does not change the difficulty or differentiate between the real student and the false. Furthermore, the motive and attitude of persons making investigations are likely to be misunderstood by the negroes, who interpret the efforts as very beneficial to them or as harmful. Finally, the student finds difficulty in holding himself to the persistent, sustained, and laborious effort that a searching investigation requires. Many incidents growing out of the efforts to secure his information are repulsive, not to say nauseous and gruesome. Only the hardiest scientific interest in discoverable facts can sustain the investigator. These conditions, together with the fact that the tendency of both the popular and scientific mind seems to be slow in rewarding such investigations, has sufficed to make most investigations general and superficial.

The student who seeks for the truth must begin at the bottom, take the position that he knows little of his subject, and welcome all true information that may come to him. Experience in this process and the results gained by the investigation lead to the hope that it is not expecting too much of the ordinary reader if he is asked to assume the same attitude. Nothing can be accomplished of lasting results unless the essential qualities of the Negro are known; it is important that the Negro should know himself. The acquirement of such knowledge must necessarily precede any effective movements for the betterment of the race or for better relations between the races. It is hoped, then, that these studies may assist to some extent in bringing about a desire for further research, a desire which must precede the attitude in which sentiment is informed with knowledge. It is well, too, for the Negro to see himself as he is seen from a different viewpoint than his own. Perhaps the majority of negroes never comprehend their situation at all. There is, however, hope that the Negro desires to comprehend the essential weaknesses of the race. Is it possible that the leaders of the race and the more intelligent among them shall permit their people to retrograde? Shall that happen, which has seldom occurred in the history of mankind, namely, that out of the darkness of race ignorance and savagery there should arise a few generations with promise of character and worth, only for the race to fall back toward barbarism, retaining only the vices of the civilization that touched their lives? To those of the negroes who are in earnest a true picture of their relation to the community and an indication of probable tendencies will be of service.

As has already been suggested, this work should not be taken as a general study and as necessarily embodying final conclusions. It is hoped that other searchers will follow and, where the facts are different from those here presented, will set them forth clearly and without prejudice. It is not assumed in this work that because certain traits and characteristics are manifested by the Negro under certain conditions, that they are therefore peculiar to the Negro. The facts are stated in their order; the entire conclusion can be reached and interpreted only through the entire picture as portrayed in the total results. The whole discussion is necessary before arriving at the meaning of the whole situation; and it is not a part but the complete picture that should be seen. If there are those who have come in contact with the better negroes only, or have had a very limited experience, and yet assume to know the whole subject in its practical application better than those who have lived in touch with its most vital problems, and have come to feel the full significance of every phase of the subject, to such, these glimpses are respectfully submitted, with the hope that they may investigate the truth or falsity of the assertions and come to see conditions as they are.

While in the South the Negro is permitted a wide range of employment, at the same time that exacting requirements are placed upon his conduct, still there is little interest felt, little knowledge had, concerning his home life and private conduct. But there is apparently a growing desire to know more of the Negro from impartial sources, more respect for earnest study of the situation, an increase in the number of persons downright in earnest in the study of the Negro, and a gratifying gain in the number of those inclined to impartiality, firmness and fairness, who feel the full significance of at least the immediate situation. The relations between the better elements of both races seem to be improving and there seems to be a growing tendency on the part of leaders to make every effort to get together. It is surprising and gratifying to note the co-operation of the best element of the negroes in systematic inquiry when once they are assured that the purpose of the work is friendly. This fact gives hope that impositions will cease and the attitude between the races may approach a normally desirable one. There is still opportunity for an understanding between the races. The situation calls for wise and positive action; the demand is for sincere utterance based on reason and knowledge.

Nor can the importance of a proper study of so vital a problem be doubted. Much has been said and written concerning various " solutions " of the problem. It is extremely doubtful if there is sufficient evidence as yet to permit a prediction of the outcome. The problem is one of time, subject to unforeseen social, political, and industrial influences. It may be possible, within a comparatively small number of years, to ascertain the direction which the solution will take. In the meantime, it is but reasonable—it is essential—that the problem have, for the present, more study and less discussion. It is but right that the Negro Problem be given the same consideration and study with the practical applications given other social and industrial problems, and that the racial element be recognized. The study which follows has special reference to such a policy, and the tentative conclusions are given with a partial view to popular interpretation.

CHAPTER I

NEGRO SCHOOLS AND THE EDUCATION OF THE NEGRO

THE question of the mental and moral training of the Negro has constituted the greatest problem to be solved in all efforts to improve the negro race. Southern leaders have sought to know the duty of the South in the matter of educating the Negro; they have earnestly desired methods by which the best results might be obtained and have sought the means of reaching these ends. Northern philanthropists, too, have sought to assist in educating the negroes and have given liberally to the cause. At the same time, there has been no phase of the Southern problem in regard to which there has been a greater difference of opinion, more discussion and harangue, more fanaticism and misguided philanthropy, and upon which there has been more wasted energy and means. And to-day the situation is scarcely changed; after years of work under the methods which have been used, after all the experiments that have been made, and after all the changes that have been suggested, wherein sentiment has often played too important a part, the situation still remains a puzzling one. While the schools for the negroes are in many cases apparently doing good work, they are not producing and have not produced results which were expected of them. To-day the problem is more serious than ever before and each year renders it more complex and unyielding to any definite solution.

Inquiry into the problem of educating the Negro suggests several important aspects of the situation. First, the question of the results of past efforts to educate the negroes, judged by the younger generations, is of immediate importance. Second, what are the present school conditions which obtain among the negroes and to what extent and with what degree of accuracy can they be said to apply? Third, what is the exact problem of race inheritance and conditions of negro children? What is their capacity for education, and what sort of education is best adapted to their needs and capacities? Fourth, what are the possibilities of the future and what are the essential needs of the situation? Finally, will education save the Negro from his weaknesses?

The extent to which education has succeeded in helping the Negro may not yet be known fully. It is possible, however, to estimate the general results which education in the past has had upon the negroes of the present generation. Such an estimate will be found, not only in the study of negro schools and education, but also in the careful study of the Negro's home life and morals, his record of crime, his industrial and social status, his social and religious life, and his general conduct, traits and tendencies. Likewise, the question of race inheritance and capacity for education, and the general possibilities of the future can be fully stated only in a thorough consideration of the entire problem of negro life. In this beginning chapter, therefore, the problem involved in the various aspects of the subject will be stated only briefly, the present conditions and facilities of negro schools described in a general way, and the question of adapting special methods of education to the negroes will be raised. This main problem should be kept in mind throughout the discussions and the facts related in the studies herein presented should be applied to its consideration. The total problem may then be estimated and considered at the conclusion of the work.

The scope of the entire problem of educating the Negro in the South is measured by the total number and condition of the negroes in the Southern States. The numerical extent to which an immediate beginning may be made through the younger generations is determined by the number of educable negro children and the proportion of those attending school, with the degrees of regularity, to those who do not attend. According to the special studies made by the Census Bureau from the last Census there were in the Southern States—Texas, Louisiana, Mississippi, Alabama, Georgia, Florida, Tennessee, North Carolina, South Carolina, and Virginia—2,369,621 negroes of school age. Of these only 717,130 were enrolled, or, of all the educable children among the negroes in these states, only thirty per cent attended school at all. Of this thirty per cent, again, a little over thirty-four per cent were in attendance from two to three months during the year; a little more than thirty-one per cent from four to five months; twenty-eight per cent for six months, and six per cent were in attendance for only one month in the year. In Alabama, Georgia, North Carolina and South Carolina, the average was greatest for those who attended from two to three months in the year; in Florida, Mississippi and Virginia from four to five months; and in Louisiana, Texas, and Tennessee for six months. Georgia had the largest number of negro children of school age of any state, having 356,667 enumerable colored children; of these only 110,586 were in attendance. Mississippi, ranking second with 315,422 negro children, had 125,850 in attendance, the largest number attending school in any state. In every state considered there was an excess of females over males in the school attendance of the negroes; the average ratio was forty-seven males to fifty-three females. From five to nine years of age the males were nearly as many as the females. Among the whites the males were in excess of females about four to every thousand. Among the whites, again, only one-fourth of the teachers were males, while among the negroes from one-third to two-fifths were males. Among the negroes the teachers were older than among the whites, the average for the negroes being thirty-two years, while for the whites it was much less. Likewise young male teachers are far less numerous among the negroes than among the whites.

Results to be obtained in the effort to educate the Negro through the present school system are further conditioned upon the school facilities offered to the negroes, the degree to which they take advantage of them, and the character of their teachers and the quality of work done. The schools described in this work are those of the better class which are found among the negroes of the average community. They do not include the negro colleges and special schools on the one hand, nor the poorer schools of the rural districts, on the other. Negro schools differ widely in particulars according as they are affected by the ideals and practices of the negroes, the facilities available, and the supervision of the whites. It is possible, however, to indicate much of the general nature of working conditions among the average negro schools. The negro school house is usually located in or near one of the negro sections of the town.[1] Most communities of the kind studied have only one building so that many of the children who do not live in the immediate vicinity must walk some distance, not infrequently from the opposite part of the town through the business portion, to attend school. A private school with a small enrollment is not uncommon. Likewise a few industrial and charitable institutions are found; but the gen-

---

[1] For the location of negro sections of the town see Chapter IV.

eral conditions in such schools do not differ materially from those of the ordinary schools. The school buildings of the negroes do not compare favorably with the negro churches of the same community. The former are erected by the whites, and the funds are appropriated from the general educational funds, the greater part of which is contributed by the whites, while the churches are built by the negroes with the assistance of the whites. The school houses of the negroes are simple and plain but usually comfortable with a seating capacity for nearly half of the negro children of the town. The crowded conditions in which negro children are often kept in school furnishes one of the most unsatisfactory features of negro school conditions. Altogether school facilities for the negroes may be said to be about one-fourth as adequate as those for the whites. Still the necessary equipment for the working of the school is increased in most cases as it is judiciously used by the negroes. The white board of education often finds it necessary to limit the negro schools in supplies, owing to the tendency toward unnecessary wastefulness. In most cases the negroes receive whatever facilities and appropriations are given them apparently with little interest, and they do not undertake to increase these facilities by their own efforts and contributions. Negro teachers are selected, salaries named and appropriations made by the white board of education. The management of the school generally is supervised by the superintendent of the white schools. It is true, however, that many of the whites are careless and negligent in selecting teachers and in equipping schools, and the white superintendents, as a rule, show little interest in the work of the negro schools and teachers.

There is an average of one teacher for every fifty to seventy-five pupils enrolled, and for every thirty to seventy in attendance. The principals of the schools, the majority of whom are male teachers, are paid an average of forty-seven dollars a month; the assistants are paid an average of twenty-four dollars a month. The length of the school term is usually the same as for the whites. Tuition is free to all resident students of the town, and non-residents pay only during the months—usually September, October and April—when the public school fund is not distributed. In the majority of instances the school facilities and the number of teachers are reasonably adequate to meet the actual demands of the negroes, but there are numerous exceptions. A town in which the negro school enrolled two hundred and sixty-two pupils, with an average attendance of one hundred and forty-six, employed but two teachers. That is, for each teacher there were enrolled one hundred and thirty-one pupils and seventy-three were in actual attendance. The building, which was inadequate, was rented for the negroes by the whites. In a larger town there were enrolled five hundred and seventy-five pupils, with an average attendance of three hundred and twenty; for this number six teachers were employed. Thus, there was an average enrollment of ninety-five pupils and an average attendance of fifty-three for each teacher. There were in the town seventeen hundred and seventy-three enumerable negro children, or, for every teacher employed in the colored schools there were some three hundred pupils in the community. The principal of this school received forty-five dollars a month, the first assistant thirty dollars, and the other four teachers twenty dollars a month each. With such averages of pay for the negro teachers, many do not earn their salaries when the value of their efforts is considered, while others earn more than double the amount they are paid. In all cases it is to be expected that such teachers would be of only ordinary ability and it is not surprising that the superintendents of the white schools should express the opinion that the negro schools are not doing good work.

The average attendance of pupils is sixty-four per cent of the total enrollment. The highest average attendance found was eighty-three per cent and the lowest was forty-six per cent. These figures represent the average attendance of the entire school for the whole year and are obtained from reports of the teachers, in which any part of a day is counted as a full day. It is apparent that in some cases the actual attendance is not so good as reported by the teachers, but in many cases careful records are kept and the teachers make out their reports with pride. Examinations of reports for an entire year show that few pupils attend school with any degree of regularity. The enrollment for each month, although differing little in numbers, is not infrequently composed of almost entirely different pupils. Usually, however, there are a few pupils in each school who attend for the greater number of days in each month in which they are enrolled. A few are not absent from school during any days for several months; such pupils usually come from one or two families in the community, indicating that the head of the family is interested in the schooling of the children. They are the most neatly dressed pupils in the school and most attentive to their school duties. But the great majority of negro children attend school regularly only for the first few weeks after their enrollment, or for the first few days following the opening of a new term. Some days the teacher finds almost a full attendance while the very next day may witness the absence of nearly half of his pupils. Many negro children do not attend school at all. This irregularity of attendance and non-attendance is one of the chief obstacles in the way of effective teaching even where the teachers are good.

Many men of the North and some Southerners have assumed that the only reason for the lack of attendance on the part of negro children was a lack of equipment in the schools and that thereby an injustice is being done the negro. They have not ascertained whether the negroes are using the opportunities given them, nor to what extent other causes operate in causing small and irregular attendance. It is important that an impartial inquiry be made. Inquiries among the whites produce little definite knowledge of the situation. The general opinion is that the negroes do not contribute means for their own education, do not use what facilities they have, and do not comprehend in any sense of the word the purpose of education. Inquiries and observations among the negroes reveal some of the prevalent causes for poor attendance.[1]   It is the consensus of opinion among

[1] Something of the attitude of mind in which actual conditions are viewed by negro principals of schools may be learned from a study of the reasons assigned by them for poor attendance; likewise much may be learned of actual conditions. The following are exact quotations: "Parents indifferent to needs, hence cannot be reached." "A lack of appreciation of the value of an education on the part of the parents." "Parental indifference as to compelling children to attend, parents catering to whims of children." "False notions as to pride in dress." "Distance of house too far for smaller children." "Poverty." "Lack of interest." "Public school facilities not good." "Children work out as nurses, etc." "Ignorance on part of parents." "Only one house—not large enough for all, in northern part of city." "I do not know the reason." "Leave school to work." "Poor school comforts and attractions." "Too small a number of teachers." "Indifference on the part of city officials." "Parents' objection to proper school room rule enforcement." "The tendency of the age toward ease and superficiality." "Parents of children take no interest in the schooling of their children, they seem to forget the main things or truths that will make a race out of the youth." "To a great extent our people do not see really the benefits of an education." "Parents who are totally ignorant fear that his child will be ruined by education." "A lack of interest on the part of school officers and teachers." "The town boy goes to school until he is 12 or 14 and then he feels that a job can not do without him." "Some of my people have not yet learned the value of school privileges." "They would come, practically all of them, but I would not have a place to put them or extra teacher to teach them, as the appropriation is small

the majority of the best negro teachers that the greatest
obstacle lies in the weakness of the race rather than in a
lack of facilities.   Thus one of the principals of a colored
school analyzed the causes for unsatisfactory attendance:

Many of our children don't attend school because *we
teachers* are incompetent; because many of the parents simply
dislike their teachers; because some parents prefer Baptist
teachers; because many children have their own way about
everything they do; because many children do not like a strict
teacher; because some parents contend for a fine brick building
for the school; because as a whole many parents are too
ignorant and niggardly and prejudiced and contentious to do
anything aright.   *Yet we here have enrolled about one hundred
and fifty pupils this session in spite of the Devil!*

Observations and studies seem to show that the causes just
mentioned are the principal hindrances to efficient school
work among the negroes.   The limitations and ignorance
of the black man make the saddest story that is told in all
his life.   There is no knowledge of the truth and no interest in its teaching.   With such ignorance there can be
no proper conception of education or ideals to which the

and space limited, we are crowded to death with the present situation."
" Ignorant parents and inherited tendencies on the part of the children."   " Lack of incentives from surroundings—seem to think little
or no education is required to do what the colored people can get to
do.   Not more than one child in a hundred seems to want to be a
preacher or teacher and think education is not needed to learn trades
and few even desire to learn them."   " Slothfulness and negligence on
the part of the parents."   " They do not want or desire to be brought
under proper control."   " Environment about the school house, no
furniture, maps, desks, etc., as they should be."   " Children becoming
breadwinners on account of death of the father."   " Few do not attend some part of the nine months, they will come some part of the
term."   " My people are not prepared educationally, a large percentum
of them, to know the real importance of education, for which reason
in my mind is the cause largely for their children not attending."

school should develop. Poverty and misguided conceptions of life, jealousy and distorted notions in general—all combine to keep the children away from school and from attending regularly. Denominational prejudice and personal interest determine much of the teacher's popularity, and rarely, if ever, does the question of his equipment enter into the chief consideration. An example will illustrate: In a town where three teachers are employed in the colored school, a petition was signed and brought to the board of trustees in behalf of a candidate for the position of principal. Three years previous to the circulating of the petition the negro whom the patrons wanted for principal had committed a murder—a white man—in the same town and was cleared in the courts on some technicality. He had been away from the town, but had returned and wanted the school; his case, too, was a well-known one among the negroes and had attracted considerable attention. The good teacher, on the other hand, is not appreciated. The negroes further complain that they are not given proper facilities, and because they are displeased they refuse to make use of those which they have. They desire that everything be given them and wait for this end; yet they are not willing to improve or increase what has been given them. They show little pride in keeping the school buildings and grounds clean; the houses and yards are not improved. Were the average community to devote the same kind of interest and energy that is given to church and lodge to the school, within a few years the negroes would find their interest in the schooling of their children increased many fold. This apparently is given little serious thought among the negroes.

The average of intelligence among negro teachers *in town and country* is low, and their education is meagre. A small per cent have an accurate knowledge of spelling and reading and the simpler principles of Arithmetic. One may read dozens of examination papers, handed in by negro teachers in vain to find one free from ridiculous blunders in the simplest spelling and usage. The prevailing ignorance is nothing less than astonishing; and the conditions would seem incredible were it not for the fact that the evidence is incontestable. Page after page could be filled with such evidence gleaned from the school room and examination papers of those upon whom rests the responsibility of teaching the negro youth. The negro teacher has little reasoning power or depth of originality. There is little of the principle of honor among them—they do not comprehend it. They do not regard cheating on examinations for license to teach as a serious offence; and whereas a white teacher discovered cheating on examination is disqualified for teaching, the cheating of the negro is often countenanced.

The colored teachers employed in the schools of *the towns studied* are of a much higher order than those just mentioned. The average of intelligence is higher; they are better educated and more earnest in their work. They have a broader conception of the needs of the children whom they are to teach. They have an honest purpose to serve well their people. It is doubtful if any worker among the negroes has more difficulties to overcome than has the negro teacher. He must fight day after day against ignorance and superstition, himself a victim. He must struggle against prejudice and irregular support from parents and pupils. He must fight his way for the most part alone. He must face inadequate facilities and know that he is failing in his work as it is reflected in the great majority of his pupils. The earnest negro teacher is good in so far as he knows how to be. He often has false ideas of knowledge and education but it is because of false ideas in the race. And the negro preacher whose highest ambition is often to

preach with the " big words of the elements of knowledge "
is responsible for a great part of this conception. The
better negro teacher is the most honest and sincere leader
to be found in all the race.   Patient and persistent, earnest
and honest, humble, yet sensitive to all interests of his people, following the best guidance he has, often vainly seeking for light, striving to increase his efficiency, conscientious
in his work, and appreciative of all true co-operation and
criticism—this man deserves the highest tribute that can
be given him.

In the average school among the negroes there is a general lack of order in the routine of daily teaching in the
school room.   There are many, however, which follow a
definite schedule and are systematic as far as conditions will
permit.   The school often begins the day with order but
ends in disorder ; a class is begun in an orderly way but often
ends in confusion because of a lack of restraining power in
teacher and pupil.   There is much noise—pupils moving
their feet on the floor, moving from one desk or seat to another, studying aloud, and consulting each other.   Often
the pupils must be permitted to study in an undertone, inasmuch as their motor habits of study scarcely permit them
to study intelligently otherwise.   During the winter months
there is almost constant coughing because the children
are continually affected with colds.   Borrowing and lending
books, asking the teacher questions, and various little irregularities keep the teacher busy at all moments.   In the
school room methods of discipline are not infrequently crude
but often very effective; in several instances there has been
a decided improvement in this respect.   Those superintendents of the white schools who carefully supervise the work
of the colored teachers testify that, relatively speaking, the
work done in the colored schools is good, notwithstanding
the disorder.

The day in school is one full of interest to teacher and pupil. The company of pupils gathers in the morning but slowly. There is little uniformity in dress among the negro children; for the most part the children are poorly dressed. But with all the varied attire and imperfectly fitting garments, there can be seen in the dress of almost every child a hurried attempt at thoughtfulness. But there is less evidence of pride in the dress of the children than is the case with the older negroes. With this company of pupils ranging in age from six to fourteen the average negro school opens. The exercises are generally begun with prayer and song; many schools have song books which they use regularly. The children do not sing as heartily as would be expected, nor are they attracted by the music of the organ or piano to any great extent. The text books in the negro schools are the same as for the whites, and while most of the colored schools are not graded as are those of the whites, the graded books are used with the negro classes. The teacher follows his text closely, and " hears lessons " much after the old-fashioned way. The classes are well organized and are often divided into groups which recite as they are ready. Sometimes they compete in the daily recitations—a method which the children enjoy. They are usually quick to criticise each other's work. When the work is over they are always eager for the recess hours and make no attempt to conceal their eagerness; when dismissed the children make a rush for the doors with much noise despite the fact that the teacher has carefully instructed them to march out in an orderly fashion. At recess they play games and are noisy and intent with their play. Besides regular " lessons " the schools are accustomed to have special exercises on Friday afternoons.; these consist of spelling matches, " speaking " and similar methods of entertainment. At most of these exercises a few songs are sung by teachers and pupils. The recitation or " speeches " are usually short, and consist of simple rhymes and sayings, or poems. They are often " funny "; not infrequently they are very creditable to the children. There is much amusement in the audience while the children say their speeches. The spelling matches are conducted in the old-fashioned way; " sides " are chosen by the leaders, preference being given to the supposed best spellers. There is much noisy rivalry in these matches, and each side is clamoring to win. On such afternoons secretaries, critics, and other officers are appointed who often read interesting reports. Such entertainments are not enjoyed by the patrons of the school; it is a rare occurrence for the school to be visited at any time by the patrons. The whites never visit the negro school. Consequently there is little known of what is being done in the colored schools except by the few superintendents who carefully oversee the work of the colored teachers.

Negro children are easily interested, attentive, eager and alert. For the most part they are bright and learn easily. In many cases they appear brighter than white children of the same age. They learn from memory easily and retain little things for some length of time. Notable examples of this faculty exhibited to an unusual degree have been found in special cases. They are quick to learn simple phrases and rhymes; they often remember entire songs and stanzas after having heard them a single time. Their wonderful capacity for thus learning is apparently explained by the fact that things heard in sequence cohere in the same order in the memory naturally. An example of this kind will illustrate: Four boys the oldest of whom was scarcely more than thirteen years of age recited in continuous order over two hundred songs and rhymes, each of which was recognized by each of the boys. The reciting of one recalled another in rapid succession, and apparently they possessed an even greater supply as they manifested no desire to stop, although they seemed to know only the more or less indecent ones toward the last. Similar cases in which even younger children were involved might be given. The mind of the Negro is easily sensitive to sound, and words which are sounded in sequence, similar sounding words or words of alliterative sound are retained by the negro child. They are very fond of riddles stated in rhymes and take delight in remembering the answers to them. They learn readily to do things by imitation and become comparatively skilful in a short time. They remember names and faces well. However, there are many negro children who have an almost total lack of mental perception, whose minds are so dense that they can scarcely learn anything. The percentage of such cases increases with age.

In the school room such qualities as have been mentioned are manifested in interest and attentiveness. Negro children study diligently for short periods, and are quick to try to think. Exceptional cases of the extremes are more marked than among the whites. Reading, writing and simple arithmetic are readily learned by the negroes; spelling is more difficult, perhaps because of their tendency to follow sound only. History in the simpler stories is easier for them than geography. In their language lessons they compose interesting sentences but they can not overcome their habits and forms of speech gained at home and the inherent tendency toward mingling thoughts to a degree that outruns the ability for any continued expression of separate ideas. They have vivid but general and vague imaginations; as far as they go they form mental images quickly. The brightest students are those from nine to thirteen years of age; the clearest minds seem to be found from ten to twelve years of age. Few are found over fourteen years old who display any ability or clearness of mind on the one hand, or any brightness on the other. Experiments with negro children seem to show that the age of greatest brightness is later than that of greatest ability. By brightness is meant quickness and aptness in the doing and learning of simpler things; by ability is meant the power to grasp and hold that which confronts the mind. In both boys and girls among the negroes the highest brightness seems to be thirteen years; the highest ability for boys was found to be eight years and for the girls nine years. With white children ability increases and brightness decreases with age. As a rule, after negro children become older than ten or twelve years, their development is physical rather than mental; whatever of mental ability in the child gave promise of worth to be recognized in later years is crowded out by the coarser physical growth. In the small community few negro children over thirteen years of age attend school. It thus happens that with all the brightness and other good qualities of negro children, they attain little in the intellectual way beyond childhood. Even with better advantages offered, and under competent instruction in all cases, they would face tremendous odds.

Before considering further the negro school and its work it will be well to note the condition of the child when he enters the school room. Reference has been made to the attitude of the parents in regard to sending the children to school. The teacher and child must cope with odds against which they are ill matched. Inherited tendency and environment of the race conditions constitute a powerful influence in the education of the negro child. Against these he must gain whatever of good he is to receive, and it is to help him overcome these that the best efforts and most careful study should be put forth. In proportion as this can be done, to that degree will the next generation be stronger than the present.

Back of the child, and affecting him both directly and indirectly, are the characteristics of the race. The Negro has little home conscience or love of home, no local attachment of the better sort. He does not know in many cases for months or years the whereabouts of his brother and sister or even parents, nor does he concern himself about their welfare. He has no pride of ancestry, and he is not influenced by the lives of great men. The Negro has few ideals and perhaps no lasting adherence to an aspiration toward real worth. He has little conception of the meaning of virtue, truth, honor, manhood, integrity. He is shiftless, untidy, and indolent; he would live " coolly in the shadow of his skin." The migratory or roving tendency seems to be a natural one to him, perhaps the outcome of an easygoing indolence seeking freedom to indulge itself and seeking to avoid all circumstances which would tend to restrict its freedom. The Negro shirks details and difficult tasks; he is incapable of turning his mind toward any other subject when once morbid curiosity holds his attention. He does not know the value of his word or the meaning of words in general. He utters phrases suited to his own fancy without regard to their meaning and forms conclusions in his mind which give him pleasure. He recognizes no causal relation between stability and prosperity, whether it be in reference to his local abode or his work. The Negro is improvident and extravagant; lazy rather than industrious, faithful in the performance of certain duties, without vindictiveness, he yet has a reasonable amount of physical endurance. But he lacks initiative; he is often dishonest and untruthful. He is over-religious and superstitious. The Negro suspects his own race and the white race as well; his mind does not conceive of faith in humanity—he does not comprehend it.

While for the most part negro children are cheerful, the older negroes are less so than formerly. Instead of the one-time good-nature, a spirit of moroseness and sullenness is developing. Negro children are easily susceptible to all influences brought to bear upon them. It has been observed that the Negro is lacking in morals, so far as personal purity and chastity are concerned. All phases of indecent subjects are discussed in the presence of children. As a matter of fact, the prevalence of habitual immorality is understood by all—the children grow up after the manner of the older ones, feeling that the situation is but a natural one. Take an illustration: " Uncle Tally " writing for a negro newspaper published in a small community, has this to say:

I have seen the time when it was a disgrace for a young girl to go out of the church at night alone, but you can see them do it now, but when a girl does it now the best people know that she is not straight and if they had half as much character as they had clothes on their back morality would reign supreme. I be dog my cats if I don't want to see the time come when I tip my old hat that I will be satisfied that I have tipped it to a lady but the way things are now I feel better satisfied when I tip my hat to a girl with a basket of clothes on her head than some of them with a fine hat on, because most of the time there is more virtue under the basket of clothes than there is under a fine hat.

He continues about girls in "big meetings" sitting out with immoral young men and adds: " and hang me if some of them don't try to be school teachers." And many of them are school teachers. One of the crying weaknesses in the negro school is the lack of moral strength on the part of the women teachers. It is but natural that children accustomed to gross immoralities at home and sometimes seeing indications of the same tendency on the part of the teachers, should be greatly affected by it at school. Thus with mental stupidity and moral insensibility back of them the children are affected already in practice and thought, in deeds and in speech. Furthermore, they come to the teacher, as will subsequently be shown, having antipathy toward their own race and disappointed at " being a nigger."

When the conditions in the school room are seen in the light of actual conditions obtaining, they are easily understood and little surprise is felt that the results have not been better. It is easily observed that these obstacles have not been overcome, but have rather set the bounds for the school's effectiveness. Because of this the growing generation of negroes is not superior to the negroes of a generation ago, as a race, rated according to religious and moral standing, and according to their economic value to the community. The schools do not appear to have improved within the last decade nor do the results appear in so favorable a light as a few years ago. Much has been attempted but there are certain characteristics of the young so-called educated negroes which work great harm to the race. It is true that as far as actual mental illiteracy is concerned, a great deal has been done, but it seems that the whole current of mental improvement has reached unhappy results.

The young educated negroes are not a force for good in the community but for evil. The Negro quickly outgrows the influence and control of his instructors; especially has this been noted in cases where the whites have taught them. These young negroes are not in sympathy with their parents; they appear to neglect them more than those who are not " educated." They feel that manual labor is beneath their dignity; they are fitted to do no other. They sneer at the idea of work, and they thus spread dissatisfaction among the members of their race. They imitate the whites and believe themselves thereby similar to them. They love only the show of apparent results and do not care for the details of attainment. They have not rejected vicious practices in their own lives nor condemned them in theory; on the contrary they have chosen to practice them and to condone the vices which are increasing in the race to its rapid deterioration. They uphold immorality and wish to ostracize any who assist the white man contrary to their own notions, thinking all the while that they are manifesting a spirit of race loyalty. It is clear that their moral natures are miserably perverted. Such a statement should not be interpreted as abusing the Negro; for, considering the putrid moral air he breathes and that there is no light to nourish his spiritual instincts, there could be no other outcome. Despite the excuse, however, the facts remain unchanged. The negro schools taught under present conditions have not produced the desired results; conducted according to the white man's own methods they have been unsatisfactory. Even in those schools which have been given ample equipment and have employed the younger educated negroes at better salaries, the results do not appear to be lasting; but it is in the acquirement of modern superficial methods wrongly applied that they seem to surpass.

The problem is indeed perplexing, and from the viewpoint of the Negro the way must appear a difficult one. Many remedies have been offered and many methods suggested for the attainment of better results. Some of these may be noted. Ex-Governor Jelks of Alabama has suggested that Southern white men should teach the negro schools. To this there are such serious objections that it would appear to be inpracticable. In the first place, the negroes offer serious objections; their objection is thus stated in a leading editorial of one of the negro church papers:

Governor Jelks of Alabama, in his article on the school question and in discussing Negro education in particular, is

very careful to suggest that only white men should teach in
these schools.   This raises a very fine point from our standpoint, namely, this—unless there is a very careful selection of
white men the Negro would have great hesitancy in entrusting
his children, particularly the girls, to their care.   Not all white
men of the South, but a very large percentage, are very bold
in asserting that the Negro women cannot be chaste and virtuous, and hence they are open to desperate attacks from a
source that ought to be helpful.   White men of the South have
opened themselves too largely to criticism to at once be ushered
into unquestioned leadership of the intellectual, moral and religious life of the Negro in the South.   Governor Jelks's keen
and decided drawing the line raises the question and since it
is raised let it be met in all fairness.   Do Southern men respect
us enough in our race life and in our hopes for the future?
Can our children be entrusted to them?

The negroes would object further because it would deprive
their best educated men and women of the field of labor
which they think they can most effectively occupy.   They
would object to being robbed of an occupation.   Besides the
objections offered by the negroes there are additional reasons why such a plan is impracticable.   The Southern white
man is unwilling to teach in these schools.   As conditions
are now, most boards of trustees are careless in selecting
teachers for negro schools.   With the present supply and
the existing prospect for a future supply of white teachers
the negro schools would get only inferior men.   And none but
the best equipped in training, endurance, and moral stamina
could ever teach faithfully and efficiently in a negro school.
The average Southern white teacher is not prepared to
teach negro children.   Certainly there will not be, even for
generations, thirty thousand such men.

It has been suggested that only Southern white women
can effectually teach in negro schools.   And it is doubtless

true that they could teach them quite successfully. But under the present relations between the races, nothing would seem more improbable than such an undertaking. It has been suggested by both whites and blacks that agricultural and mechanical schools should be established for the negroes. It has been suggested again that half of the curriculum be given over to industrial studies. Military discipline has been advocated as the best way to direct the education of the Negro youth; strict methods of discipline in many forms have been suggested as a sufficient corrective of the evil conditions. The kindergarten system has been urged for the development early in life of manual dexterity. While these systems have much to commend them, is it probable that they will be adopted? If adopted, has the negro at present a sufficient foundation for effective results? In the light of the whole situation and in connection with the many proposed plans, the following observations are offered.

It is clear that, at least for some time to come, the Negro must have his own teachers in the school room. The school is the only place where a change of home life can be affected to any marked degree and where moral, physical and hygienic education can be obtained. This must necessarily take more than a generation. And it must be begun by the negroes under the supervision of the white man. It is furthermore true that the negro teacher should have means and methods for his use which are specially adapted to the proper training of his children, and he should have the careful co-operation and supervision of the whites. There are certain conditions which must be met by the negroes which do not obtain among the whites; and it is but just that white supervision, recognizing this difference, should better adapt means needed for the colored teacher's use. Here are children who must cope with tremendous odds in inherited tendencies and environment. They are different in every particular from the white children; the basis on which their education must rest is different from that of the white children. And yet under white supervision, they are given the same books, the same methods and the same grade of methods, and are required to learn as the white children do. The Negro is condemned because he thinks himself the white man's equal, and still we say to his children: You must use the same methods and the same degree of perseverance if you are to get anything out of school. It is complained that they learn too much, and it is complained that they can not learn at all and are incapable of receiving an education. In each case the Negro is compared with the whites. The logic of the situation is all wrong; the methods would appear to be wrong. In addition to the fact that the children of the two races have lived under such different educative influences and therefore need different matter and methods, the text books used in the first grade are especially suited to the whites and not suited to the negroes. To illustrate, turn through the pages of the first and second or third grade readers used by negro children in the schools. Such books are used for reader, spelling book, for writing exercises, and they often use no other text. The pages are illustrated with pictures in colors, and in every case where persons are involved they are pictures of white boys and girls with rosy cheeks and pretty features. These children have toys and pets and comforts, and all that luxury without labor could demand. The simple stories are of these boys and girls at play, of their dolls and toys and friends. The stories are varied, and are illustrated with the view to interesting children; and properly so. But what is the state of interest with which the negro child reads of things which are not his and can never be? Or what must be the recoil to his feelings when eagerly enjoying the scenes, his imagination has transported him into that wholly ideal life, he suddenly remembers that it is only the white boys and girls that he reads of and that nothing of his own life is mentioned, and that he can not be like the white child?   Certain it is that the bright mind of the child conceives some idea, and there can be but one result in his mind, even though it may sometimes be indefinite.   Is it surprising that the negro child, as he gets the daily lesson, begins to wish that he were white, or is it surprising that the new world which dawns upon the brighter negro children is a wrong conception of life?   Is it surprising that the girl cherishes and fondles, as with some motherly instinct, the white doll and refuses to have aught to do with a black doll?   It is little surprising that early in life these children begin to aspire naturally to be like the whites and that they seek every opportunity to gain any similar traits or appearances.   They do this whether they attend school or remain at home—it is unfortunate that the school should be a means for cultivating this tendency. Again, is it surprising that the older negro boys, already affected with criminal impulses, begin to formulate those malignant and voluptuous thoughts which turn to criminal aspirations?

The negro teachers, as they follow the text book closely, can but long for the beauty and light which is pictured in the more favored life of the whites, naturally making it an ideal for his pupils.   The current feeling among the children as well as older negroes is well illustrated by the consolation offered by a negro teacher to one of her pupils: "You write so sorrowfully about being a negro.   My dear Dulce brown skin and kinky hair are nothing to distress you; the trouble lies much deeper than that.   If you were a little pale faced, yellow haired girl, and all the rich, well-educated people about you had brown skin; if those who rode in carriages and autos had kinky hair; if the dominant, cultured, successful race were Negroes, you would long to be a Negro also, brown skin, kinky hair and all. It is a matter of education, morality and money; and just as soon as the majority of negroes acquire these, the question of color will begin to drop out. Are you doing what you can to hasten that day?" The idea among all classes of negroes —teachers and pupils — is monstrously wrong. For the most part they seek only to be like the whites rather than to obtain the qualities which make the white man superior. The question of color will not drop out. On the other hand, the Negro is encouraged in imitating the white man and then abused because he does it; we expect him to imitate the good in the stronger race and not the bad. We give the white children lessons which we desire to be incentives to learning, culture, and high ideals; when the Negro reads the same lessons, if he should aspire to the same ideals, he is accused of being criminal. Perhaps he can not aspire; he imitates.

The suggestion made here is that the text books of the first years for the negroes should be very different from those of the white children. It is hoped that the suggestion will merit serious consideration and to this end brief explanation is given. No outline of the proposed books will be given here but the general plan may be indicated. New text books are desirable for two main reasons: First, books are needed which are especially suited to the negroes as a race, to develop the negro child *within his race*. The second may be stated more fully: Text books are needed which are especially adapted to the negro *mind*, texts based on the most accurate and sympathetic knowledge of the characteristics of the Negro, which comprehend the peculiar needs of negro children, which are carefully planned and graded to teach the things fundamental in their proper education. It is essential that details be taught from the very beginning, and by constant drill the habit of doing things with accuracy be forced. The constant repetition of little things, done in order, might overcome much of the tendency in the Negro for carelessness and instability. But if any such results are to be hoped for, they must be obtained before the pupil goes beyond fourteen years of age; here the physical brain in the Negro reaches its maturity, and nearly all that can be done for a generation must be done by methods suited to the children.

(1) Let the influences upon the negro child, at least so far as the school is able to effect this end, lead him toward the unquestioning acceptance of the fact that his is a different race from the white, and properly so; that it always has been and always will be; that it is not a discredit not to be able to do as the whites, and that it is not necessarily a credit to imitate the life of the white man. Let him not measure his work by the white child's achievement. If there were no impossible fancies of being like the whites, or the constant thought of being below them, slight progress might bring the teacher and pupil to some consciousness of the degraded condition of their race. Let the negro children read stories of pioneer days, and of those who have worked their way up through the years; let such lessons be designed to teach that labor is honorable and idleness degrading. He may learn from reading stories of Africa how much better off he is than his cousins. Let him read stories of his own people, of whom there are hundreds of stories told of fidelity to duty and trust; stories of little homes with the family, and what attractions are possible for the clean negro home; of neat cottages and houses, descriptions of rooms and yards; of cleanliness and its necessity; of everyday life and what to do in the home, of fresh air and sunlight—stories of health and happiness, of labor and honor, of things interesting in the telling, but of vital import as they pertain to the everyday life of the children themselves.

Then there should be many nature stories, of animals and crops, of planting and growing seed, of birds and country life. Simple rhymes and poems specially chosen for the purpose would be inserted at frequent intervals—all of which could be arranged with proper illustrations and the same pedagogical principles of teaching the reading, writing and spelling. This would have its positive value and it would have its negative value. While the negro child is interested in his own matters he will not be incited to wish for the white man's conditions of life or for his nature. Until some such methods have placed the negro child on a firm basis, the Negro can never achieve permanent results in his civilization.

(2) Little experiments in the school room indicate that it is almost impossible for the negro child to do anything with continuous accuracy. The scorning of details is clearly seen in the habits of the children. For instance, if, after careful instructions, the child is given the task of drawing ten straight lines, two, three or four, will be well drawn, while the others will be carelessly done. This tendency may not be overcome in a short while; but the negro child learns to do little things easily, and, when made to do so, can do them well. The one fundamental need, then, of the child is constant drill; nothing will take its place.

Exercises for facilitating the teaching might be offered at the end of the several chapters or lessons in the text books. With the reading lessons squares or other figures should illustrate the story and the child should be required to draw these figures; with examples in arithmetic, exercises in drawing parallel and perpendicular lines and adding them, or similar exercises, would be given constantly. Notes at the end of each lesson might assist the teacher in enforcing accuracy and effectively teaching the lessons. Again, after a story, the note might suggest that the pupil read aloud the lesson at home; so with a lesson on hygiene, instructions for simple exercises at home or at school might be given. In all instances they should be repeated often enough in the proper way for the child to recognize a practical application. If the negro home standard is to be raised it must be through the child. Nothing short of constant drill and the habitual performing of details can ever make good home keepers of negro girls. In all exercises the methods should be reasonable; the negro child needs simpler exercises than does the white child. However, each should be designed with a special purpose in view. Negroes are rarely open to reason; here they need to see things in their details rather than in the total appearance. They need to learn the real meaning of a few words rather than the sound of many. Boys and girls who are sent to the board to write sentences illustrating the meaning and use of common words like *are, the, boy, girl*, compose many sentences containing admonitions as to boys and girls stealing, telling lies, and similar sins. And yet they manifest no practical knowledge whatever of the meaning of the words; they think of the sound of the words and the entire sentence and of a pictured favorable impression made upon the teacher, or their own sense of " oughtness " and what they know to be the right sentiment. So it is with *right* and *wrong, heaven* and *hell*, and other words commonly used by negro children. Here again this method may help to resurrect the conscience of the Negro and move his intellect, and if it is possible to eradicate the criminal tendencies, it can best be begun in the school room. Special passages selected from the Bible and placed in the back of the book for morning reading or home reading might greatly assist in teaching the scriptures to the negroes, and perhaps in time, moral principles would be inculcated. Such exercises as have been mentioned, with suggestions for improving the school grounds and keeping the building clean, would not only be effective in results upon the children, but also in the discipline and management of the school.

It will be objected that the above plan is theoretical and in the practical test would fail of results. No one, however, would claim that it would be less effective than present methods and it would imply only the ordinary change brought about by the adoption of text books. It would, besides meeting the needs of the negro children already mentioned, meet the requirements of superintendents of white schools who have indicated in their reports the defects of the school work among the negroes. Furthermore, the negro teacher follows his book closely and as a rule teaches what is found in it. He can be depended upon to do so in this case. The simple exercises because of their newness would be of interest to the teacher, and it is probable that the average teacher would find pleasure in preparing each lesson, and the pupil look forward to each new exercise. This change would put new life into the work and new interest into the teacher's field of labor. Like the children, he would reap benefit. It will be objected that the Negro will protest against such a change; it is assumed, however, that the illustrations and contents of the books would be judiciously chosen with the view of pleasing the children and at the same time instructing them. Many negro teachers are willing to affirm that they approve of the plan. It would, of course, be impracticable to require separate texts for negroes above the grammar grades; but it is only in the formative period, when the pupil will be in the elementary subjects, that special texts are needed. Students whose ability and ambition carry them into advanced studies will most likely be intelligent enough to understand their position. Such a change in elementary studies would not be cutting off the Negro's present advantages but an essential aid in preparing him for better things. If the plan is properly interpreted no negro leader who aspires for his race to reach the best results will offer objections. There should be no objection on the part of the whites if they desire the negro to be trained for usefulness.

The great obstacle in the way of the Negro's industrial efficiency as well as in his mental and moral character is his lack of sustained application and constructive conduct. Such a state of being is, however, but natural to a people of the Negro's temperament. He easily responds to all stimuli and is controlled, therefore, by present impulses, which leads to almost complete lack of restraint. The pleasurable yielding to impulses in the breaking-down of restraint and in the habit of non-exertion make the negro very inactive on the one hand, and the carrying of pleasurable responses to an extreme exhausts and degenerates his vital powers, on the other. The negro is therefore weak in social and self control and in self-direction, and has little capacity for sustained control of any sort. With such a predilection and predisposition the Negro does not lend himself to the development of deep and permanent qualities through the working-out of essential processes. Through habituation, facility, inheritance and temperament, therefore, the Negro is superficial and irresponsible. It is easily seen, then, that in order to help the Negro most effectively not only the content of his mind must be improved but also his mode of applying the intellect and feelings must be changed. If the Negro has latent powers they can be developed and retained only through some such processes as have been suggested, together with selection. Even if the various methods should be adopted, or any parts of the many plans already suggested for the education of the negroes should be carried out, the elementary branches must still be taught. Efficiency in application is the first essential to any permanent results. Such specially adapted methods would greatly facilitate matters as well as assist in making a proper beginning. Uniformity would be had, as now, by the adoption of satisfactory texts, edited and selected with special care, and the cost of books would not have to be increased.

A careful study of the Negro's habits and traits of life will reveal the extent to which the facts just related apply. In connection with such a plan as has been suggested there is need of some method by which regularity of attendance may be had, otherwise the basic principle of the method would be thwarted. Some regulation is needed whereby compulsory attendance is required, not for any specific number of months, but for the time during which the pupil is enrolled. The work of the negro schools should have the co-operation and interest of the whites of the same community. Furthermore, supervision by white teachers of ability is absolutely essential for the present. Many negro teachers have been known to put new life into their work and new interest in their schools because white men have shown a real and practical interest in the work. The negroes thus reap both the benefit that comes from white supervision and the encouragement offered by others who work in similar fields of endeavor. A careful consideration of this phase of their duties is earnestly asked of school superintendents throughout the Southern States. The negro can be assisted in obtaining a substantial training easier than he can be given a superficial education.

CHAPTER II

The Negro Church and Religion

The Church has been called the central point around which all negro life revolves. It is certainly a great influence in the life of the negroes and furnishes them with the greater part of their better life and the outlet for much of their energy. The function of the negro Church is rather to give expression and satisfaction to social and religious emotions than to direct moral conduct. The Negro is well-known for his religious nature and the richness of his experiences. The question has often been raised whether or not the Church could be used effectively to assist the Negro in overcoming his weaknesses. What the possibilities may be and what the Negro's needs are can best be known through a study of the Negro's churches and church life. Such a study should reveal the main facts concerning negro churches, membership and attendance, church services and methods of worship, religious feelings and beliefs, the moral qualities of the negroes, and the relations existing between the white church and the negro church. In this chapter the effort is made to present and interpret in a discriminating way such facts. The results of the concrete experiments made by the whites among the negroes are especially significant in their bearing upon the entire question of negro religion and life.

There are among the negroes in the South church organizations in the following denominations: Baptist, African Methodist Episcopal, Colored Methodist Episcopal, African

54   [358

Methodist Episcopal Zion, and Methodist Episcopal. In some of the states there are a few organizations and churches among the Congregationalists, Colored Cumberland Presbyterians and African Union Methodist Protestant, with a small number of special or " sanctified " organizations. The white Presbyterians of the United States have established a number of churches among the negroes and exercise a supervision over them. The Protestant Episcopal Church has many communicants throughout the South. The Churches most commonly found among the negroes in the South are the Baptist, Methodist Episcopal, African Methodist Episcopal, and Colored Methodist Episcopal, known generally as the Baptist, the M. E., the A. M. E., and the C. M. E., respectively. Most communities have more than one church, generally three or four. Where only two churches are found, one is commonly a Baptist and the other some form of the Methodist. There are, however, more organizations among the Baptists than among all others combined.

Negro churches are usually located in or near the negro sections of the town. If there are communities of negroes segregated in two or more parts of the town, the churches are accordingly not infrequently located in different negro divisions. If there are, for example, four negro churches, three will perhaps be located in the same vicinity and the fourth on the opposite side of town, or two will be located together and the others in a separate section each. The negroes exercise much care and judgment in selecting and obtaining lots upon which to build their churches so that the locations of the negro churches compare favorably with those of the white churches. Through the industry and energy of the negroes and the co-operation of the whites the church and parsonage are often located in most desirable parts of the town. The church edifices, too, reveal considerable industry and pride. Measured by the property owned by the negroes and by other ordinary standards, the negro churches are, thus relatively speaking, far superior to those of the whites. The whites, however, assist the negroes in many private ways and contributions. In one place, at least, namely in his church, the Negro does not suffer by comparison. The exterior of such churches presents a pleasing appearance. Most churches are constructed of wood, are painted, have a simple but creditable steeple, and the windows are usually of stained or painted glass. The interior is comfortably and neatly furnished with substantial pews, pulpit furniture, an organ, and a bookcase for church and Sunday-school supplies. As a rule the church is kept neat and clean to a reasonable degree and much pride is manifested in the keeping of the church. The bell is an important part of the church building, since it appeals to the negroes with unusual force and serves to remind them of church hours. The externals of the negro church, the building, the bell, the equipment and furnishings are pre-eminent in the Negro's thoughts for the success of his Church. These and successful collections are causes for the heartiest congratulation. There are, however, quite a percentage of negro churches which reflect little pride and thrift. Many are poorly equipped because of lack of funds and poorly kept because of lack of interest and pride. A neat but poor building does not appeal to the majority of negro worshipers; it then represents only a place to meet, and the same habits of filth and carelessness are found as in other activities of the Negro's life. Taken as a whole, the average value of the churches studied with their properties is $2710.00. Each church receives, in addition to the names of the town in which it is located, also a special name, *e. g.*, Woodville Grace M. E., Thompson Bethlehem Baptist, Jackson St. Paul A. M. E., and other scriptural names.

The membership of negro churches is large, although it is scarcely more than sixty per cent as large as the total membership of the fraternal orders in some communities where the Lodge has been well organized. The average membership of the churches studied was one hundred and ninety eight. The average in the Southern States was only one hundred and twenty at the time of the last census and for the entire United States the average for the negro churches was only one hundred and fourteen. The smaller average, on the whole, is due to the fact that many negro churches are situated in localities where the colored population is small. Thus when several denominations have organizations in small communities, the membership for each must be small. The churches studied, then, represent the more prosperous churches. Of their membership some two-thirds are female and one-third male. In many cases the percentage of males is smaller, ranging from one-tenth to one-half. About fifteen per cent of the membership are over fifty years of age and only about five per cent under twenty years. Perhaps most of the church members co-operate in church services and fifty per cent are willing to lead prayers. From two to four church papers are read in each congregation. Although superficial in many respects, such papers are well conducted on the whole and are enthusiastic in their reports and suggestions. Each church has from two to six church societies and benevolent associations of which the women constitute the greater part of the membership. The churches pay their pastors an average salary of $469.00 a year, with such other assistance and hospitality as he may receive. The highest formal salary paid any pastor was $900.00. The churches pay liberally toward general collections and are assessed for missions and other items an average of seventy-eight dollars; some were assessed from three to four hundred dollars.

Religious services and church activities mean much to the Negro. The question has been raised whether the Lodge is not supplanting the Church in a marked degree and hindering its work. Many colored preachers openly hold that the Lodge is coming to be an evil because of its interference with the work of the Church. Of this something will be said subsequently. However this may be, it still remains that the negroes have many church services, and that they are often well attended. The regular church services are: preaching in the morning and evening, Sunday-school, class meetings, prayer-meetings, business meetings, together with the meetings of the missionary societies and benefit associations. To these must be added protracted meetings and church conventions or conferences. There are also, in connection with the churches, funerals and public baptizings, which are also well attended. The Sunday-schools are for the most part conducted in the morning before preaching.[1] The church societies, the membership of which is chiefly women, meet in the afternoons.

The average attendance at Sunday-school is not large, being perhaps one-fifth of the total church membership. The attendance at the morning preaching is good; most negroes attend church on Sunday, though many, instead of going to church, visit their friends in which cases they do not " dress up ". The morning service at the church is conducted along the usual lines according to denomination and local custom. In those churches where regular choirs are provided, special music is rendered, and the congregation does not take a prominent part in the singing; where less effort is made to procure special music, appointed leaders

---

[1] This is apparently well suited to the afternoon plans of the negroes; it leaves the afternoon free for strolling, sitting around uptown or elsewhere. It also assists in gathering the morning congregation, which is ordinarily slow.

conduct the singing, and the congregation joins in all the songs. The worship is prolonged to a later hour than among the whites. The best attendance upon church exercises is at the evening sermon. Before the time arrives for the services to begin, small groups gather at near-by houses, often at the parsonage; other groups, composed of only men, gather around the church. They talk here at length until the church has been lighted, and a few have begun the preliminaries with singing. The groups then begin to wend their way toward the church; those about the doors begin to enter and the congregation is thus made up rapidly. However, stragglers come in and go out of the building at intervals during the entire service. The preaching begins twenty to forty minutes later than in the white churches. The order of service is: Singing, prayer—many songs and a number of prayers,—the reading of the scripture lesson, and sermon by the preacher, prayer and singing, collection, benediction. The singing is usually begun by lay-leaders who conduct the prayer and song service; this gives opportunity for a larger number of members to take an active part in the worship. After the preliminaries the pastor takes charge of the service until the sermon is finished; he generally turns the remaining part of the meeting over to one of the leaders who is sitting by him on the rostrum. Sometimes, however, the preacher himself continues through the meeting, and where special collections are to be made, he announces the purpose for which the collection is made and urges the full payment. Many announcements of a general nature, too, are made at the close of the service. The benediction is pronounced with much unction and the negroes are off.

The weekly prayer-meetings are held on Tuesday, Wednesday, Thursday or Friday night; the effort is made not to have the meetings of the different churches conflict.[1] Church services begin at eight or eight-thirty o'clock in summer—earlier in winter; the hour is placed late in order that any whose duties keep them may attend. However, the attendance at prayer-meeting is not large, varying in the different churches, the average being from five to twenty-five. This attendance is smaller than formerly, owing partly to the fact that some of the lodges meet at the same time. As a rule, men are in the majority at the mid-week meetings; most of the older men attend. The pastor is not always present at the prayer-meeting, though it is his custom to attend. Sometimes he conducts the service or makes a talk. More generally the service is conducted by an appointed leader; the hour is spent in singing and praying and talks from the members present; the service is an impressive one. The leader " lines " each song and all respond in the singing; at those services where only a few are present, the leader calls on each one for prayer, and it often happens that every person present, man and woman, has led in prayer before the service is concluded; some have prayed more than once. Their prayers are very appropriate for the occasion. There is no hurry, and the meeting extends to a late hour; often a group of five or ten remain singing, praying, and talking until eleven o'clock; after service they ask after each other's " folks ". In some localities the prayer meeting is well attended and often takes the form of a revival, but conducted on the general lines mentioned.

[1] The negroes almost invariably leave their own churches if unusual attractions are going on at a neighboring church; the chief drawing card being that of the protracted meeting in its advanced stages. A Baptist preacher remarked dryly, but with a touch of humor, to the handful gathered: " Well, we couldn't expect many to be here tonight; the big meeting over at the A. M. E. and a presiding elder at the C. M. E."

Those churches which hold regular class meetings have additional features of worship. The preliminaries to these meetings are very similar to those mentioned; sometimes the choir practices songs for the Sunday morning worship. As a rule the class meetings are well attended; old and young attend, with slightly more women than men. An appointed leader conducts the devotional exercises in which he reads a passage from the Bible and makes a short talk. After the devotional exercises the leaders take charge of their classes, the number of classes varying from five to twenty according to the membership of the church. Such classes occupy sections in various parts of the church; those occupying seats in a section belong respectively to the class numbered for that section, though it is customary for the classes to have a certain number of regular members. Not infrequently the leaders are absent and others must be appointed to take their places; these leaders are chosen from among the best church members: as a rule they are good " workers " in the church. The leader of a class is accustomed to approach members of his division and ascertain by questioning what is the spiritual condition of each; the method is effective. After talking for a short while the leader takes the hand of the one to whom he is talking and continues his interrogation until he is satisfied with the response given. He talks of the soul's salvation; he warns and instructs; he often pleads—it is his personal work. Here, too, the negroes ask for prayer and guidance to the " Solid Rock ", and exchange experiences. No sooner does a newcomer enter the building than he is approached by one of the leaders, who immediately engages him in conversation. The young fellows often smile when first approached; but the leader is not at all taken aback. Soon the youngsters are seen to become restless and a more serious expression comes over their faces; and so anxious are they to escape so direct an appeal that they often give the desired assurance to the leader, who threatens that God will punish them in this world and in the world to come. Such results are not without their wholesome effect. While all this is going on in the various parts of the church, some of those who are not actively engaged in the work keep up the singing, so that the personal work may be done more effectively. Sometimes after the leaders are through with their classes, they exchange experiences; "happy" times often follow. The secretary then calls for reports from the various classes, including reports of the number present and the collection taken. The total report by classes is then read. The collections are usually creditable. When the report is finished they sing a song or two and are dismissed. Though there is much form and superficiality of expression in the class meeting, permanent results are apparently achieved.

The four general subjects under which worship and church services among the negroes may further be described are: Songs and music, prayers, preaching, and collections. Of the negro church songs a part are selected from the regular denominational song books, not unlike those sung by white congregations, and a part are more or less peculiarly adapted to the negroes. Many of the latter consist of a general mingling of the words and music of several songs; some are local in their origin and usage. The negro-folk-songs and spirituals are still popular for church music. Both the singing of the songs and the matter contained in the stanzas are significant. In addition to the tune in which the songs are written, the Negro always puts his own music into the singing, and his own interpretation into the words. This together with the " feeling-attitude " which is unconsciously his, and the satisfaction which he obtains from the singing of his songs, puts church music among the negroes into a class of its own.

Church services are opened with song; a leader will occupy his place at a central table or chair, select a song, and
begin to sing. Others join in, and the crowd begins to
gather. This leader usually lines each hymn aloud, reading
two lines, then singing. By " lining " the songs is meant
the careful reading of the lines, so that the audience may
get the words and join in the singing. With the negroes
this is naturally a favorite method. The leader often puts
as much " music-appeal " into the reading of the songs as
he does in his singing and praying. The rhythmical, swinging reading adds zest to the singing which is to follow, and
secures co-operation, not only from those who have books
and can read, but also from others who catch up the lines.
Most of the negroes who take part in the regular services
know all the common hymns, provided they are given a start
by the leader. At prayer-meeting, the leader continues
lining the songs throughout the service; at preaching the
preacher reads the regular hymns, while the leaders start the
singing. In the class meetings, while the leaders are engaged with their classes, now a woman on this side, now a
man or woman on the other begins the song, and others
join in; the singing is conducted similarly while collections
are being made. The process is the same with all—a leader
begins to sing—another joins in—then another and another
—until gradually all are singing. A much greater percentage of negroes who attend church sing than among the
white people; there are however many negroes who do not
sing regularly; this is not because they can not sing the
songs but rather because they are not disposed to take part
in the singing, preferring rather to remain quiet. The
negroes are proverbial for their good singing.[1] A group

[1] See *American Journal of Religious Psychology and Education,* vol.
3, p. 277 *seq.*

of five negroes singing in a church will produce a volume of song which would appear on the outside to be the equivalent of thirty or forty voices in a white church. One can hardly appreciate the singing of the negroes at church until he has heard on a quiet Sunday evening from some position, say on a hill, the singing of four negro congregations, each clearly audible. It would appear to be the unrestrained outburst of ten thousand souls, or the rhythmical expression of deep human longing and feeling. Inside the church, one may watch the leaders as they line the hymns, and listen to their rich, tremulous voices; he may see the others respond and hear the music of each peculiar voice. The leader's voice apparently betrays great emotion as he reads the lines, and as he begins to sing. He appears literally to drink-in the inspiration from these songs, and his soul seems to be filled to overflowing as he sings the words telling of grace and redemption. However, he manifests the same emotion when he sings one song as he does when he sings another; the same emotion when he reads the words wrongly as when he has read them correctly; it makes little difference to him. He is consumed with the music and the state of feeling which singing brings to him. He enjoys singing to the fullest extent; and after all, perhaps one feeling dominates his whole being, and there can be no song to him which does not accord with this.

A full analysis of the music of negro church singing in its details would be worthy of the efforts of anyone who could describe it. A few details apparently characteristic in his sacred music may be noted: The singing begins slowly and with time-honored regularity; the effect made by voices joining in successively is agreeable. With tenor and bass and varied voices, the chorus-like song is pleasing and satisfying. Many times the singers begin as if they would sing the simple tune to which the song is written. But in a short

time, apparently unable to resist the impulse to give their
feelings full sway, their voices fall into that rhythmical
swing peculiar to the negroes, and all measures alike become
stately.   They continue in this strain until the song is finished.   Most negroes are proud of a good choir because it
represents a step toward a model which they seek to follow;
but they do not like the choir's singing so well as they love
their own.   The Negro's song will characterize his natural
self wherever he hears it sung or himself sings; he is loath
to give it up.   Many pastors affirm that so far as they know
not a single member of their congregation refuses to sing.
Observation, however, shows that many of the younger
negroes do not take part in the religious songs; many who
sing do not appear to enter fully into the spirit of the old-
time singing.   There are, however, many individual young
negroes who enter heartily into all the services, the singing
especially; their singing mingled with that of the older
ones adds greatly to the total effect.

The pastors do not seem to agree as to the favorite songs
sung by the negroes in their worship.   Inquiry elsewhere,
and observations show that there are a number of favorites
which are regularly sung, and that favorite themes are common, mostly noticeable in the prayer-meetings and evening
services.   One may attend week after week and hear the
same songs; the negroes know these and love to sing them.
As of old they enjoy singing of Heaven and rest where
luxury and ease abound and where Sabbaths have no end.
They love to sing the praises of the Deliverer who shall free
them from life's toils; they have learned the " good old "
songs and have placed new feeling into them and a different
interpretation.   The meaning of the words and the sentiment of the songs are transcended by the expression in the
singing.   The accustomed manner together with the responsive feeling absorb whatever attitude of pure devotion

might exist. Of the hymns, the songs, " There is a Fountain Filled with Blood ", " How Sweet the Name of Jesus Sounds in a Believer's Ear ", " Show Pity, Lord, O Lord Forgive ", " O for a Thousand Tongues to Sing my Great Redeemer's Praise ", and the others, may be heard; others not so common are sung as favorites for the simple reason that these folks have learned to sing and love them. The Negro looks always to some future state for happiness, and sings with peculiar faith the common lines: " We've seen our foes before us flee ", " We've seen the timid lose their fears ", " We've seen the prisoners burst their chains ", " We've seen the guilty lose their stains ". Likewise they sing of an eternal rest and of a Sabbath that " ne'er shall end ". Such songs appeal to the Negro's idea of the fitness of worship and accord, as well, with the ideal of rhythmical perfection expressed in music and the feeling of the worshiper.

In addition to the standard favorite hymns there are many folk-songs and spirituals which are especially pleasing and appropriate for most negro congregations. Indeed many of the old spirituals are still popular among the negroes and take the place of the church hymns. Negro preachers, in addition to the fact that they themselves enjoy such songs, take advantage of their peculiar power to sway the feelings of the negroes into accustomed channels. These are the Negro's own songs and set forth the peculiar expression of his being; they are, moreover, beautiful, childlike, simple and plaintive. Some of the old songs are sung often with little modifications; others are mixed with new and old songs, taking on new forms and meanings, but clearly the product of the negro singers.[1] Perhaps the mass of negro worshipers prefer the old songs to the hymns of

---

[1] *Op. cit., passim.*

the churches, for in them is found the truest expression of
nature and life as they are reflected in the Negro of to-
day. They are not the expression of complex life but of
simple longing. They set forth the more simple thoughts of
an imaginative and emotional worship. They magnify the
personal and spectacular in religion. They satisfy the love
of melody, crude poetry and sonorous language. Simple
thought is expressed in simple rhyming phrases. Repetition of similar thoughts and a single chorus, with simple and
pleasing music lending itself to harmonious expression, are
characteristic. The music is specially adapted to the chorus-
like singing which is produced by the informal carrying of
many parts by the singers. A single leader is often required while a swelling chorus of voices take up the refrain.
As " shoutin' sings " and " runnin' speerichils " they are
well suited to protracted meetings and " good feelin' ".
Throughout the narrative style, the inconsequential, dis-
jointed statements, the simple thought and fastidious
rhymes, the music of the songs tend to take into it the
qualities of the Negro's native expression—strains minor
and sad in general expression. With the idea gained from
the music of the songs must be joined the church scenes and
personalities freely mingled with the music. The preaching, praying, singing, shouting, swaying and the unity of
negro worship—perfection of rhythmic sing-song, together
with the throbbing impulses of the people make the negro
music what it is. Thus it happens that, for the most part,
all religious songs become spirituals and easily merge into
satisfying melodies when the occasion demands. Likewise
the negroes reach their climax in fervent outbursts alike in
all songs that lend themselves to a free expression.

Negro church music is beautiful and impressive. The
prayers uttered by negroes at church may be similarly described; moreover they are pathetic and eloquent. As the

Negro is very much of a religious being, so he appears to be specially fitted by nature and cultivation for making appeals to divine power. A large per cent of the negroes love to pray in public; some pastors testify that all will pray on most occasions when called upon, while others affirm that a majority would do so. In some of the larger towns only a small number are reported as willing leaders. It is true, at any rate, that those who are called upon, both men and women, usually respond. Passing over the well-worded and deliberate utterances of a few more modern preachers and leaders, the prayer which is common to the great mass of negro churchmen — the natural prayer — may be described. Such prayers are ordinarily appropriate and earnest; the manner is full of appeal and reverence. They are, for the most part, well worded and uttered; there is seldom hesitancy and faltering in the negro prayer. Nowhere is the rich voice of the black man more manifest than in the pathetic tone in which he utters his appeals. It would appear to be the voice of a penitent child and grateful servant crying out to the Father and Master in a darkness penetrated only by a single ray of light. However, the same tremor and pathetic eloquence is heard in a slight petition as in a more sorrowful invocation. Again the one attitude is made up of an expectant manner and general feeling.

Reduced to its particulars the negro's prayer is very formal. There are three general parts, and two general tones are noticeable as a characteristic utterance. The manner and tone of the first and third parts are the same; the first part is the introduction and consists of chosen phrases uttered in a low and deliberate tone. The second part consists of the rising fervor and climax, in which part is the body of the prayer. This is uttered sometimes in tones of most pathetic appeal; sometimes the voice of the speaker trembles as if he were too full of emotional con-

flicts for further utterance. Sometimes—often—the words
are beautifully eloquent. More often the body of the
prayer is a mean between two extremes—musical and rhythmical, it yet has the typical swing. The third part, which
is the close of the petition, is an abrupt change of voice.
There is no falling action to the negro prayer; from highly
pathetic appeal to calm and deliberate utterance, the prayer
is changed as quickly as the voice can possibly be altered.
The effect is impressive. A characteristic of these prayers
is the frequent repetition of some appellation of the Divinity;
of such expressions the negroes have many. The petitions,
too, are many; they pray for those who are absent from service, and for those who are " away in foreign lands ", by
which is often meant in a neighboring town or county or
state; they pray for " sinners ", for " gamblers ", for
" drunkards ", and for " dancin' women ". They pray, too,
for the sick, the widows and the orphans. There is much
repetition in their prayers. The special features and characteristics of the negro prayer are illustrated by the examples given below. The body of the prayer, which is in-
toned, is written in italics. The first and last of the prayer
are uttered in the most impressive and deliberate manner
which the negro can command with slow and subdued tones.

" O Lord, to night our Fadder, we thank thee for the privileges which thou has promised us to engage in this hour
for the express purpose of having us to worship thee with
reverent prayer. *Most holy Fadder*, besides thee we know
no other name whereby we can be saved. *Most holy God,
our Fadder, our Fadder, you have said in yo' most holy
an' written word that where one or two or three o' yo'
believin' servants come togedder you would be in de midst
of yo' chilluns. And Oh, Oh, Jesus, we ask you to come
into this little 'sembly an' endow us with thy spirit. We'se
but frail creatures an' evil; we doan feel worthy o' callin'*

on you to night, our heavenly Father, we doan feel worthy o' callin' on thee, but we ask you to night to come into our midst. O Lord, bless them that's not here, hover 'round them the arm o' protection. We ask you to bless the sinner to night an' the gambler an' we ask you to bless the dancin' women. We thank thee to night, our Fadder, that las' night we did not lay down on de bed o' death an' wake up this mornin' in the mornin' o' judgment. O my Lord, wouldst thou be pleased to remind me that tomorrow the sun may rise on my grave. An' O Lord wouldst thou be pleased to bless yo' servant to night who's been waitin' so long. Oh, oh, my Lord, thou divine an' heavenly Father, God of the world an' tender love, please hear yo' servant to night. Oh, oh, my Lord, sometimes we try to weep but we can't weep; come down to night an' weep wid us; O Lord, to night, our Fadder, sometimes we try to sing an' we can't sing; come down to night, our Fadder, an sing wid us——

"Now, our Fadder, when we done toilin', when we done meetin', when we done minglin' here, when we don't 'tend no mo' meetin's, when we'se done comin' to dis ole church—save our souls is the petition of yo' humble servant, for Chris' sake—Amen."

The word music of parts of the prayer is given on page 71; to the tones of the notes must be added the peculiarities of each voice and the rhythmical pathos expressed.

RECITATIVE.

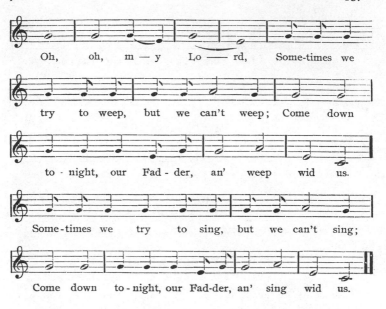

Oh, oh, m — y Lo — rd, Some-times we

try to weep, but we can't weep; Come down

to - night, our Fad - der, an' weep wid us.

Some - times we try to sing, but we can't sing;

Come down to - night, our Fad-der, an' sing wid us.

A woman prayed in most pathetic tones: " *Oh oh—Lord, to night, bless the basterin' child, wherever he is; Oh—oh —Lord, bless my mother's children scattered in foreign lands; Oh—oh—Lord, bless my sister's children to night. Oh—oh—Lord, you knows my heart an' you knows I wants to do right; Oh—oh—my Lord, my spirit's strong but my flesh is weak—Oh—oh—Lord, give me clean hands an' clean heart, an' Oh—oh—Lord, you has blessed me befo' when I prayed an' you has promised to bless me ag'in if I come in de right spirit, an' Oh—oh—Lord, to night bless me; an' you has promised to have mercy on yo' chilluns an' it does seem like we need mercy over the lan' to night. . . ."* A more pathetic appeal can scarcely be imagined; so are the majority of the prayers commonly heard at the prayer meetings.

The Negro also utters prayers which have less of the

plaintive appeal in them; they are less eloquent, though the
negroes call them " eloquent " prayers. They are more
declamatory and are uttered with much satisfaction. In
all the negro prayers, the audience enters into the spirit of
the occasion; while the leader is praying, many others assist
by their fervent sanctions. In the prayers, as in the sermons, there are many " amens " uttered by both men and
women. To each sentence, petition or marked utterance,
there are many cries of *amen, grant it Lord, Lord help us,*
and the like. Together with the prayer they assist in making rhythmic harmony. Sometimes, after the leader has
finished his prayer, he begins a song and all remain kneeling
or bowed while they chant the melody or tune in a low
monotone-like manner. With lips closed they hum the
tune most effectively; with its rise and fall the chant adds to
the perfection of rhythmical feeling and is most beautiful in
itself.

The negroes are good preachers. The majority of the
older negroes, and many of the younger ones are able ex-
pounders of moral rights and wrongs. It is not surprising
that there are many " exhorters " and local preachers among
them, nor that their preachers preach with great vigor.
Many of the sermons preached by the negroes are good, giving out wholesome advice. Many are severe in their denunciation of sin and crime; many preachers are understood by their hearers to speak in a more or less incendiary vein. But there is less concern at this point with the
matter of the sermon than with the methods used by the
preachers and the manner of delivery, with the part the sermon plays in the unit of negro worship. The college-
trained preachers deliver many of their sermons, for the
most part, after the manner of the ordinary white preacher;
they often strive to effect a similar delivery. Such sermons are not infrequently appropriated, in part or alto-

gether from written sermons. Such negro preachers are
very graceful in the pulpit and bestow great pains upon the
manner in which they are to deliver their sermons. Except during protracted meetings, and on special occasions,
their manner of preaching is not unlike that of the average
speaker, except that matter is made subordinate to manner,
There are many attempts at humor, most of which are successful in their way; the negroes laugh at every opportunity. Many of the preachers, too, are eloquent speakers.

But the average preacher conforms to no rules other than
those of natural impulse and time-honored custom. Should
he memorize a sermon and attempt to deliver it in a deliberate manner, he would find such a difficult feat. After the
prayers and songs, he too is in a state of fervor and in
most cases he abandons the set phrases and turns into
his own line of thought and expression. It thus happens
that the average sermon preached to the negroes has a pleasing effect upon the congregation and receives a hearty response. In fact, the sermon would be expected to conform
to the songs and prayers as a logical sequence. Such must
be the case in order to meet the demands of the congregation
and to satisfy the preacher's own inclination. The sermon
is composed of two general parts: the deliberate utterance,
and the swinging, rhythmic delivery and climax. The manner of the first part characterizes the beginning of the sermon; the preacher announces his text, begins his discourse,
and gradually rises to the personal appeal. The second part
embodies the greater part of the sermon; in this the preacher
reaches the climax in "true poetic height", and in regular
sing-song, he approaches musical recitative. Again, in the
opening words of each topical division, the deliberate manner is used; while in the climax of each division he reaches
the same height of sing-song. Sometimes the words are in-
distinct, and the attention of both speaker and hearers is

absorbed in the " preachin' ". Sometimes with rhythm of words and swaying of body the preacher holds his audience spell-bound, while they in turn lean forward, sometimes rocking to and fro to the time of the preacher's voice. They agree with everything the preacher says without pausing to ascertain the truth of his utterance. He often repeats a part of his sermon a number of times, the audience nodding their approval and uttering shouts of assent with growing enthusiasm. The negro preacher receives a respectful hearing, and his audience is always responsive. While he proclaims the words of his message there may be heard on all sides cries of: " Talk to 'em, preacher ", " Great God ", " Ha, Ha ", " You're right, brother ", " Yes? ", " Yes— yes ", " Preachin' ", " Preachin', now ", " Now you're preachin' ' ", " Talk about it ", " Talkin' ", " Holy Lord ", " Truth ", " God grant it ", " Good Lord, that's right ", " Lord help us ", " Preach de word ", " Dat's so ", "Amen ", " ain't de Lawd a-talkin' ", and many others. Mingled with such exclamations are frequent grunts, the sound of which could scarcely be reproduced; it would be recognized as "huh" pronounced with a nasal twang, now low, now high. The exclamations may be heard whether an old-time preacher occupies the pulpit, or a more modern one, or even a white minister. Negro preachers do not discourage this, but on the contrary they often defend it, saying that they " b'lieve in advertisin' religion when you've got it ". The exclamations increase as the fervor of the preacher rises; the utterance of these exclamations is very satisfying and greatly assists the preacher. Such responsive exclamations serve to complete the current of rhythm when the preacher must pause, or to stress those rising notes which his own voice emphasizes.[1]

---

[1] If we wish to balance the two factors, we may place the tones of

The characteristic tones of the sing-song heard in the preaching and the expressions of responses uttered by the " lay " members are almost reproducible in musical notation. An example of a common type of sermon heard among the negroes is given below. The preacher was a graduate of one of the colored theological colleges; in his sermon to a large audience, he began with a very dignified manner and made a most favorable impression upon his hearers. One would think that he is going to avoid the old-time style; but it will be seen that he reaches a high poetic pitch, though slightly different from the extreme sing-song and dramatic utterances of the more primitive negro preacher. He is arrayed in a black robe and as he speaks of the " wings of the morning " he uses his arms with the flowing sleeves for splendid effect; this pleases both the audience and himself, for he repeats the gesture with satisfaction. The sermon is supplemented richly with the shouts of "amen." The musical notation of sermon and exclamations follows.

the preacher on one side and the exclamations of response from the audience on the other. Or again, if we liken the sing-song to a series of metrical verses in which each verse has one or more caesural pauses and the end of each line is catalectic or incomplete, the exclamations may be said to occupy the time taken up by the pauses and to rhythmically connect each line or verse without loss of continuity, time or harmony. Were the metrical scheme completed, other exclamations would serve as stress or ictus in ascending and descending measures. Thus neither is complete without the other—still they must and do go on at the same time. Though monotonous, and to some extent almost unbearable to some sensitive ears, after the first few times of hearing it, such worship is nevertheless an almost perfect harmony of rhythm.

RECITATIVE.

Yes, my breth-er-in, we've been troub-led with the sin-ner

long e-nuf; then at the great Judg-ment day, we'll

see them all sent off to hell and there'll be re-joic-in'

for we won't be troub-led with them an-y

mo'; We've prayed for 'em an' we talked with 'em an' now we

won't be both-er-ed with them an-y mo'. Oh, with the

wings of the morn-ing, I'd fly to that heav'n-ly home.

Preachin'.   Yes, my Lo-rd.   Yes, yes.

Ha, ha.

At the close of a service in which there had been a number of penitents at the altar, an officer who had been sitting on the rostrum came to the front, and with his broadest grin and most polite manner, said: " The Lawd's done been here, I knows he has "; and he added, " done come an' gone away an' now we wants to get down to business—I wants some money." In this action he characterized his church more than he was aware. For, as a rule, the collection occupies the most important place in the total of church activities. Collections made by negroes are marvels; they represent a great part of the strivings of negro church members; it is not surprising that they represent much satisfaction. The church collections fall into two general divisions: those taken in the church itself at regular services, and those made outside by means of various methods. The collections made at class meetings have been mentioned; in a similar manner they take collections at Sunday-school. Other methods may be described.

No church has been found which does not use the "table" way of taking up collections in the church. This method is used for raising money for incidentals, and all miscellaneous collections called for from time to time. A table is placed in the front part of the church; after the other exercises are over a secretary and " counter " take their places by the table. The leader announces at length the purpose for which the collection is being made. One by one the negroes bring their contributions and place them on the table. They do not hurry; they do not come in groups. One would judge at the beginning of such a collection that no one would respond, and that the collection would be a complete failure. While this delay is going on, the preacher or leader urges his cause effectively, and others sing. Presently one will bring a small coin, place it on the table, and return to his place. Then another, and an-

other—until several dollars have been received. A single
individual will often " go up " six or seven times during one
collection, giving a nickel each time. Negroes usually give
the last cent they have with them. The men often give their
coins to the women who in turn carry them forward as their
contribution. The women enjoy this, and the young fellows vie with each other in furnishing their favorites with
money. The husband must furnish his wife as much as he
can obtain; much more than he can afford. Negro women
have been known to spend half the wages of the husband
in contributions to the church and various societies. It is
the woman's great desire to appear to give more than any
one else. The negroes love to display their finery before
the congregation; it thus happens that a negro will have a
quarter dollar changed into nickels and give it in this form.
Apparently they all have a mania for handling money in
small pieces. It is thus that their money is raised and the
amounts raised are surprisingly large. The time occupied
in taking these collections varies from thirty minutes to an
hour and a half. The ease and grace with which the
speaker urges more money is a part of the exercise; flattery
and pleasing speeches are scarcely to be surpassed. The negroes look forward from week to week to the collection and
direct their labors and savings to this end. Young negroes aften seek work for a few hours in order that they
may get money for this purpose, after which they may not
be persuaded to work again. Some negroes have urged
that the table way of taking all common collections ought
to be discontinued; but such a question has not become
an issue. A class-leader's remark fell with little effect
when he said: " The Lord ain't pleased with our collection.
We ought to bring our contributions to the class meetin'
and give them quietly; but my people wants to walk up here
Sunday an' show off theirselves—anyway we makes mo'

contributions to the devil than we does to the church of the Good Lord." Many admit that they would prefer other methods to be used but to stop the table way would mean absolute failure in meeting assessments and demands for money.

To raise money for building and repairing churches, and for general and miscellaneous purposes, where larger amounts are wanted, the negroes have many methods. The banquet, torch-light supper, box supper, feast and reception, are described elsewhere.[1] Such entertainments are always successful in that they succeed in raising money. The average negro will not be without the price of admission if he can get the money—which he generally does. Concerts, too, are frequent, in which many take part—reading, reciting or singing, purely under the auspices of the church; after the program is finished they serve refreshments. Musical and literary entertainments are given as often as a program can be arranged. If an unusually good one is to be given, circulars are scattered over the town and tickets circulated among the people. On the circular, tickets, and printed programs full announcement will be made, with exaggerated enthusiasm.

This brings the crowd, and the entertainment is often a worthy one. Many seek to enjoy the program from the outside. Perhaps the windows have been closed and the house crowded. After the exercises, the preacher may announce that he regrets that the room has been so warm but " we wanted all we paid for and we didn't want those who did not pay to get any, and anyway, just in a moment you can all get to the ice box and cool off." This has the desired effect, and when the ices are served the crowd buys liberally, remaining late in the evening. It is a great so-

[1] See Chapter VI.

cial event, but it is not uncommon for the negroes to clear more than a hundred dollars at such an entertainment. They look forward with much anticipation to the coming of such a concert. Their attitude toward such occasions is well illustrated by the excuses given by some negro women who refused to work during the day preceding the concert, saying: "I wants to git ready for the musical; I wants my money's wuth, I does."

When larger amounts are to be raised still other methods are devised. A favorite method will be described: Clubs are organized having captains at the head of each, who solicit money from all sources; each captain in turn appoints subworkers and seeks the honor of reporting the largest amount at the final counting. Individuals then solicit funds not only from the negroes but from the whites; they report to their favorite captain. Cards are gotten out for distribution among the workers. An example:

Club No..... Mrs. ....Captain
M ....is authorized
to solicit funds for the Bethlehem Baptist Church
Ralley to be returned th 5th Sunday June 30th 1907
Please help us God will bless the cheerful giver

---

5 5 5 5 5 5 5 5 5 5 5 5 5 5 5 5 5 5 5 5 5 5 5
5 5 5 5 5 5 5 5 5 5 5 5 5 5 5 5 5 5 5 5 5 5 5
10 10 10 10 10 10 10 10 10 10 10 10 10 10 10 10 10
10 10 10 10 10 10 10 10 10 10 10 10 10 10 10 10 10
25 25 25 25 25 25 25 25 25 25 25 25 25 25 25 25
50 50 50 50 50 50 50 50 50 50 50 50 50 100 100 100

A. D. SMITH, *Pastor*

The amount given is checked off on the card and when the

first card has been exhausted, another is taken. Thus each individual co-worker has his or her name and the amount obtained handed in, while the captain reports her total amount by cards. The above card was used by the congregation of a Baptist church having less than two hundred members; they raised in a short time seven hundred and fifty dollars.

One other method may be mentioned; this illustrates well an underlying principle and spirit of giving among the negroes. A representative from one of the church colleges recently preached from town to town, speaking to large audiences. Before closing his services he announced that a special collection would be made at a specified time—" three weeks from to-day." He announced further that their college had now paid every cent of its mortgage, a copy of which he had in his possession. He would present this mortgage to that person who should bring the largest amount of money at the stated time. This person is to burn the mortgage in the presence of many people. He adds: " Be a hero among your people; let's see now who will get this mortgage and destroy it and thus go down in history as a hero to your people."

It will be seen that all church functions and services are agreeable to the negro's nature. The church satisfies as much as anything else his social wants, and relieves his psycho-physical cravings. His worship is music to his soul, whether it be in the word-music of prayers and sermon, or in the natural music of his song, or in the rhythm of all combined. It is all freedom from restraint, and the gratification of impulse, and the experience of sustained languor. Although the Negro expends a great deal of energy in his religious devotions, it is nevertheless resting to him. He appears to manifest the same tendency and principle as one who is tired, or grieved, and finds no relief so immediate as giving way to feeling, loud singing, or crying out; or as one of weak mind constantly whistles or sings regardless of words or tune. What the negro thinks to be total confession and contrite submission has a very soothing effect upon him; the songs are even more satisfying to his nature. Many older negroes may be seen with heads resting backward—sometimes forward—and their eyes closed as they sing vigorously their favorite songs. Their senses are all turned toward the perception of one attitude, and besides a wonderful tranquillity of feeling, they also see visions. The Negro is at ease and can give expression to his feelings among his fellows without hindrance and interruption, and without incentive to action. Is it surprising, then, that after a day's hard work, while he has passed the hours away in emptiness or misguided thinking or perverted notions, that he finds sweet rest in some melodious songs and rhythmic verses as he rests his body in the pew? Is it surprising that he does not want to leave until a late hour, when he has little to attract him to his home, where he must begin again to think of work which is disagreeable to him? Is it to be expected of him that he would desire to hasten when he can stay here in the crowd and listen to songs and sing, hear and offer petitions in which he feels some kind of communion with the mysterious? Likewise it is little surprising that the attitude of the negroes is often one of listless apathy when they have finished their worship.

The protracted meetings of the negroes, church conferences, and baptizings are yet to be mentioned. No attempt will be made to describe them in every particular. The revival services held during the protracted meeting may be said to be a series of meetings like those already mentioned, except that they are carried to a greater extreme. There is more preaching, more praying, and more singing, and with it all more shouting and perfect unity of negro worship —perfection of rhythmic sing-song as it is found in the re-

ligious services of the negroes. There are many altar services; " propositions " are popular—at least they are numerous—among the colored people, though they do not always
easily respond to an appeal. At the altar there is much
manifestation of concern, though it is doubtful if there
is much of real salvation. At these meetings, too, there
is much shouting during which those who have become
" happy " must be " held down." This is done in various
ways, for instance, by one negro standing directly in front
of the one who is shouting and placing his hands firmly upon
his shoulders. He thus holds him as he attempts to jump
up; presently one will see the spectacle of two jumping instead of one—first the one leaping into the air, then the
other, both shouting all the while. Other manifestations
are evident; crying, laughing, and general exuberance are
accompanied by general movements of the body.[1] Many
negroes testify that not infrequently these occasions are
used for personal abuse by those who are evil-minded, or
those who have " malice in their hearts ". It may take the
form of slapping or running into each other violently; in
the case of women, " accidentally " using a hat pin or sitting on the new hat of a " sister ". No attempt will be
made to describe their trances, though there is much of
reality in them to the negroes.[2] The penitents are not al-

[1] One may observe a negro congregation thus wrought up with some
satisfaction from a distance, provided the windows be raised. Men
and women move to and fro, their bodies swaying backward and
forward; arms are seen waving, and with all this comes the rhythm of
sound—songs, shouts, and preaching. Inside the observer notices more
of the individual performances.

[2] The nature of the " trance " may be indicated by the use of extreme
examples: During a meeting of much fervor, a woman is smitten
down and suddenly topples over on the floor, apparently unconscious. Nothing the negroes do will restore her and she must bide
her time—usually from twelve to twenty hours. Another woman

ways converted during the church service; many times the
" spirit comes upon them " wherever they may be, at work
or variously occupied—in either case they begin to shout,
and all who are in hearing distance and who can possibly
get off come running to hear the " experience ".   The
preachers, too, take prominent parts in such meetings.   They
encourage undue manifestations and go to various extremes;
they often profess great power and revelation.[1]   Some of
the preachers are sincere in their misinterpretation of the
scriptures; many are not.   During these " big meetins' "
services sometimes begin at daybreak and continue through
the day and in the evening till midnight; the same is sometimes true of the church conventions.   One who lives near
a church in which such meetings are being held will often
wake up in the morning at the sound of the negroes singing;
and the last sound which he hears at night will be the songs
of these same singers.   The meetings are well attended and

suddenly leaped into the air and rushed out of the building; after
searching for some time she was found in a ditch in a nearby grove,
apparently unconscious.

[1] Recently during one of the great negro revivals in a small town,
the report became current that the preacher and some who had been
converted had received the gift of tongues and could speak the message of the spirit in many languages and could commune directly with
God. This report was generally believed by the negroes. Investigations brought out these facts: The preacher would begin his sermon
as usual, but would presently raise his eyes heavenward and begin in
gutteral tones something like this: Lub-dub-a-bub-a-gud-a-lub, etc.
This inspired great awe throughout the congregation and he was drawing great numbers. Further inquiries into the life of the negro
preacher proved that his allies were instructed in the business; the
preacher had already amassed considerable property by his own
methods; he had just built a fine church in the town. He received this
latest " revelation " in California where he had attended some meetings. A few years previous the same negro had preached the easily
received doctrine that it was no harm to " pick up " anything one
wanted, for it was not stealing.

here may be seen many " distinguished " looking negroes.
The delegates and preachers are well dressed and talk and
walk with much dignity.   As many as can do so speak at
the meetings; they have at the night services many " big "
sermons preached by a divine " who can speak in seven languages ", who has " traveled all over the world ", or who
is a D. D.   The communities show much cordiality to the
visitors and all enjoy life for the week.   The welcome addresses read on these occasions are elaborate, but reflect
much of the negroes' disposition.[1]

The negroes flock in large numbers to witness the public baptizings, whether few or many are to be immersed.
They prefer the stream or pond of water, and use artificial
pools rarely.   They desire to be baptized " like Christ was
baptized " after which the " spirit comes upon " them.   The
applicants for baptism are assembled; the preacher is ready
and leads the first one into the water.   To one who has
not witnessed these cermonies, the question will arise as to
why several attendants wade out with the participants.   One
is not kept in doubt long, however, for as soon as the candidate has been immersed, he or she begins to struggle,
beating the water right and left, and four men are kept busy
holding the newly inspired applicant.   It is understood that
each one is to have a similar experience, though all are not
effected in so extreme a manner.

Any comment on the religious views and moral code of
the negroes must begin with mention of the negro preacher;
he is perhaps responsible for much of present conditions.
The greatest need of the church seems to be for preachers
whose lives do not give the lie to their teachings, and who

---

[1] In a long welcome address read by a young negro woman were
these words: " We welcome you to our humble homes, our tables, our
beds, and to our cool shades and to our watermelons."   And they were
all welcome.

realize something of the responsibility resting upon them.
As a rule the average pastor does not begin to grasp the
situation nor recognize the crying needs of his people.   The
majority of negro preachers are superficial in their work and
in their reports; they suspect any attempt of the white man
to assist them, and consequently they give the most un-
reasonably unsatisfactory responses to requests for co-operation.   They are unwilling to properly co-operate with any
who would study conditions, and their statements are often
farther from the truth than those made by any other class
of negroes.   This is a hard saying, and it is gratifying to
note that there are notable exceptions to the rule.   Many
do not think of their work in any other phases than the material; if asked to mention the most vital need of the Church,
they answer in regard to the various needs of the building.
The pastor who answered, " Money, money, money, money,
money," was typical of many who seem so utterly unable to
get away from the standpoint of big things that they fail to
do the little things.   They will not commonly give information concerning the ordinary facts that are vital to
the welfare of their church.   Among the negroes there is
much respect for all that the minister says in public and
private; his actions are sanctioned.   He carries with him a
sanctity frequently ill-deserved and ill-won.   His position
and grace of manner give him a complete entrance into
every home, and win for him the favor of the crowd.   It
is a great honor to that member of his flock who stands first
in his favor, and upon whom he bestows his most graceful
salutation.   He strives to please the people, and is master of the art of successful flattery among the negroes.   He
seldom cares for high principles in his life.   Many cases
of gross immorality among negro preachers have been noted,
which though of the lowest and most corrupt nature, elicit
no surprise among the negroes.   For it is not expected that

the average negro preacher will always be pure in his life; rather his position gives him freedom to do as his inclination dictates.   Open and hidden deception, the drinking of spirituous liquors, illicit relations with members of his congregation—such a state of affairs is not unusual.   The ignorance, too, of most negro preachers is appalling; many are without accurate knowledge of the simplest truths of the Bible. But it may be assumed for the time, that the notable exceptions, of which there are many, constitute the majority, and that the negro preacher only reflects one phase of the weakness of the race.

In spite of pretensions and superficiality, there is nothing so real to the negro as his religion, although it is a different " reality " from that we commonly expect in religion. The Negro is more excitable in his nature, and yields more readily to excitement than does the white man.   The more a thing excites him, the more reality it has for him.   So, too, the quality of arousing emotions, of moving or exciting him, has as much to do with his belief in a thing as does the quality of giving pleasure.   The religion of the negroes gives them much pleasure and satisfaction, they also are very much aroused in their worship.   Their belief in the reality of religion is, then, almost a natural acquirement. And although the greater part of the religion of the Negro is pleasurable excitement, it is nevertheless, perhaps on that very account, the reality of all realities to him; his faith comes in this way rather than by knowledge.   It is not surprising, then, that the Negro's religion is not one of practical application, and that a scarcity of thoughtfulness and will-power is everywhere predominant.   Although he has a ready knowledge of right and wrong, the Negro does not do the right nor condemn those who do the wrong.   The attitude of both races tends to take it for granted that all negroes may be morally unaccountable.   The question of morality does not enter into the consideration of employers, even those that hire all kinds of domestic servants; they have little knowledge of the lives of these people and put forth little effort to make them better.   So, too, among the negroes there is no social ostracism for those who are habitually guilty of gross wrongs.   There is, generally speaking, no deep conscience in the race.   The criminal instinct appears to overbalance any consciousness which makes for righteousness and the Negro has little serene consciousness of a clean record; he is ready to " run " at any surprising or suspicious turn of affairs.   The Negro does not value his word or honor; he apparently can not always tell the truth.   Only about one in every ten will keep an important engagement made in seriousness.   Honesty appeals to the ordinary negro as the best policy, but his interpretation of honesty and policy is that which permits his natural self to fittingly appropriate things not his own.

The Negro's conception of heaven and hell, God and the devil are very distinct.[1]   Heaven is an eternal resting-place where he shall occupy the best place.   He sings of his heavenly home in striking contrast to his earthly abode. Perhaps for the very reason that the negroes have little satisfactory home life, they expect to have a perfect home in the next life.   The Negro wants that which is ideal and perfect but he is unwilling to put forth efforts to receive it. In slavery days it was perhaps natural that he should look to Heaven for his home.   The same ideas intensified by the Negro's emotions and self-pity still predominate.   He expects to be with the angels and to talk and associate with God and Jesus.   There are many means of getting to Heaven, and the Negro's fancies of "Heaven's bright home" are scarcely exceeded by any fairy tales.   There are silver

---

[1] *Op. cit., passim.*

and golden slippers, crowns of stars, jewels and belts of gold.   There are robes of spotless white and wings all be-jeweled with heavenly gems.   Beyond the Jordan the Negro will outshine the sun, moon and stars.   He will slip and slide the golden streets and eat the fruit of the trees of paradise.   Not only is this home to be a happy one, but it is to be exclusive; only the most fortunate, of whom he is chiefest, will go there.   With rest and ease, with a golden band about him and with palms of victory in his hands and beautiful robes, the Negro will be indeed a happy being.

Hell is a place for thieves, sinners, drunkards and liars, but such persons are far removed from the negro individual. The Negro does not dwell upon thoughts of hell as he does of heaven.   It is a place of torment and fire, it is deep and wide.   It is the place where sinners go.   But the negroes make much of the day when God shall come to " wake up the dead who's a sleepin' in the grave."   The day of judg-ment is a terrible day, and may mean everything that could happen of death and terror at the end of the world.   But it is also the destruction of the sinner and the glory of the righteous.   The gruesome awe and terror which the Negro pictures together with the assurance that the saved shall come into their own, make the judgment scenes especially attractive to the Negro.   Nor does he hesitate to affirm that the righteous in heaven will shout amen to the sinner's dam-nation.   The sinner in hell will see his friends in heaven. While the negroes speak of the " po' sinner " and while they exhort to salvation, there is little human sympathy felt in the portrayal of the eternal punishment which the damned will receive; rather it is the glory of the righteous.

The devil is the constant terror and proverbial enemy of the Negro.   He is alive, alert and concrete.   He represents the demon trickster incarnate in man.   He is the opposite of God but much less powerful.   He is the enemy against whom a personal battle is always on. The devil meets the pilgrim at every turn of the road, but somehow he is usually outwitted. Satan howls when defeated. He throws rocks in the way of Christians, wears an iron shoe and is a busy old man. He throws a ball at the sinner, gets in a rage when he misses him, he rides iron gray horses. Satan is also a consummate liar. It is with such pictures as these that the negro sinner is warned, doomed and damned. Such warnings have little practical bearing upon the permanent thoughts of the negroes in relation to conduct, and it is always offset by the better pictures of heaven and God.

On the other hand, " King Jesus " is the bosom friend of the Negro. He comes in to intercept Satan and save the sinner-man from hell. He works wonders and miracles, takes the sinner's sins away, rides and flies, and comes to wake up the dead. He may be found in the wilderness, on the hillside and in the valley, or " settin' in de kingdom ". He buys the negro's liberty, plucks his feet from the miry clay, and raises man from the grave. He wears a snow-white robe and rides a milk-white horse. The negroes sympathize much with the Christ of the crucifixion. God is often synonymous with Jesus. He is King Jehovah and walks the heavenly road with fire and sword breathing from his mouth. The Lord listens all day long, He unlocks the prison door, He comforts sinners, He sits in Heaven and answers prayers, and He rides all the time in his chariot. The negro and God will walk and talk in the heavenly land.

To find a happy home, to see all the loved ones and especially the biblical characters, to see Jesus and the angels, to walk and talk with them, to wear robes and slippers as they do, and to rest forever constitute the chief images of the Negro's heaven. He is tired of the world which has been a hell to him. Now on his knees, now shouting, now sorrowful and now glad, the Negro comes from " hanging over hell " to die and " set by de Fadder's side ". In this life he will weep all he can for his Lord, do what he can and fight the battle in the struggle of life, in which he has a " hard time ". A sense of sin and guilt is ever present in the struggle between himself and some imaginary. But this sense of guilt is less practical than it is an expression of emotion. In all phases of the Negro's religious beliefs the emotional and imaginative transcend the practical application. His religion is essentially dependent upon feeling and the stress is placed upon the supernatural that lies beyond his present sphere. A religious attitude is scarcely conceived by the Negro aside from the fundamental conception of the next world. Thus it is that this life is contrasted with the next, the sinner contrasted with the righteous and the devil contrasted with God. The Negro is not to be censured, therefore, because the moral and ethical in his religion does not exert so strong an influence as it should; such is inevitable with a religion of this kind and among a people of the Negro's habits and temperament. He is no weaker in his religion than elsewhere; perhaps he is no stronger. It may be possible, however, to turn his religious nature into channels which will assist in leading him to a proper development of his better qualities.

The casual observer does not realize the conditions which obtain among the negroes in their worship, because he does not see them. To know real conditions one must work with these people in their churches or see them week after week as they gather to worship. Then some of the difficulties which must be overcome may be seen. The testimony of those who have thus made careful observation is expert. The most thorough and effective organized church work of this kind done by the whites among the negroes is that done in the Sunday-schools. Many well-organized schools have been conducted by white leaders and teachers among the negroes of smaller communities. The best organized and most systematic work of this kind has been under the auspices of the Presbyterian Church in the United States. The results of schools thus conducted for several years in towns in Texas, Louisiana, Mississippi, Alabama, Georgia, Florida, Tennessee, North Carolina, South Carolina, and Kentucky are here given in a general way.[1] The list of white leaders in the schools includes prominent lawyers, professors, teachers, preachers, physicians, and business men, while many private workers of the highest intellectual attainment have not only put their best efforts into the work but have also given liberally of their means. The spirit of the work is missionary; the methods " are governed by plain Southern principles ". There are now in operation a smaller number of such schools than a few years ago.

On the part of the white people at large, there has been some opposition to the work, and a general lack of faith in the outcome. There was no co-operation on the part of the negro churches, but they rather looked upon the movement with some suspicion and jealousy. There was little disposition on the part of the parents to send their children to the schools; a few individuals approved of the work. The enrollment was small at the beginning but increased to larger numbers, while the average attendance remained the same, generally speaking, after the school was fully organized. The attendance was always uncertain; in good weather in summer the attendance was likely to be small; and always

---

[1] The total number of Sunday Schools thus organized by the Presbyterian Church is twenty-eight; they enrolled 1,965 pupils and there were one hundred and ninety-two teachers. The number from which reports were made included fourteen schools. The reports were much more extensive than is here indicated; the general summary is made from the combined reports. I am indebted to Rev. W. D. Hedleston, of Oxford, Mississippi, for assistance in obtaining data for this report.

when there were protracted meetings, lodge meetings, basket dinners, funerals and other similar attractions in the neighborhood, a small attendance might be expected. In cases where the enrollment is small it often occurs that there will be no pupils present, while the next Sunday will witness the largest attendance for weeks. In the management of such schools few offices have been given to negroes, and collections were rarely taken. The attitude of those teachers who have taught faithfully for a number of years has not changed materially. Some have felt the hopelessness of the situation so far as visible results go; some have been much encouraged; all have been astounded at the prevailing ignorance with which they have to contend. The courses taught in the schools are made up from the catechisms and the Scriptures. The children are quick to memorize their lessons and appear to enjoy the Sunday-school. Many of them learn passages of scripture and the catechism easier than white children of the same age, while some are too dense of mind to learn at all. The brighter ones not only memorize well, but retain for some length of time what they have learned. The children love all music alike and appear to show no special favorites in the selection of their songs. Curious interest, habit, and " just to be together " seem to be motives for prompting attendance. Years of patient work show no visible results in the schools, though there is apparent improvement on the part of individual pupils. No change in the religious condition or improvement in the moral status can be traced to this source, and there is little visible effect upon the colored churches of the town. The negroes show no gratitude for the work done in their behalf, but think they are doing the workers a favor if they attend the school at all. They do, however, have respect for the leaders and their work. If the school should be closed in each community, there would perhaps be no effort on the

part of the negroes to get it back.   In the classes composed
of older men, there is, however, often real interest manifested from Sunday to Sunday.   The personality of the
teachers has much to do with the work in general.

These are discouraging facts; but perhaps further particulars of existing conditions, as brought out in these reports, will serve to explain them.   The negroes are ignorant of the Bible and its teachings; they do not know in practical life of the moral law, but have a vague idea that it
applies only to " white folks ".   They reflect no home training and must follow their inclinations in the crowd.   Hence
any kind of serious appeal is by nature subservient to pleasure, and must overcome a rooted love of pleasurable sensations.   They have apparently no motive for living; stylish
white people are the ideals to which many look and their
ideas of " stylish " are rather vague.   Some would do right,
but are kept in doubt by the conduct of their own pastors,
and by seeing devout ones daily practicing the most disgust-
ing sins.   Their ideas necessarily become a confused mass of
instability.   Both old and young seem almost irresistibly
drawn to the various gatherings which benefit them in no
particular, leaving those who would teach them better things.
Few realize how great are the obstacles in the way of such
work for the negroes.   But it should be not forgotten that
there are exceptions to the generalizations above outlined.
In a few instances the white workers have found gratifying
results; they have found co-operation and earnestness.   The
pupils seem to have attended only for the real good they get.
The workers have found gratitude, appreciation of the work,
and improvement in numbers of those who have attended.
None of the white workers have regretted the work done
among the negroes.

Besides the Sunday schools mentioned, there are sixty-
four colored Presbyterian churches under the general super-

vision of the white church. They have a membership of 2046 and there are 1828 Sunday-school pupils, with two hundred and twenty-three officers and teachers.[1] The colored churches pay a total pastor's salary of only $1511.00 and congregational dues to the amount of $2395.00. Fifty-three colored pastors serve these sixty-four churches. The work grows slowly; during the last year the churches received a membership of only one hundred and twelve by profession of faith and twenty-six by letter. Thirty of the sixty-four received no additions by profession, and twenty-four received no additional members. Rev. J. G. Snedecor says in his report: " It is possible, however, that too much is expected of these men. Few of us realize how fearful are the obstacles which confront these faithful men when they seek to raise the standard of church membership and home life. Their work, like that of the foreign missionary, can not always be fairly estimated from statistics."

Other denominations are showing an active interest in the work of the negro churches. A number of workers have undertaken to assist the negroes in various ways. In many towns preachers of the various white churches are disposed to preach to negro congregations in negro churches. The negroes in turn welcome them and receive their messages with good attendance and respectful attention. They invite frank criticism given in the proper spirit. They feel an unusual amount of encouragement and fellowship when assisted properly by the whites. Many negroes have expressed the wish that relations between the colored and white churches could be more practical, expressing the belief, too, that such an interest on the part of the whites would

[1] See *Fifteenth Annual Report of the Executive Committee of Colored Evangelization.* Rev. J. G. Snedecor of Tuscaloosa, Alabama edits these reports and is general secretary of the Conference on Colored Evangelization.

be extremely beneficial to the negroes.   Likewise many of
the whites manifest a growing interest in the negro churches.
It is difficult to see why such an interest and assistance
would not be helpful.   While it is true that the Negro must
work out much of his own salvation, it is nevertheless expedient that he have as much direction as possible.   And
there is a large field for church workers and a large measure
of responsibility upon the white churches if they are to take
advantage of the opportunities before them.   The results
will be slow and the obstacles are many, but the best informed leaders among the whites express the belief and
hope that much good can be accomplished through co-operation with the negro churches.

CHAPTER III

Fraternal Organizations and Benevolent Societies

Perhaps no phase of negro life is so characteristic of the race and has developed so rapidly as that which centers around the secret societies and fraternal orders. In the chapter which follows the effort is made to present a general view rather than exhaustive details, many of which it is not possible to obtain. The facts here presented are representative and typical; they combine the essentials that are embodied in the fraternal organization as a social factor among the negroes, and indicate the position it holds in the Negro's estimation. This phase of negro life has grown to such an extent that in any study of the negro community it must be ranked as an influence with the home, the school, and the church. Indeed it has become an institution and at times is ranked by the negroes above the other institutions, in part combining these with business and personal interests. The business of the fraternal orders is ranked along with the trades and commercial interests; they are given a prominent place on the program of the business leagues. The success of such organizations is rated with pride as a distinct business achievement. Church members often leave the church for the lodge; business hours are arranged to meet its demands, and school is dismissed that the children may attend the meeting of the juveniles. The Negro esteems a prominent official place in his lodge a greater honor than a position of trust in his work. Managed by members of his own race, the lodge offers the

Negro a place wherein to indentify his interests with those of his own people; even more than the church, it is an institution that appeals to him as his own. It thus satisfies a natural social want.

The growth of fraternal and benevolent societies among the negroes has been phenomenal. Since they became free the negroes have turned naturally to numerous organizations among themselves. It is often stated that prior to 1890 there were more benevolent societies than at the present time; it is perhaps true that a greater total number of local organizations might have existed, but the secret societies, carrying benefits and insurance, managed entirely by negroes have mostly arisen within the last twenty years. Form and ritual have increased with an accompanying pride in their functions. Such societies prosper alike in town and country and city, and when once organized they immediately become a vital part of the community life, often its center. Scores of different orders are represented in Southern towns, with hundreds of local chapters. A special feature of the colored organizations is found in the local character of their orders. The majority have their home offices in the state in which they do business. Few extend over much greater territory. Hence a comprehensive view of the fraternal organizations of a state is essential to an adequate conception of the workings of the negro orders. At the same time, such a view gives an insight into both the general and particular facts obtaining. Mississippi is perhaps the most typical state and combines a large membership with enthusiastic workers and the societies have been well organized. The status of the Negro's societies in this state will be given therefore, before going into details of their operation. Out of thirty-four organizations licensed to do business among the negroes of Mississippi, only four do not operate from some central home office within the state.

These organizations are not identified with those of other states, except in the case of a few prominent orders, which practically become local in their nature, as local branches of the larger order. Of twenty-two similar organizations among the whites of Mississippi, only two operate from a home office within the state. The majority of colored organizations have been organized since 1902 and others are being successfully organized each year, while efforts are made for still others that are less successful. In 1904 five were licensed to do business in Mississippi; in 1905 fourteen were licensed and three ceased operations. Those recently organized have prospered and have an aggregate of upward of eight thousand members. This means that new chapters are being placed in many new towns. The financial report of the fraternal organizations among the negroes of Mississippi for 1906 follows.

BENEVOLENT SOCIETIES

Name of Organization	Certificates			Assessments and Dues Collected
	Issued	Ceased	In force	
American Woodmen	24	13	58	$363.90
Benevolent Association of Mississippi	30	246	118	719.65
Benevolent Industrial Association of Alabama	1,021	404	696	2,081.19
Colored Knights of Pythias	3,066	130	11,326	71,741.85
Colored Woodmen of Alabama	1,958	158	1,800	14,428.00
Earnest Workers Laborers' Union	220	256	664	780.25
Eastern Star Benefit Association	2,050	358	7,197	50,597.28
Grand Court of Calanthe	1,637	278	3,941	11,969.12
Grand United Benevolent Order	20	18	295	368.75
Independent Order Sons and Daughters of Charity	......	26	71	246.75
Independent Order Sons and Daughters of Jacob	2,763	4,705	5,620	55,427.71

BENEVOLENT SOCIETIES—*Concluded.*

Name of Organization	Certificates			Assessments and Dues Collected
	Issued	Ceased	In force	
Independent Sons and Daughters of Charity, U. S. A.	250	10	3,454	1,727.00
Industrial Mutual Relief Association........................	80	....	80	94.45
Knights and Daughters of Tabor of Mound Bayou	770	62	3,374	16,720.00
Knights of Canaan	1,259	505	1,283	3,799.34
Knights and Knights and Ladies of Honor of World	1,519	683	6,155	14,820.78
Knights and Ladies of the Temple of America...................	509	300	684	25,563.70
Lone Star of Race Pride.........	688	623	192	240.15
Masonic Benefit Association.....	2,410	697	10,655	105,502.15
Mississippi Benevolent Society ..	187	....	187	112.50
Mississippi Benevolent Mutual Aid Association	633	253	380	3,646.00
Modern Workmen of Alexandria.	437	330	320	4,416.94
Mutual Benefit Association, United Brothers of Friendship, and Sisters of Mysterious Ten..	282	18	1,380	10,764.75
Odd Fellows Benefit Association, G. U. O. of O. F..............	4,000	1,790	11,110	129,385.06
Old Dominion Protective Ass'n .	303	1	302	652.71
Royal Benefit Society	12	3	9	
State Golden Rule Societies	166	190	406	447.25
Supreme Lodge Financial Union.	276	262	1,245	8,489.75
United Brothers and Sisters of Benevolence of America.......	462	805	1,262	9,370.23
United Reformers...............	1,391	288	1,500	7,412.14
United Woodmen Benefit Ass'n ·	2,175	930	3,512	21,865.16
Universal Brotherhood, Silver Key Commandery No. 1.......	15	25	100	650.70
Woodmen of Union of Nachez...	841	104	737	1,955.60
Mosaic Templars of America	51	2	110	258.87
Total	31,505	14,273	80,223	$552,601.88

The total amount of losses incurred in 1906 by the colored societies in Mississippi was $454,880.34, and the total paid was $430,719.06, which amount was paid out of $552,-

601.88 collected in assessments and dues. The remaining losses were paid later or refused according to the merits of the cases; but in most cases they are always paid. The total amount of insurance carried by the colored insurance organizations in December of 1906 was over thirty million dollars. With the 31,505 certificates issued among the negroes in 1906, compare the 13,515 members which were added to the organizations of the whites during the same year; and with the 80,223 certificates of the negroes carrying thirty million dollars of insurance, compare the total number of certificates in force among the whites, 44,595, carrying insurance to the amount of $64,992,784.00. The comparisons show the relative amounts and values of certificates. The total membership of the negroes is double that of the whites; the amount of insurance is less than half. Among the colored organizations, the losses paid in 1906 exceeded those paid in 1905 by $79,832.44, and the assessments and dues collected exceeded those of the previous year by $153,-079.61. With the whites the losses paid in 1906 were $35,340.44 less than in the former year. For the negroes the average annual assessment and dues collected was $6.75 for each member, while for the whites the average was $21.00. The lowest assessment among the societies of the negroes is fifty cents annually for each member, while the highest average for any negro society is about fourteen dollars. Five of the colored organizations did not increase their membership during the year and had a greater number of certificates cease than were issued during the year. These figures are given from the official report of the insurance commissioner of Mississippi. Careful inquiry and compilation of data obtained from the individual societies, and checking of results, show some inaccuracies, but no results could be obtained so satisfactory from every standpoint as those given. The total membership of the negro societies, paying and non-paying, is nearly equal to the total church membership, while in many communities the total membership of the societies is more than double that of the churches. The fraternal organizations in Mississippi operate from headquarters in eighteen towns in the state, having a population ranging from one thousand to thirty thousand. Vicksburg is the home office for six societies; Greenville has four.

In addition to the activities of their insurance and social life, the societies of the negroes in Mississippi support ten newspapers published in the state. The official organs of their respective societies are: *The Benevolent Banner, The Jacob Watchman, The Mississippi Odd Fellow, The Blade, The Taborian Leader, The Southern Forum, The New Light, The Calanthian Journal, The Signal American Grand Reporter,* and *The Financial Union Journal.* These papers issue the official information, notices, orders and news of the organizations which they represent. They often issue a roster of their subordinate lodges with the principal officers and location. Special news and reports are given prominent places. Local news of the town in which the paper is published is also given a prominent place in the social items. Special articles and editorials with comments and letters complete the news of the publisher. The greater part of the paper, however, is furnished with the patent sheet; sometimes only a half dozen columns of local matter is given, while in a few cases the whole of the publisher's news occupied less than four columns. For the most part, the matter published is of a wholesome nature. Enthusiasm can be felt through it all and the Negro's interests are well looked after. Good, wholesome advice is often given, and opinions exchanged. The managers offer attractive terms to agents for their papers and solicit job work from their constituency. They support the interests of their societies, which in most cases are identical with their own private interests. They lend their influence to the support of such educational institutions as are encouraged by the fraternal societies. On the whole they are a very positive influence and add much to the Negro's self-interest and pride.

Investigations show that other societies are in operation in Mississippi besides those chartered and recorded on the official lists. Some of these operate under secret rules and assess members according to their own agreement. The total number of such organizations, including the many little ephemeral societies operated wherever groups of negroes are found, would run into the hundreds. Sometimes they continue for a year, sometimes only for one or two meetings. The passing of one makes room for the coming of another and their variety is measured only by the Negro's love of devising means and methods of social life, with leadership and entertainment in the foreground. Among such societies are numerous church and charity organizations, women's societies and literary clubs, debating societies and the like. There are, however, a few more prominent organizations that have more than a local field, that are not included in the official list. Among them the most prominent are the Evening Star Benevolent Association, Victoria Star, Zion Aid Association, Wide-awake Benevolents, Mutual Aid, Home Benevolents, Sons and Daughters of Gideon, besides branches of the larger orders and imitations of a local nature, growing to a large degree out of the older orders. A study of the names of the societies already given will reveal much of their nature as well as the Negro's methods of naming them. They pay burial expenses, sick benefits, and small amounts to beneficiaries of deceased members. Such amounts in many cases are determined entirely by the number of members, the assessment plan being the most common and most practical one.

Members are admitted variously according to a flexible constitution made to meet the demands of the largest number of people. There are non-paying members who receive only the advantages coming from the fraternal society; there are those who take insurance for sick benefits only, while others wish burial expenses also. Still others take life insurance, while some combine all benefits, thus paying the larger assessments and dues.

The subordinate lodges are organized throughout the territory wherever opportunity is favorable. Either an agent perfects the local society or a local person is authorized to organize. There is much freedom in their operation. The subordinate societies are called variously *lodges, fountains, unions, tents, tabernacles, camps, cabins, households, councils, meets* and so on, according to the head organization. The usual officers are appointed, with slightly more naming and titles than the whites, and with a full quota of officers to be elected. The local subordinate lodge is then named according to the pleasure of the members. The naming of the lodges indicates much of the Negro's nature and pride as it is revealed in his newly acquired social institution. An inquiry was made into the particular reasons for special names given local organizations, but not a single answer was found to be reliable. In general the names are given at random, at the suggestion of a leader. They are often selected with general satisfaction because of a good sounding name or for special local associations. A great many are named for places in general, like Philadelphia, America, Africa, Tallahassee, Pennsylvania. A greater number are named after the town in which they are located, as for instance, Woodburn, No. 99, Mound Bayou, No. 144. Many are named for historical characters: Washington, Jefferson, Franklin, Napoleon, Webster, Pythagoras. Quite a good many are named in honor of noted negroes, Brown, Turner, Dunbar, while a larger number are named in honor of negroes of local reputation or of less wide repute, such as Maggie Scott, Ed. Jones, No. 14, H. C. Holbrook, G. F. Bowles. The favorite names, however, and the large majority are given more promiscuously from scriptural names and places, from names of abstract qualities, terms denoting pride and honor, names indicating the nature of the society, and some from a sense of humor. In the latter class are Sheriff's Ridge, Lightfoot, Tillman's Home, and Hard Cash. The list shows a remarkable vocabulary of appropriate names and is well worth a careful perusal. While only a very partial list is allowed in the space here given, the number is large enough and the examples fully characteristic, so that a view of a rostrum may be gained. Take, for instance, from the Pythian Lodge Roster of the Knights of Pythias, including over four hundred subordinate lodges, the following list, which excludes names of persons, towns and more general and common-place appellations. In order that the full force and application of these names may be felt naturally, they are not classified according to themes, but given exactly as they occur over the state; the reader may then classify them if he chooses.

Eureka, Mt. Helena, Beacon Light, New Light, Evergreen, Rising Star, Beulah Star, Morning Star, Damon, Bright Crown, Pride of South, Pride of Natchez, Bell of Delta, Pride of the East, New Moon, Forest Home, Eminence, Carolina Star, St. Pythian, Knighthood, New Hope, Queen Esther, Crescent, Lilly of Valley, Vestal, Progress, Climax, Friendly Brother, Golden Ridge, Dionysius, Rose Bud, White Hall, St. John, Golden Leaf, Avondale, Mt. Pleasant, Pilgrims' Rest, Pride of Delta, Rose of Sharon, St. Elmo, High Grade, Sweet Home, Queen of Valley, Silver Lake, Rose Hill, Traveller's Rest, Utopia, Mizpah, Sunlight, St. James, Silver Shield, Lilly

White, Pride of Onward, Blue Banner, Excelsior, Pride of
West, Rising Sun, Pilgrims' Rest, Weeping Willow, Salem.
King of Night, Light Wilderness, Rosedale Star, Triumphant,
Pride of Life, Golden Grain, Seven Star, Melodia, Bear
Garden, New Prospect, Beilus, Good Water, Good Tidings,
Rose Bank, Cora Esther, Southern Beauty, Fidelity Monitor,
Bonhomie, Corner Stone, Farmers' Rest, Golden Gem, Mis-
sionary, Sharon, Golden Crown, Bold Pilgrim, Center Beauty,
Progressive, Hill of Zion, Canon, Valley Home, Acme, Victor,
Mt. Nebo, Dominion, Annette, Banner, Waveland, Gold
Wreath, Swan, Eclipse, Grand View, Breaksville, Buckhorn,
Sunflower Bell, Hickory Tree, White Oak, American Beauty,
Mississippi Valley, Free Will, White Cloud, Golden Rule,
Beatrice, Aurora, Rose Bud, Nugent, Progress, Pine Grove,
Black Bayou, Bethume, Waterloo, King Davis, Isola, Choice,
Helm, Soul Chappel, Silver Globe, Honita, Dralloo, Sweet
Home, Golden Gate, Dixie, Silver Ring, Welcome, Farmers'
Pride, Sea Shore, Clearfield, Leaf Rivers, Arborvitae, Saving
Farmer, Friendly Farmers, Shady Oak, Gold Eagle, United
Farmers, Light of Meadville, Pacific Banner, Marvel Rock,
White Cedar, Zion Traveller, Brownsville, Champion's Hill,
Child's Chapel, Prosperity, Purity, O. K., Single Star, Good
Will, Sweet Pink, Sprangle Star, Lone Star, Gloomy Rose,
Prince, New Era, Paradise.

Many of the most popular names occur several times
even in the roster of the same organization; a separate number differentiates them. Thus St. Paul, St. John, Shiloh
and other Scriptural names are popular. So are such names
as Rose, Silver Leaf, Loving Brothers, Home, Pride, and
different names embodying the words star, rest, sun, leaf
and so on. If this list be compared with the roster of other
societies, it will be found to be very similar; in fact, for the
most part the names are very much the same. Likewise the
names of subordinate lodges in other sections of the South
resemble those just enumerated.

The essential characteristics of the colored fraternal organizations are not unlike in the different states of the South. There are branches of the same orders operating in different states, with home offices in their respective states, thus making practically separate orders. Others operate from one office into two or three states, while a few, as has been indicated, operate in more. Agents are constantly planning to extend their societies into wider territory. Leading teachers, preachers, and business men among the negroes are continually planning and organizing new societies, each modeled in general after some well-known one, but having a special feature through which it claims excellence. Such a society is not infrequently originated in a small town and extends further, if successful. Competent lawyers are employed to draw up its articles and a suitable charter, and the encouragement of the whites is sought. In other instances, the secret societies belong entirely to local organizations of negroes, and not even its meetings and purposes are to be known by the whites. The names of other common orders reveal the same general purposes and nature of the organizations as those cited from Mississippi. Typical ones are: Brothers and Sisters' Aid Society, Charitable Brotherhood, Colored Brotherhood Company, Giddings and Jollifee Union, Golden Rule Benevolents, Good Samaritans, Grand Fountain United Order True Reformers, Grand United Order of the Sons and Daughters of Peace, Lincoln Benefit Society, Living Stream Brotherhood, Negro Christian Brotherhood, People's Independent Order True Reformers, Royal Knights of King David, Sons and Daughters of Refuge, Standard Fraternal, Loving Sisters, Consolation, Sisters of David, Humble Christian, Daughters of Rebecca, Moral Reform.

Besides the subordinate adult lodges, many of the organizations make provision for children's societies. Such

" juveniles " are ordinarily superintended by one or two officers elected from the senior organization, in most cases from among the women. Each community as a rule has one or two children's societies and in larger towns they are more numerous. They usually meet once a month, less often fortnightly. They include on the roll the majority of children of the requisite age, usually from six to seventeen years. The attendance at the meetings is good and the children find much pleasure and pride in them. At such meetings they play, drill, talk and sometimes sing. They are taught to keep the pass word, which they do with pride and consummate skill. No inducement will lead them to give the word to a white man. Like the older members, the children are taught the benefits of the societies; the juveniles are training schools for the children. Dues and assessments of small amounts are collected and an initiation fee of fifty cents is charged. The proceeds go for sick benefits and burial expenses. The childrens' societies are, however, entirely subordinate and hold no conspicuous place in the total of lodge operations.

Some of the characteristics of the negro lodge may now be inferred. A single town having not more than five hundred colored inhabitants not infrequently has from fifteen to twenty subordinate lodges, each representing a different order. Many negroes belong to from three to five each, and the majority [1] belong to more than one. Indeed it is a source of great pride to be able to hold office in more than a single order, but as a rule every negro has a favorite one to which he is most loyal; this may be changeable, differing from year to year. The negroes ordinarily have one or two central meeting places where the lodges may meet, a Masonic or Odd Fellows' Hall, or rooms rented over a store

---

[1] That is, a majority of the regular lodge patrons and enthusiasts.

owned by negroes. Such halls are owned by negroes and are used for various assemblages. The pro-rata for each society in rents is thus reduced to a minimum, inasmuch as they arrange different nights for their meetings; a single hall will thus serve for a half dozen societies, or even more. The social and fraternal features occupy the greater part of the Negro's time and interest in the lodge. The common hour for meeting is eight o'clock in the evening, with special hours arranged to suit occasions; such meetings often last far into the night and not infrequently into the morning hours. This is true especially when extra features are on the program. The attendance is rather full, although at times it falls off for lack of interest, such a state preceeding the disorganization of that special lodge. As a rule, however, the average negro does not love to miss a meeting, and will set aside church or family duties to attend the lodge function. However, meetings are often neglected or postponed by mutual agreement for some other special event; for with the Negro any new special feature is better than an ordinary one. At the regular meetings the members attend to the usual round of business, consisting of receiving or soliciting members, discussing the lodge affairs and its members, the trial of such members as are deemed questionable, learning the rules of the society and enjoying special talks and debates and the like. In the discussion of measures and means every member wishes a prominent part with his speech. The learning of the rules and regulations, the keeping of the secret and learning others, with the attendant pride and entertainment, make up the attractive features of the regular meeting. The election of officers gives additional interest, and a large number of offices makes it possible to honor a large portion of the membership. The social feature is thus stressed in an indirect way, the members " have somewhere to go ", and the total social life is greatly increased by the meetings. Above all, the secrets of the society are not disclosed. From the youngest member of the children's societies to the oldest veteran in fraternal circles, complete silence is maintained on all things pertaining to the secrets of their society. Leaders and preachers who have responded readily with information in regard to other matters, become silent on all alike when questioned in regard to special phases of lodge life, although there is a minority who are willing to express an opinion concerning the advantages or disadvantages of the secret societies.

The chief characteristics of the fraternal organization may be learned from the enthusiastic claims of their agents. The Negro stresses the feature that appeals most to his constituency, each organization maintaining that it has special qualities that render it unquestionably the best in the world. Typical examples of advertisements will serve to illustrate. The following announcement is printed regularly in the official organ of the society, besides being distributed in circular form.

READ EVERY LINE OF ME.

THE

INDUSTRIAL MUTUAL RELIEF ASSOCIATION: Home Office, Brookhaven, Miss. Chartered in the State of Mississippi in 1901.

Its object is to Intellectually, Morally, Financially, and Religiously elevate the Race.

This organization has no equal. Why? Because it provides to pay its members when totally disabled, to earn support, a pension of not less than $12 or more than $36 PER QUARTER, to members holding $1,000 policies. Pays doctor's bills out of pension if previous arrangements be made with the Master or sick committee. Pays from subordinate lodge $8 PER MONTH AT $2 PER WEEK for sick benefits and buys medicine. Will educate members of the order free. FURNISHES A $25 FUNERAL. Puts a $15 TOMB-STONE at the grave of the dead. Loans money on policies. Makes all loans at 6 percent. Will aid in buying lands and building homes for its members. Pays all assessment money back every five years, in cash to each member, or if any member wishes he can draw a paid up certificate for five years and remain in the order without paying assessments. Members cannot lose if they stick to the order five years. All claims settled promptly. Either sex eligible from 5 to 65 years of age, if in perfect health, for $3.00. Children from 5 to 15 years of age at $1.50. It is the purpose of the Association to furnish educational protection to its members, and to assist them in time of need. Therefore it is the desire of the Society to secure the cooperation of all who have the interest of their fellowmen at heart, in order that the sick, disabled, widows and orphans, and any legal representative may be protected. Members holding $500 policies will get a pension for total disability of not less than $9 or more than $18 per quarter. In writing members state what policy wanted. Assessments per month on $1,000, $1.00; on $500, 50 cents.

$200 for 35 cents per month. Members holding such policy shall be known as contributors to the Old Folks and Youths Distribution fund. The fund both in the subordinate and grand lodge shall be kept entirely separate, as there is generally more sickness among the ones expected to hold this policy than any other.

Anyone though can hold this policy that wishes.

This policy can be held by all persons wishing to join this Society from 50 years of age up, children may hold it if desired from 5 years to 16 years of age.

This Association is to elevate the Race by building Industries that will better employ each and all who want to do something. Aside from the benevolent part, we expect to establish ·Banks, Drug Stores, Build Homes, and do many other good things as stated above.

After Death : When You Have Robbed Your Family.

When men think of their death, they are apt to think of it only in connection with their spiritual welfare, and not of the destruction in the household which will come from their emmigration from it. It is selfish for you to be so absorbed in the heaven to which you are going, that you forget what is to become of your wife and children after you are gone. You go out of this world not leaving them a dollar yet you die happy. You can trust them in the hands of God, who owns all, but if you could pay a premium on a policy and neglect it, then it is a mean thing for you to do to go up to heaven rejoicing, while the family goes to the poorhouse. When their elbows, feet and knees are bare, the thought of your splendid robe in heaven will not keep them warm. The minister may preach a splendid sermon over the remains, and the choir may sing with tongues of angels, but you have robbed your family. You could have provided for your household, and you neglected it. To this end we wish to interest you, that you will not neglect to join a good society.

The president of the above society is an industrious and law-abiding negro, owning some property and taking great interest in his leadership. He maintains that " you don't have to die to win in his society, but win while you live ". He wishes to extend the territory of his organization into other states. He and his wife conduct a school for the industrial training of members of the lodge, but open to any who have the money. Instruction is given by these two in " Kindergarten, English, Normal, College Preparatory (Classical), College Course (Classical), Industrial, Sewing, Cooking, Fancy Work, Bicycle, Umbrella and Furniture Repairing, Mattress Making and Upholstery." The wife, who is principal, the husband being the president, " Solicits Donations for Purpose of Building Dormitories for Girls and Boys, and for other general necessities such as Desks,

Apparatus, and other school supplies. We are out for the good of the race and will be thankful for any amount contributed by the lovers of education, morality and industry. We want to raise $50,000." The expense account then is given, including instruction in " Music Department—Eight Grades ", which is given by the " lady-Principal." Special items are: " Positively, payments must be made monthly and in advance." " Recitations will be suspended from students who fall behind in their accounts. Members of the I. M. R. A. will be provided for an entrance into the school. Board $6.00 per month." An advertisement, on stiff cardboard, is the means of extra solicitation for the school. On one side of this card is the photograph of the " president ", covering one-half the face of the card. With the photograph and covering the other half, is written: Prof. ————, President of the I. M. R. A., The I. M. B. I. I. & C. of T., Editor of The Peoples Relief and Sec. of the Y. M. C. A. Box 251 Residence 413 E. ———— St. On the opposite side of the card is inscribed the " School of Information " giving rates and courses and in addition the following card:

JOIN OUR ORDER
THE INDUSTRIAL MUTUAL RELIEF ASSOCIATION
And be benefitted. See the President, or
write for information. The best
in the world
Subscribe for THE PEOPLES RELIEF, one of the
leading negro papers
AGENTS WANTED FOR EVERYTHING. BIG Salaries Paid.

The above illustrations show something of the enthusiasm and remarkable energy and faith that is put into these societies and their undertakings. They show also one of the secrets of their marvelous success. The Negro believes in advertising; he does not object to figures or world-wide comparisons. Enthusiasm is contagious and members come in rapidly. They are all honest in their beliefs, in a way; his order succeeds, then why is it not a great one? He wishes to teach everything that can be taught and his people need it, why not teach it? And indeed he must have his running expenses and these are forthcoming. Take another illustration, published in the *Southern Forum*, the official organ of the Lone Star Race Pride, Friendship, Love and Help:

GREATEST IN THE NEGRO LIMELIGHT.

The following are a few of the many reasons why the ORDER of the LONE STAR RACE PRIDE is the greatest before the fraternal limelight today:

First—It is purely and absolutely a colored order from start to finish—the product of the brain of the race.

Second—It aims to reach the unreached masses, as well as the classes, of the race, thereby placing the lever where it is most needed to elevate the manhood and womanhood of this race.

Third—It pays a weekly sick benefit, from $2.00 to $5.00, to all sick or disabled members.

Fourth—It furnishes a funeral outfit, from $15.00 to $100.00, to all deceased members.

Fifth—It pays a $300.00 death benefit, ninety days after the death of a member in good standing.

Sixth—It gives relief to all members who are financially distressed from loss of home or household effects etc., caused either by fire, wind, water, or other natural agencies.

Seventh—It operates an ART, TRADE AND LITERARY COLLEGE where the members can have their sons and daughters educated at a minimum cost.

Eighth—It has a MILITARY or UNIFORM RANK DE-

PARTMENT under the management of a MAJOR GEN-
ERAL, where its male members may receive such instructions
that they will be prepared to serve their country in future
emergencies.

Ninth—It has a JUVENILE DEPARTMENT under the
management of a MATRON and CHAPERONE where the
boys and girls, from 6 to 16 years of age, are prepared to
enter the Mystic Temple of Light and Knowledge.

Tenth—It has a BUSINESS DEPARTMENT, in which
the members are taught business—how to save and invest their
money and thus have something in this life.

This order is presenting ITS CLAIM and TAKING HOLD
on the race everywhere, and we need DEPUTIES, GOOD,
HONEST, ENERGETIC men and women in EVERY
STATE to represent it. ONE who is a HUSTLER can
easily make $200 or more a month and expenses. When writ-
ing for deputyship, send REFERENCE and your PHOTO-
GRAPH.

The claims of such an order are indeed enormous; to
some extent, however, they are all fulfilled. There is a
trade school, a juvenile department and business suggestions made in plenty. They do drill and train sometimes in
uniform under a " major general " such as they choose;
plans are made to relieve suffering of all kinds. It thus
claims to be a panacea for all human evils and the only way
to perfection in the individual and the millennium of the
race. The above society besides furnishing such benevolent aids is also the " Mystic Temple of Light and
Knowledge." Its school is a " Trade and Literary College "
with two teachers and a small number of pupils, like the
one just mentioned, varying from twenty to fifty. The
school is situated " in the heart of the Delta, the Modern
Eden of the world, offers unsurpassed opportunities for the
colored youths of the South ", and gives courses in

"English, Normal and Collegiate, Industrial courses for boys—Carpentry and kindred trades, Agriculture, care of Live Stock, &c., For Girls—Sewing, Mexican Drawing work, Household Economy, Horticulture and Millinery."

The success of the negro fraternal orders in obtaining money enables them to make such offers as the above. The chief elements entering into their finances must be reserved for another place, but some of their demands may be noted at this point. Here are some of the requirements in brief as they are given in the orders of commanders:

All Grand Writers must collect endowment, $1.00, in December from every member of their lodge. Each Grand Writer shall collect the Supreme Lodge tax, 25 cents for the last half of the year and report in December . . . also collect the first half of semi-annual distress tax, 5 cents, from each member. . . . This is in accordance with a late act of the supreme lodge. The school tax, 25 cents, for the first half of the year must be collected from each member. The Grand President of each subordinate lodge shall see that semi-annual pass word money, 10 cents, is collected from each member by the Grand Writer. Each subordinate lodge shall be held responsible for each member on its roster and must forward in its report 10 cents for each member. No lodge that is chartered shall make or initiate persons into the order for less than $5.00, nor more than $10.00 without a dispensation from the Great Supreme Grand President. The last supreme Lodge passed a resolution making it compulsory for every subordinate lodge to subscribe for the lodge paper and also have its lodge, location, nights of meeting, and chief officers advertised for the whole year in the lodge directory, for which each lodge must pay $2.00. Each lodge, therefore, must collect the money at once and send it to the Great Supreme Grand President. If the Grand presidents of each subordinate lodge will urge upon the members that each purchase a copy of the constitution and by-laws there will be less trouble among the members in the local lodges. The Supreme Lodge ordered that every subordinate lodge at an early date give a special entertainment for the benefit of the SCHOOL FUND the proceeds of which must be reported forthwith to the treasurer.

The officer closes his instructions as to " extras " with an enthusiastic tribute to the lodge, which is well calculated to inspire absolute confidence in the worthiness of the causes for which the Negro's money is to be spent.   Says he:

Our order is springing up here, there, and in fact everywhere, as if touched by some magic wand. In short, its development is the greatest wonder of the hour. People everywhere instantaneously appreciate the inestimable worth of its aims and objects, and fully regard them as the " key " to the solution of the negro problem the world over, hence are joining our ranks by thousands daily.

Other items of possible extra fees are numerous, and are flexible.

Deputies and lodges can charge $1.50 for membership or renewal in the U. S. and S. of B. of A. but must send to the grand secretary and treasurer, fifty five cents for new members and one dollar for renewed members. If a member does not pay assessments by the fifteenth of each month he or she must renew by paying one dollar. All members missing two assessments in succession must take out new membership by paying $1.50 and changing policies. The Bond Tax for each lodge is seventy five cents, which amount secures the local secretary and treasurer and is cheaper than making personal bonds. Just send in seventy five cents and the Grand Lodge will do the rest. You do not have to hunt up any sureties or go before any officer of the law, nor do you need any bond blanks. All you need to do is to send the seventy five cents in at once.

Likewise, another lodge charges more for blanks and forms, another for ritual and another for various incidentals. Guides containing the ceremonies are sold at from seventy-five cents to a dollar and a half with the exhortation that " every lodge should have several copies and every member should be in possession of one copy and keep up with the ritualistic work ".

One of the most prominent items in the expense entailed upon the members by many of the lodges is that for dress regalia. Badges, buttons, signs, uniforms and robes contribute much to the pleasurable expenses of the members. And the supplies are usually bought from headquarters or from an individual prominent in the order. Take the following illustrations:

Keep Your Eye On This Article

To all Subordinate Lodges throughout the Supreme Jurisdiction, Greeting:

I, ————————————, Great Supreme Grand President of the L. S. R. P. of E. L. & H, by authority invested in me, do hereby designate Sunday, August ninth as the day and date on which to observe our aniversary, and call upon every one of the lodges to assemble in their temple or some house of worship, and observe the day with appropriate religious ceremony. Official program will be mailed out to all lodges in time

Dress and Regalia

All gentlemen must wear black pants, black coats and black hats and white vests and white gloves. Ladies must wear black skirts and white waists and white gloves and plain white sailor hats. All officers must have on a collar, except the Grand President, who must wear a crown, white robe and collar; the Grand Writer must wear a crown, blue robe and collar. All other members may wear collars but must wear badges. All officers and members must be in full regalia on that day. For collars, buttons, badges, banners etc., each lodge should send in its order now that there may be no delay in filling it in time.

Again another lodge rules: "All subordinate lodges are required under penalty of law, to celebrate the Grand Lodge Anniversary on the 4th. Sunday in April. Fail not. On this occasion and on all public occasions, every member must participate and have on the regular lodge badge. Better send in your order in time." So again: "Every lodge should have a full set of dress regalia and the lodge seal". And no one objects to the regalia. Indeed it is the chief joy of special occasions to march in uniform with banners and colors. Such a procession is indeed an interesting and also an impressive spectacle. It is with pleasure that the local lodge reports the ceremonies to headquarters, services being carried out "with members sitting with badges on" or "when members marched in full regalia".

In addition to such expenses as are entailed by the regular fees and such extras as have been mentioned, the lodge undertakes to raise much money by social gatherings. Special meetings always "raise" a collection and rally days are numerous. The box suppers, musicals and literary entertainments, dances and the like combine the social features with the raising of money. In this way the sum total of money raised approximates large amounts for the Negro; much of this is never returned to the members because of the great percentage who drop out after a few payments. Enthusiasm is wild, but wanes. So too there is some discontent and rivalry among the lodges and members. Some of the secretaries and treasurers apparently appropriate some of the collections to their own dispensation, while as a rule they are allowed great freedom in expending it. The attitude of the Negro toward the actual and probable misappropriation of lodge funds is noteworthy.

The penalty for such offence is not heavy, as a rule.   The
pointed locals from the editor's pen illustrate the situation.

M. A. Thomas who was secretary at Pleasant Hill Lodge has
been suspended from office, because of misappropriating Grand
Lodge Funds.   Some other secretaries are pinching off the
Grand Lodge funds and misappropriating Grand Lodge
moneys, who if they do not stop will receive the same medicine.
Better accept this timely warning and " come across."
   There is a certain local secretary in Warren county, won't
call his name just now, but if he keeps up his habit I will, who
has been nibbling off the Grand lodge money for a year or
two.   If he does not quit we will have to pull the cover from
off him.
   Some of the secretaries are still appropriating the assessment
moneys to their own use, which is a violation of the laws of
the order and of the state.   Such an act is a penitentiary offence and yet some of our secretaries will take the risk.
   If some of the secretaries who have appropriated the lodge's
money to their use do not " come across " at an early date,
their names and acts will be published in the May number of
the Banner.

And thus frightened, the secretaries " come across " at a
rapid gait; indeed some make amends who have perhaps
appropriated no funds illegally.   As has been noted elsewhere the Negro assumes an attitude of guilt all the time,
both toward himself and toward his fellow man.   He may
at least be guilty of something.   On the other hand, it may
be said that after all, aside from the general graft of lodge
leaders, which is considered by all parties thoroughly justifiable, the amount of lodge funds appropriated would seem
to be much smaller than one would expect.
   It is often difficult for members and for subordinate
lodges to bring forward their assessments on time.   Hence

ample provisions are made for paying them later, by an increased fee. For two or more delays renewal is necessary, for which one-half of the original fee is usually added. It often happens that there are more renewals than new members. Again, individual members, as well as entire subordinate lodges permit their policies to lapse for weeks or even months, thus giving up all claim to the amounts paid in, until some speaker pleads the cause of the order, when enthusiasm is again aroused and all join again. Nor do they regret the necessity of having to pay again; this happens not once but often, and not infrequently several times in the life of a single subordinate lodge. It is to be expected, then, that petty difficulties may often arise, and attempts to avoid paying and yet keep their membership. There is, however, much leniency at headquarters, lest the lodge be lost, and rules are not always enforced. The following items from the column of instructions and warnings will illustrate the general as well as the specific attitude.

A certain Lodge at B. always straightens up in time to represent in the Grand Lodge every year and then never pays another assessment, but renews again just before the next Grand Lodge meeting. They tell us the members pay assessments regularly during the whole year. Now the secretary of this lodge must "come to time" or we will publish his lodge.

If you take a notion to become delinquent or the money is hard to get to pay your dues, don't lay the blame on the Grand Lodge or some of its officers, but act the part of a man or woman and just back out.

If several other lodges who are behind in paying assessments do not report in a few days, they will be suspended and published. All must comply with the law alike. We cannot bend the law to you but will have to bend you to the law.

So, too, letters from former members indicate the renewed enthusiasm as well as the desire to again get in the " lime-light of fraternal society." Sometimes it is a desire to become the leader in the new lodge and thus receive certain emoluments; sometimes it is a desire for approval from the Supreme headquarters and from the race in general, for each writer thinks everybody else reads and knows his or her letter. Sometimes it is apparently pure enthusiasm and faith in the good work of the order. Pride goes far toward culminating such enthusiasm. The following is a typical attitude:

Dear Professor B.—This, I suppose, will be a surprise to you, but I trust it will be an agreeable surprise. The Benevolent Banner reached me today and after perusing its columns with much care my mind went back to its first obligation, which was made in the Benevilent Society some years ago. So I write that I may get authority to reorganize the lodge at this place or to organize a new one. Now if this is satisfactory, please send me a constitution and full information that I may become acquainted again.

I am now carrying $3,700 worth of fraternal insurance in other orders but the Benevolent is my first love and reading the Banner has renewed my affections for it. Please explain fully, as my school will close on the 22inst and I can do much work for the Grand Old Order by the next session of the Grand Lodge. Much love to you and yours. Yours for Success,   Mrs., ——————— etc.

" Chips from the Grand Inspector's Ax " are interesting reports and insight into the lodge life and ideals of the negroes. Here are found bright, sparkling and newsy enthusiasm, which reflect all too plainly the popular and pleasant manners and methods of the lodge workers and the laymen. The inspector reports:

I visited St. Paul Lodge and was nicely received and entertained. We had a regular Benevolent Covenant meeting and all delinquent members to promise to renew, those in promised to stay in the field and those out promised to get in as soon as possible. Good Benevolent talks were made by Brothers so and so and sisters so and so etc. I responded in my humble way in behalf of the Grand Lodge. A royal banquet was spread and all enjoyed it beyond description. A *nice purse* was presented to to the Grand Inspector. The St. Paul Lodge is up to date.

Having arrived at Arcola Saturday morning I was met by Hon. L. J. Taylor who carried me to Manhatten to the home of Hon. Brother C. M. and Sister M., a Christian lady. Dinner being ready, I sat down at that large and tempting table and wondered whether I had arrived in the Land of Canaan or the Garden of Eden. Horses being furnished us by the President we rode to several plantations preaching the Benevolent gospel. We also walked the streets of Arcola doing the same. Rev. E. D. W. our grand deputy is doing good work in this neck of the woods and expects to send in ten lodges before the grand lodge meets. Sisters M., T., and T. are good working members. Having arrived at the hall President M. called the meeting to order. Rev. L. I. T. chaplain ascended the sacred rostrum and read for the opening the 2nd. chapter of Matthew, and sang "A Charge to Keep I have ", after which prayed a spiritual prayer. Addresses was then delivered by Brothers and sisters etc. President M. in a most stylish and flattering way introduced your humble servant. My benevolent spirit being at its highest degrees at the good treatment of these I spoke until I was carried off in a benevolent trance. I was nicely entertained at the home of Rev. I. T. that night and was escorted to the train the next morning by a committee composed of brothers. A thousand thanks to Arcola. Go forward.

Another, after the description of various particulars as above concludes in an equally joyous manner:

Devotional exercises being over, I was introduced by the vice-president and I informed them that all great things has its ups and downs but stand fast in the benevolence that was handed down to Hon. P., Prof. B., and Father R. After this a nice purse was presented to me. After the meeting adjourned these loving brothers went to Sawyers Hotel and rented the best room and paid board and lodging for me. Three cheers for Pride of Leland No. 190.

While in some localities much strife and jealousies exist between rival orders, for the most part they are noticeably lacking. The contrast between lodge and church is here apparent; the lodges manifest more of the fraternal spirit than do the churches one toward another. In no phase of negro life, home, school, church or lodge is he free from petty rivalries to some degree, but in the lodge, members are often in good fellowship and standing in several orders. A leading " light " and the editor of the official organ of one order was also the most prominent local leader in another. He published the rival orders' meetings and proceedings in a column preceding those of the one represented by the paper. He also refers with pride to the two orders when speaking of his work. Local lodges often combine to celebrate a special day, each sitting in a section of the hall or church. Many letters report with pride the harmony existing among the two or more orders, and much fun and ribaldry is indulged in at each other's expense.

Perhaps enthusiasm is nowhere more marked and wild than among the lay members and officers of subordinate lodges. Their sentiments are less often given to the public than are those of the supreme officials, and as a rule, their enthusiasm is of shorter duration, but it is nevertheless not less marked. Reports from secretaries of the subordinate chapters are solicited for the official papers and many are published. Statements from individuals give characteristic zeal in conversation and in writing. Something has already been seen of this feature of lodge life. Typical letters from members are here given for further illustration. They indicate the specific points noted and at the same time sum up many of the features and details of negro lodge customs and operations. Much, too, of the Negro's nature is reflected in such expressions.

Dear Editor: Please allow me space in your valuable paper to speak of our excellent Grand Lodge Aniversary, which was observed by St. Paul Lodge, No. 81. The Lodge attired in full dress uniform, accompanied by Zion Hill Lodge No. 100, who was also attired in full dress uniform, formed procession at school house and marched to the church where an anxious crowd was assembled to witness the ceremonies.

The meeting was called to order and a fervent prayer service followed. Everybody seemed fairly enthused and the singing was beautiful. Brother J. M. T. read for introduction the 61st Chapter of Isaiah and lined while the congregation sang, " I heard the Voice of Jesus Say etc ". Brother S. C. W. fervently petitioned the Throne of Grace. President W. J. B. preached an able sermon from a selection of the 13th chapter of Cor. He struck a death blow to the theory of fraternal benefit societies being a hindrance to the race. He showed that a man had a right to live and die for his God and his family, and that a man could not better live and die for his family than by joining endowment societies and leaving a benefit to his dear ones when he crosses the river. Brother D. B. executive officer of the local Jacob Lodge made an able address defending the good name of fraternal orders. Many persons in the audience were heard to exclaim, " I am persuaded to join this great order." Cloths were spread on the beautiful grass, a feast was had and all ate till they were filled. Collection $9.50. All went home exclaiming in the

language of Peter of old, "It is good for us to be here."
Yours in B. L. etc.

Every letter from subordinate lodges furnishes many points
of interest; only a few, however, can be included here. Differing somewhat in details from the above reports is the
following characteristic letter, coming from the Pythian
circles. It presents a complete general view of a typical
meeting with the consequent effect upon the negroes present.
While the form and language is less correct than the ones
already given, it is still typical and full of enthusiasm. It
is nearer the average attitude of the great majority of
members.

Sir. John W. S,
   Dear Editor:—Please allow me space in your paper for me
to say that Belmont Lodge No. 51 held its memorial service
on the above date, with the grand lecturer P. C. D. with us
on his official visit. Making his lecture and helping us to
conduct the service. The lodge was called to order by Sir.
J. W., C. C. after the members had been seated with their
badges on, then Sir. Whitney explaining to the lodge the cause
of the extra session, that it was to pay the loss due respect
to our lamented an sainted S. P. C., S. W. Starks, who had
fallen from our ranks by the hand of death. He then gave
the lodge into the hands of Sir. P. C. Dowan, who taking the
stand. Then he sang a hymn. No prayer was offered by Sir.
John N. Pempleton. Then the grand lecturer proceeded. I
am glad to say that never was a man gifted as that man, for
taking his text from the 5th. chapter of Ephesians, the 14th
verse, "Words Was Wake thou that sleep." He held closest
attention for two hours. He taking that holy scripture and
men cried that they was going to wake up, the members said
they was going to wake up to the sense of their obligation.
He had us to know that the order had been ever since the
creating of man, and would be as long as God would let man

live on the earth. Dear Sirs I will say that the G. C. Sir. John W. H. did know his business when he appointed Sir. Dowan for a field man, for he is a Pythian missionary to go and carry the Pythian gospel if Belmont Lodge had been a Pythian engine, Sir Dowan would have been the engineer to blow the whistle at every station. Wake thou that sleep to your obligation. Then he spoke along the life and death of Sir. S. W. Starks and made things awful sad then closed his talk. Song was sang by Sir. Steve Tucker the prelate of his Lodge. Happy day when Jesus washed my sins away. Then Sir. John Pembleton responded. Then song was led by Sir. Dowan, " There is Rest for the Weary ". Then the lodge was called in secret prayer by the prelate for five minutes. Then Sir. Chas. Wood spoke on the line of Pythianism. Then song led by Sir Tucker, " Let Us Walk in the Light of God." Then Sir. C. Grandison spoke on religious principles, saying that he hoped to meet the S. P. C. S. W. Starks in the kingdom of our God, where we would all sit in the halls of heaven to part no more. Song led by Sir. Dowan, " I will Follow Jesus ". Sir Ben McCoy spoke on the death of S. W. Starks and at the meantime he cast the evergreen upon the alter of the lodge in memory of our sainted S. P. C. Then Sir. John Whitney, C. C., made the closing talk which made things very sad on the death of Sir. Starks. Then the lodge turned the vote of thanks and gave the grand sign in honor of the grand lecturer and asked him to come again. Then a memorial supper was served with bread and wine in remembrance of Sir. S. W. Starks that we all hope to meet him again, and feast with him around the banquet table with Jesus to hunger no more.

From observing the ceremonies and regular services, it is seen that opportunity is given for many individuals to participate in the exercises. This gives the greater degree of satisfaction and adds to the total of the social values offered by the lodge. Ritual and ceremony, ranging from simple form to the most elaborate details carried to ridiculous extents, regalia, including hats, caps, robes, collars, badges, buttons, tassels, spears and swords, with gavels at the desk, these features are easily the popular ones. And like them are the officers with their titles. There are grand presidents, vice-presidents, secretaries, inspectors, counsellors and legal advisers, wardens, marshals, chaplains, inner and outer sentinals, orators, speakers, writers, with special forms of " great grand " as often as distinction is necessary. Then there are the same officers who are " supreme " and " great supreme ", " grand supreme ", " masters " and so on. There are " ladies " and " gentlemen ", " honorable ", " Sir " and " brother ", " sister ", " knights " and so forth. Such officers feel greatly honored by these offices and make much of them. They are also honored by their fellow members and " given a good time ".

The pride which the negro leaders have in their offices and duties is noteworthy. Perhaps they feel much of social self-feeling but, nevertheless, this constitutes a peculiar factor. A principal of the city colored high school has his letter-heads prepared with " ORATOR OF THE MOST WORSHIPFUL STRINGER GRAND LODGE OF ANCIENT, FREE AND ACCEPTED MASONS OF THE STATE OF MISSISSIPPI " in large and bold lines across the page, with " Principal of Colored School " in small letters in the left hand corner. Others have their photographs inscribed on the stationery with the titles attached. Nor are they alone in valuing their positions. The lay members as a rule put absolute confidence in them. A single leader often dominates an entire conference by his eloquence and thus secures passage for measures which suit his own interests. More frequently two or three or perhaps a half dozen men dominate the entire delegation. Their claims are enormous, but they are rarely doubted. Field leaders and grand secretaries are usually presented with a " purse " at each lodge and they are entertained royally.   Gifts of more value are presented to higher officers.   In the report of Biennial Minutes of the Supreme Lodge of the Independent Order of the Sons and Daughters of Jacob of America is the following " Preface " and " Presentation " details concerning such a gift:

Hon. Supreme Grand Master, and friends of this honored Guest:

On the 25th. of October 1906, while all was busily planning the future destiny of our Order, in session of the Supreme Grand Lodge which convened in the city of Greenville, Sister Lettie J. Walker, a member of the Board of Grand Directors, still and deeply thinking as she is, saw very wisely what a beacon light of wisdom the Sons and Daughters of Jacob of America has as its official head; and how wisely and honestly he has brought the Order of Jacobs from a ridiculous to a sublime standard, that a spirit of highest appreciation was prompted to the extent that a resolution was presented by her to the Supreme Grand Lodge requesting the presentation of a diamond costing $150.00 to our Supreme Grand Master, as a testimonial of our honor and confidence in him.

All honor to Sister Walker for this beautiful thought.

Just what the diamond stud actually cost is not known.   It was presented as well as bought by the committee of ladies. Like the preacher, the negro leaders of the Lodge are popular with the women.   It is not surprising that he should accept all favors and consider himself an important factor in his race and a great man of the hour.   Nor is it surprising that many negroes abuse their privileges and take undue advantages of their less watchful brethren.   With the the chief officers of the grand lodges, this abuse is chiefly in the form of exorbitant demands and misuse of money and power given into their keeping.   Few peoples have been able to furnish more skilful tyrants, if one is to judge by observable data. The officers of the subordinate lodges manifest their abuse of office in the same manner, only to a smaller degree. Their chief fault and abuse lies in their over-bearing disposition toward fellow members and those who wish to apply for membership. Such leaders are often governed wholly by personal motives and refuse membership to any whom they dislike. Consequently much strife arises and not infrequently ends in more serious difficulties, some of which are referred to the Supreme Orders. Again, the officers of subordinate lodges are boisterous and severe in their rulings at regular business sessions, often abusing and belittling members of the order, for the simple reason that they are in a position to do so, and wish to show their authority; they thus feel their positions more weighty. Few more ridiculous acts could be imagined. This state of affairs, however, is not entirely neglected by the supreme officers. In a conclusion to his annual address before the Session of the Grand Lodge of United Brothers and Sisters of Benevolence of America, the Grand President said:

Permit me to note here that we are informed reliable that a great many of the Presidents and other officers of our Local Societies are very rude in their rulings and treatment of members, or in other words, are of the opinion that they are the bosses of the societies instead of the servants which they are. That state of affairs should not exist, yet on the other hand they should be kind, obbliging and courteous at any and all times under the most trying circumstances to give good and wholesome instructions. Such treatment to the most illiterate, boisterous and obstreporous person will have good effect.

Again officers are often elected without due process and then they refuse to be governed by any law save their own wishes. One of the chief violations of the law is refusal

to give bond for the holding of money belonging to the
lodge; still they are retained as officers, chiefly, perhaps,
because there are no others, and because this state of affairs
is quite common. Many other complaints are made of local
officers, such as ignoring the rules and regulations, failure
to dress properly and to conduct the meetings and operations decently.

Before coming to a final summary of the features which
are determining factors in the negro fraternal organizations,
it is well to note certain general conditions under which they
operate and the general relation fraternal circles bear to
negro life and opinion. A partial glimpse of the many
phases of the Lodge may be gained from the facts cited
above. It is to be expected that anything which occupies so
prominent a place in the life of a people would be vastly
beneficial to them and would have the support of the leading members of the race. Nor is our expectation disappointed, for a comparison of the church membership rolls
with those of the fraternal orders shows that prominent
church leaders are in most cases leading lodge members.
The majority of negro preachers are prominent in fraternal
circles. The secret society finds its ablest advocates in the
teachers of the schools and those prominent in negro business circles. Practically the entire professional calling, including the few lawyers and physicians, are enrolled as leaders. Again, non-church-members are intimately associated
with church members both as officers and as " lay " members of the lodge. But while the majority of the negroes
value the relations made possible by the fraternal organizations more than all others, there is a minority, however,
that is agreed that the secret society is fast becoming an evil.
Close students of the situation are undecided whether the
centre of negro life is not being shifted from the Church
to the Lodge. If such is the case, it is to be expected that

there would be found serious objections to lodge life as it
is now being developed.   This objection is maintained
chiefly by certain negro preachers, among whom are some of
their ablest workers.   The question which must be answered, then, is: Does the good overbalance the evil?   In
answer to this inquiry, certain important considerations
should be noted.

The majority maintains, as may be observed in the claims
of the secret orders, that through such societies many
benefits come to the members of the race that are rendered
necessary by the conditions under which the colored people
live.   The lodges care for the sick, look after unfortunate,
bury the dead, and give funds to the family of the deceased
members.   In return for this each member pays only a
small assessment, entirely within his means, varying according to the benefits received.   All assessments are paid in
installments, either weekly, monthly or quarterly.   The
dues for membership vary from ten to twenty-five cents
a week and from ten cents to a dollar a month.   They
hold further that these expenses are not draining upon the
Negro and return him many times their original value, and
that the fraternal order is of practical benefit to the Negro
both in the quality of service rendered and in the methods of
collecting dues; it thus renders a racial service.   It is a
great consolation to the Negro to know that he will be buried
with proper ceremonies and his grave properly marked.
This appeals to a fundamental principal in the Negro's
nature; there are few greater events than the burial, and
none which brings the community together in more characteristic attitude.   The funeral is a social event, for which
the lodge appropriates the necessary expenses.   Here the
religious trend of the Negro is magnified and with praise
of the dead and hopes for the future he mingles religious
fervor with morbid curiosity and love of display.   But the

society not only buries its members but also cares for them while living. Many cases are cited by the negroes of assistance rendered at the critical moment. Persons, sick, old and feeble have been known to be left alone to die within a short distance of neighbors, and were buried by the town authorities. Nor were they more destitute of friends before they became sick than are hundreds of negroes everywhere. The Negro is thus willing to admit the condition of his people, knowing that some obligation must be brought to bear upon them if they are to become brotherly and sisterly in the true sense. The lodge undoubtedly approximates this, for the Negro regards the obligation placed upon him by his society as binding; no member must lack burial, and the sick committees go far toward helping the helpless.

Furthermore, the negroes are a working people and depend entirely upon their wages for a livelihood. They have little or no property which would render them funds for the " rainy day ", and are therefore helpless and dependent in times of sickness or accident. It is essential that the negro and his family be protected by his membership in one or more of the lodges. Such membership will insure him against starvation and dire want, at least, will assure him of visits from his people which he would not otherwise get, and render him secure in a reasonable degree. No one will deny that under such conditions as the negroes labor to-day there is urgent need for just such organizations among the negroes. Again, in addition to the relief features and the social phase of the fraternal orders, the secret societies furnish the Negro a means for united effort. It satisfies a social want, which is unceasing in its demand; it satisfies an imperative demand for benefits, and it satisfies the craving of the Negro to exert his racial and individual ambitions. Here he may rule his own affairs and plan his own business; he is more nearly united here than elsewhere.

He may discuss subjects of interest to his race; he becomes informed of events and discusses them without the white man's knowing it.   The rapidity with which information is diffused throughout a negro community is scarcely less than marvelous, especially when the news relates to matters of racial interest.   The lodge is a means whereby this interchange of information is facilitated; this is an essential benefit, according to the Negro's ablest advocates.   Again, the Negro teaches himself to speak, to debate, to become an " orator " in the halls of his secret society.   He learns the rules and regulations of his society as he learns nothing else. He reads or listens to the news of his lodge paper when he would otherwise not care for the reading.   He is thus being educated slowly and this training appeals to him when no other school interests him.   So the secret societies, combined, offer an effective medium through which the negroes can move with facility and satisfaction.   They offer pride and enthusiasm.   Here are found opportunities for organization and business.   They may organize and drill after the manner of armies.   Their children are trained for future service and their women are united with their men.   The lodge more than anything else offers means for the uniting of communities, counties, states and the negroes of the nation.   Such are some of the advantages claimed by the majority of negroes.

It is claimed, too, that the fraternal associations are helping to solve the race problem.   And well might they assist in so great an undertaking.   Here is opportunity for teaching honesty and diligence; they might teach forbearance and persistency and the doctrine of damnation to criminals and those who shield them, and that no criminal should have a place in the brotherhood of associations.   Here better than any other place they can teach true race pride and encourage honest endeavor toward proper advance-

ment in all lines. But do they do this? It is encouraging
to note that many orders draw up and endorse fitting resolutions at their general meetings and these are given to the
public in good faith in the great majority of instances.
They are the result of proper enthusiasm. Such resolutions
at both general assemblies and local orders, backed by the
members will assist much in bettering the present conditions
that exist in the relations between the races. They will assist
greatly in raising the standard of civilization among the
negroes. Recent utterances of the leaders at these meetings
have voiced the proper sentiment.

"Above all the Negro must uphold law and order." "We
are willing to join the better class of white people at any
time in putting down the criminal class." "Tell it so all the
world may hear—print it in the heaven's blue, so that he
who runs may read it, that the negro of this land will frown
down, cry down, hunt down and strike down this crime and
these criminals, until not one shall be left in all the land, and
a black face be a badge of truth, of peace, of protection to
innocence." "It is our duty to seek the haunts and the influences that produce crime and criminals, with the whip of the
law and the gospel of righteousness scourge them until vicious
idleness shall give place to virtuous industrial intelligence, and
thus purge ourselves and wash away the foul stains of dishonor
from a glorious record transmitted to us by our fathers, although but poor slaves." "We cannot afford to apologize for
crime—we cannot afford to sympathize with the criminals.
We can only afford to do right and fear not before God and
the laws of our country. All of this we can do. We can become the little leaven that shall leaven the whole lump; the
grain of salt which preserves your whole community, your
ward, county, state, until your whole community becomes
known as a center of health-giving energy for the race."
"What a negro will be depends entirely upon what his attitude

is toward himself as well as toward other people. The negro must develop in his own sphere as a negro, after his own nature, and then he will succeed. He should not attempt to get away from his black skin, discard his kinks, be ashamed of his physical features in general. But let him strengthen his face on the inside, whiten his face through his heart, adorn his physical features through his intelligence, magnify and exalt himself in the recognition of the civilized world. He will be respected in proportion as he respects himself."

These are commendable utterances and should the inward meaning be greater than the outward form, these orders would deservedly win a permanent place in the life of the Negro.

But the Fraternal Orders must meet certain serious objections which are offered by members of both races. Reference has already been made to one of these. The Lodge is interfering seriously with the Church and conflicting with many of its services. A minority of leaders among the negroes hold the view that the fraternal organizations are for this reason an evil, but a minority which includes many of the most sincere men and some of the clearest thinkers, who are themselves members of fraternal organizations. The greater part of this number is to be found among the pastors of the churches. The charge is thus stated by one:

The evil effect of secret societies upon the church of God here in the South is becoming to be a serious problem. We should study this problem closely and prayerfully. In the first place the Christian people and members of our different denominational churches have gone into these societies mixed in such a way with sinners and whiskey drinkers and with women whose garments have been dragged in the ditches of immoral despair and degradation until you can't tell one from the other. Even this degraded sinner thinks himself as good as the Christian, consequently the Christian is forced by his obligation to call that drunkard and whiskey-head brother. Hence the standard of religion is lowered and the sinner exalted in all his un-repented-for sins; therefore both are injured. Come out from among them and be ye not partakers of their sins. Many of these little dupe societies give public balls and disgraceful dances to advertise their society interests. In many cases sinner men and women are the "head bursters" of these societies and the Christian people who join them must come in at their command and do whatever they say, right or wrong. If it is to violate religious principle, the chief has said it and his orders must be obeyed. Christians should lead sinners in all things and in all places until they are led to the Cross of Christ. Christians, open your eyes and let not the blind lead you. In nearly all of these societies the Holy Bible is used and sinners are to handle that sacred book whose hands and hearts are unwashed. This seems to be almost sacriligious and downright profanity. We must not be ignorant of these awful sins that are confronting us in our everyday life. This is a serious problem. Sinners and halfway Christians are now saying that their reason for supporting so many of these little dupe societies is that they will do for them what the church will not do, namely: bury them and give them sick benefits; they have an endowment for them or their family. In answer to this trashy saying, let me say this: if they will put all the money in the church that they put in the secret societies the church will be able and will bury them when they die, give them sick benefits when sick, and care for the widows left and educate and care for the children left as orphans. Put all of your grand lodge money and expenses to and from all your supreme lodges in a common church treasury and the church will meet your every demand and need at much less expense.

Another shameful evil is this: Our Class Meetings are growing dull with but little Spiritual fervor, because the members are all gone to meet their society. They cannot go to the class meeting because Brother or Sister So and So will fine me.

Therefore the class leader who tries to be faithful must go and lead the benches—a sad spectacle indeed: The prayer meetings are nearly all dead because deserted by the members gone to the lodge, the prayer meeting having to be upon his lodge night; therefore he shows to the Church and to his God that he loves the lodge better than communion with God. The Ladies' and Stewards' meetings, the Quarterly conferences, and even our revival meetings are all affected by these societies. A brother or sister will tell you at once that they must meet their lodge or had to go to their lodge. These are serious sins and a sad problem now before the church of God. Must this state of affairs continue to exist? or shall we now in the name of Christ stop and reform? God grant that our people will stop before it is too late. I appeal to my race: Stop now and return to God, else we perish and the societies will perish with us. Some people are so ignorant as to say that the society is as good as the church. Oh, my, what ignorance: No one would say that but a poor, blind, ignorant sinner whose eyes are blind with scales. I have been criticised for writing my convictions on these things, but I wish to say to the public that I am paid a salary. The people I serve pay me what they promise and I am not on a beg, and I ask for nothing more than a comfortable support. I write this because I see the awful pit into which my poor people are being thrown, duped and dumped. Now, Brother Preachers, let us return to our pulpits and give ourselves wholly to the service of God and the salvation of the sinners, the sick, the dying, the poor, the needy, the widows and orphans need our attention daily. Get the people to come back to the church. Let us have a great revival of religion.

Many pastors have stated privately the opposition already expressed. A single statement will be given:

Against these societies we have our churches whose total membership is less than half the total membership of the societies. From my own experience, I can safely say that they hinder the church in every way. I was compelled to move my official board from a week night and hold it on Sunday afternoon as there is not a single week night in the month that some of the official members are not called by some of the societies and they almost invariably go to the call of the society when they will not to the call of the church.

It is charged by the whites that these societies are hotbeds of vice and that incendiary views are promoted; that they not only do not help to solve the race problem, but daily make the situation worse. It is charged that these meetings are often plotting places where groups of negroes devise plans and encourage thoughts against the white man; that they go beyond race pride and interest to race antagonism. In answer to these charges it must be said that some of these meetings do discuss improper subjects, and that indecent pictures are sometimes hung on the walls, and that there is little or no restraint upon criminal instinct. It is true that in many cases the tendency is toward unrest in matters pertaining to the relations between the races. But in the ordinary meetings in the smaller communities this is not true. Except in particular sections and under particular circumstances, there are not the agreed councils against the white man; many of these meetings of groups of members are purely proper enjoyment of their own personal rights and pleasures. The lodge meeting is naturally regarded as a place where all matters may be discussed but for the most part the glaring headlines in the newspapers describing negro lodges as storehouses for ammunition and plotting places against the whites, are written by men who know little of the real facts about the Negro and who are willing to distort the truth for the sake of a sensational report. But it should be remembered that so long as any number of lodges make a practice of such agitation as has been mentioned, the above charge will be true. Perhaps there is yet a noticeable fruitage of that old organization known as the Union League which followed the war having as its basic principle the consolidation of the negroes against the whites. There are traces and remnants in many of the Southern towns and passing talk of organizations similar to the Before-day clubs which regularly train their members in incendiary motives; which prescribe immediate death as a penalty for divulging the secrets of the organization. These are a menace to all good societies and the sooner all traces of such groups are obliterated the better it will be for all concerned. There are many negroes who advocate extreme measures in their excitement, and they easily obtain a following. Such negroes are doing their race more damage than can be eradicated. And on the other hand the misguided doctrinaires and the greedy fools who instill incendiary ideas into the minds of the negroes, regardless of the wreck and carnage which must follow, are the leaders most dangerous of all to the race. It is of prime importance that the negroes be free at all times from all appearance of evil in this respect. The Federation of Women's Clubs, if they desire to accomplish what they profess, should keep this tremendous fact in mind and stop the present-day tendency toward unrest, which is prominent in many of the secret societies of which women constitute the membership. If they will assist their men in substantial achievement, they will, among many other things, see that agitation against the whites need not be a characteristic feature of their local meetings. The height of folly and idiotic thoughtlessness is to be found in such agitations; putting aside the purposes of the benefit societies, and not knowing that they are utterly incapable of discussing any revolutionary measures relating to labor or any other topic, these groups bring untold permanent hurt to the race.

Other serious objections are offered. The lodge is a waste of time and energy for the negroes. It takes them away from home and work and renders them useless for anything else, while the lodge itself offers no permanent substitute. The lodge is an unreasonable drain upon the Negro's money. He must attend the local meetings, pay the assessments for membership, local extras imposed by the whim of some tyrant leader, the extra fees for the supreme and grand lodges, and the dozens of other expenses involved from time to time in regalia and special functions. Representatives must attend the general sessions and for this they must have certain requirements and must pay their expenses to and from the convention. Foolish gifts and appropriations are made on every hand; the expenses of these must be met, and there is no material benefit from them. The handling of money and the power to make assessments encourages the spirit of dishonesty and graft among the negroes. The present methods of the lodge encourage, to the fullest extent, superficiality and display, the very things which need to be regulated among the negroes. While the rules and regulations are good, there is little conformity to them, hence the increased disregard for drill, order and systematic action. In fine, the lodge is the greatest of those factors which lead the Negro to neglect the substantial groundwork of his economic and moral salvation. It shifts his efforts from the detailed accumulation of property and the attainment of individual worth to the popular general achievements. It leads him to magnify and overvalue the outside without due consideration of essential qualities.

Again, however, it is but just to give the negro's interests full consideration. Even though the defects seem much in the majority, it is but fair to sum up the better qualities and the purposes for which the societies are founded.   The constitution and by-laws of the several societies differ only in details and are for the most part very much alike.   The length varies from ten to fifteen thousand words, according as particulars are stressed or features are added.   There are great possibilities in the fraternal order conducted according to the constitution and by-laws.   All of the societies incorporate in their requirements for admission to membership that persons shall be moral and upright, dealing in no illegal business and of good reputation.   The purposes of the orders are thus seen to be of the highest order and would seem to be the exact essentials for the race.   Religious devotion is an important feature.   Their societies are devoted to many virtues.   One holds that " In union there is strength " another, " At the bar of universal justice right reigns supreme "; another, is devoted to " friendship, love and truth," while still another is devoted to " Virtue, Purity, Honesty and Prosperity."   Others are devoted avowedly to the same purposes and incorporate the best sentiments possible in their mottoes.   For instance, take the closing ceremony for the laying of the corner stone as an example of high and noble purpose expressed in words :

In the name of virtue I scatter this earth on this stone typical of the moral excellence and charity of our Order and as a reminder that we are of the dust and to dust we shall return. In the name of purity I sow this grain in this earth typical of the manner members of our Order who are of themselves free from dirt enter walks of life and force moral cleanness upon men. I in the name of honesty and to promote prosperity sprinkle this earth and this grain with water, may the favors of God rest and be daily with the people of this building and those of this community as they go into abide within and pass out of its portals. As the moments of time pass away may all men especially all Jacobs love, worship, and adore Thee, and the four principles of Jacobism, virtue, purity, honesty, and prosperity, hold in esteem the name and teaching of God.

And indeed many of the local leaders profess to rule by standards of morality and claim that they expel or suspend members who are unworthy of the lodge. As a fact the records show that many are actually suspended. Reproof is most common for violating the laws of the order, for misappropriation of funds, for non-payment of dues, for immorality, for unlawful co-habitation, for disturbing harmony of order, for theft, for fighting, the time of suspension varying from two weeks to twenty-five years. Expulsion occurred for murder, theft, receiving money on false pretense, misappropriation of lodge funds, unlawful co-habitation, and one case was recorded of expulsion for ninety-nine years for burglary. Many of these names are published, and the Negro has no sympathy or mercy when he once begins upon an unfortunate brother.

Attention should be called to the Federation of Colored Women's Clubs which holds an annual meeting, in much the same way as do the whites. While it would seem that little practical work is done by these women, it is necessary to note the better side of their work. Here enthusiasm is as evident as at the other clubs and they rise for the moment "above the petty affairs of the world." They might well do a great work under better environment; perhaps the value of their labors is not felt and will in the end work much good. They are not excelled by the fraternal organizations, at least in the expression of noble purposes. The following is a statement given out from the state meeting of Mississippi:

These women with human hearts and souls that reach up to glorify a pure Creator are being awakened to a moral and true virtuous consciousness that has been lying dead more than two hundred years. The colored women of the state met in convention declaring to the world that Negro woman stands as high and firm for true moral virtue as any other woman that lives. The meeting was so enthusiastic that every woman that was present wished that her absent sister were there. It was an encouragement to every struggling sister for true womanhood to meet others of her kind. No class of persons could be more elated than Negro men to know that ere long they will not be scorned because of the immorality of their women. Many a young lady was made virtuously strong in that meeting and each would do untold good should she go back to her home and community and there be a shining light among the others in an attractive way. There can be no better way of establishing virtue among both women and men than through the medium of the Federation.

If this were only true and if practical lives could only bear out the enthusiastic word testimony, how rapidly would the race begin to rise. It is thus seen that the outward purposes of the Negro organizations are of the right sort. What then is lacking?

What is a true estimate of the Negro fraternal organization and benevolent society? What accounts for their marvelous success and growth? Wherein do they fail in fundamentals and essentials and how can they be made better? A proper estimate is scarcely possible with the data in hand and at this stage of their development. It may be well, however, to note the essential characteristics of the main operations. The outside student is astonished at the remarkable benefits paid by the insurance and benevolent societies. How can they make and sustain such claims, even with double the amount of assessments charged for membership? And yet few claims are unpaid and few instances have occurred of failure of the society. And this is in the face of the undisputed fact that many funds are used by the chief officers and others are badly managed and often lost in a business project. The officers are paid good salaries, ranging from four hundred to seventeen hundred dollars per annum. A number of records show that amounts varying from one hundred to fifteen hundred dollars have been misapprpopriated. How then does the lodge meet its demands? In the first place, the first assessments and the regular membership fees are only a relative part of the demands. Reference has already been made to the numerous extras that are demanded constantly. Fines from subordinate lodges go to swell the total amount. Charters are sold at from five to fifty dollars; seals range from two to ten dollars and every lodge is required to have one. The official organs in some instances assist in raising this money. From the beginning of the year to its end, the poor negro lodge member is beset with calls for money on all hands. In the second place, perhaps one-half of the members who join the orders do not remain in good standing long enough to receive the benefits therefrom. As their enthusiasm wanes and times become harder, they allow their dues to lapse and thus forfeit what they have already paid. They thus receive no benefits and cause the supreme lodge no outlay, while at the same time they have contributed much to its support. These funds remain in the treasury. While the total membership of the lodge is usually on the increase, it is quite a different membership each year. The field workers keep enthusiasm up from place to place and gain new members. And almost as large a number of renewals is made each year as of new members. Such members pay extra assessments for the privilege of renewing, which also helps to increase the treasury fund. Again, many of the lodges provide that, when they are unable to meet the payment to the beneficiaries of the deceased, a pro-rata assessment is made upon each member, thus insuring the amount. Perhaps one-half of the societies are " mutual " in this respect and are governed according to the jurisdiction of their leaders. In this way and by combining all the forces, the negro lodge pays its insurance and benefits with comparative ease.

The question naturally arises as to the degree to which the purposes of the Lodge as set forth in the constitution and by-laws are adhered to in the practical working of the lodges. And the question is both important and difficult. The majority of subordinate lodges are wholly unable to interpret the constitution and by-laws as they should be known. They are rarely a practical factor as a whole; certain parts are learned as favorites and the local lodge supplies the rest according to its own pleasure. Thus it is with the organization of lodges, the giving of bond for the officers, and the receiving and retaining of members. The average negro is incompetent to enact any of the requirements strictly and continually. He may do so for a few meetings, but he soon grows careless. Consequently the headquarters must needs send constant threats and warnings in order to keep the lodges going at all. And too often, the supreme officers themselves are equally careless and incompetent, caring only for the general appearance and the possibility of getting as much money for the lodge as possible. In fine, the evidence shows that the great majority of irregularities are unnoticed; regulations are thus a farce. So it is with the moral influence which the lodge exercises over the community. While cases are tried and members are actually suspended, the great majority go unnoticed. Personal dislike and malice, jealousy and the sense of superiority have much to do with the officer's action.

The matter may be stated by saying that principles are subordinated to an occasion, and as a moral factor in practice are worth little.   Like the church, in practical life, the lodge excuses the criminal instead of raising the moral standard.   There is strife and discord abundant in the internal workings of the lodge.   Here again, the poor Negro must battle with his inheritance and with his environment. He follows the lines of least resistance and his battle is lost. Like the problem of the home, church and school, the problem of the lodge may be explained by saying that the maximum good, which might come from these organizations under better circumstances, is turned into evil or at least the minimum good by the overwhelming odds of environment.   The Negro at his present stage cannot help his superficiality and love of display.

Can the Negro begin to apply himself through the medium of his societies to the individual and home?   Can he learn that he must solve the fundamental problems of his race on a small scale rather than long for world-conquest?   Is he willing to face the situation, give up his superficiality and devote himself to the betterment of his condition?   Is he willing to take the problems one by one and meet them face to face?   One of the negro leaders sets forth a great motto, "A Black Face a Badge of Truth, of Peace, of Protection to Innocence ".   And well might they strive for such an attainment.   In this school of adults in which the Negro finds most of his politics, he might also find a great school for moral training where a higher ethical standard can be raised.   To the Southern white man, the face of an innocent and industrious colored person appeals as few other things do; assistance and encouragement are always the rewards of such individuals.   The finer type of Southern white stands firmly for justice to such negroes even to the jeopardy of the protector's own interests.   The good white man's respect for such negroes is little short of admiration and he is anxious to help him along. Can the negro secret societies of the present day assist in raising the average of negro character, institute simple campaigns for industry and hygiene, and strive to better the relations between the races by effectually instilling principles of moral life into the race? The negroes have a noble inheritance in the deeds of many fathers and mothers, whose principles of fidelity and application are worthy of copy. Will the fraternal organizations and benevolent societies at least study the situation and become followers of the faithful fathers?

CHAPTER IV

THE HOME LIFE, DISEASES AND MORALS OF THE NEGRO

INDIVIDUAL character is inseparably connected with pure homes, and to the social and political organism the home is the first essential. The home is the most cherished possession that we have; it is first in our hearts and in our actions. For home and loved ones we live and work; we love them better than ourselves, and because of them we attain whatever of worth is consistent with the best that is in us. The scenes in the home bring to us the brightest pictures our hearts can fancy and awaken the tenderest feelings of which our beings are capable. We do not forgive the stranger who enters, not knowing the traditions and habits of the inmates, and criticizes the arrangement of home or looks upon any part of it with contempt. For the home and the family are one; they constitute the " fundamental problem of civilization," the first institution that makes for the higher development of man. With the home preserved intact, a race is safe and ready for individual and national greatness. In proportion as the home life of a community is of a high order, to that degree will the community make for moral and civic righteousness; with the home and family neglected, nothing can long uphold a race. For no people can live above their home life.

If the circumstances and conditions which make up the basis for home life are almost wholly lacking in a people; if there is no deep impulse to cherish the home with parents, wife and children; if there is no desire to find true

homes and improve them, surely the leaders of such a
people would recognize the dire necessity to which they
have come.   What strivings ought there to be for knowledge of these dangerous conditions and for the realization
of any aspirations for better things on the part of leaders
and those most interested!   What efforts would be put forth
to make race leaders capable of establishing models of purity and ideals of life!   And yet, is not such a people in our
midst?   Side by side, worshiping the same God and serv-
ing the same commonwealths as the whites, the Negro's
life may almost be described by saying that these fundamentals are thus lacking.   Their first and crying need is for
home life and training.   And while there is much unpleas-
antness and dissatisfaction in criticizing as a " stranger "
the habitations of these people, it is necessary for all concerned to paint the picture from life, to see things as they
are.   And to speak truthfully concerning the Negro at home,
the purity of plainness must be observed.

The majority of the negroes, as a rule, live in the inferior
sections of the town and occupy inferior houses.   There
may be distinguished three subdivisions of negro inhabitants of the community: those who live in a better negro
section of the town, those who are segregated in a poorer
and more barren negro division, and those who live in the
midst of the whites in servant-houses or cottages near the
white residences.   In the first class are the majority of the
more prosperous negroes in the community, some twenty-
five per cent of whom own their homes.   The proportion of
better houses occupied by negroes is greatest in this section.
Such sections of the town, being in the nature of a negro
town, often receive various names: Freeman's Town, Liberty Hill, Macedonia, Improvement, Rising Sun, and so on.
In the second division, the houses are more thickly grouped
and the majority of them are inferior in size and condition,

if compared with those of the first division, though many of the best negroes live in this section. Few own their homes; they rent from whites, many of whom have built cottages purely for the income which may be derived from them. Sometimes the houses are rented from negroes. In this division of the negro inhabitants may be found the most typical common life. The houses are not good and are often far from comfortable; the windows are without glass, the coverings let in wind and rain, the rooms are small. Few of the houses are painted either externally or on the inside. This section, also, receives various names, such as Rabbitskip, Sheriff's Hill, Gullensville, Shakerag, Needmore. The two negro sections mentioned are ordinarily in opposite parts of the towns. The third class, numbering some twenty per cent of the entire negro population of the community, includes many of the most industrious negroes; among them may be found many of the best homes and much of the best negro life. Taken as a whole, the average negro house presents an exterior with the appearance of neglect; the yards are not kept and rubbish of various kinds is much in evidence. Except for the woodpile, the axe, the clothes-line and utensils for washing, the appearance of many negro houses would indicate that they were unoccupied. The inmates are, however, apparently satisfied.

The houses of the community may be described under three divisions. Number one will represent the best quality of houses, number two the medium, and number three the sorry. If the houses of the whites be divided into three classes according to quality, number three is as good as the best houses of the negroes. If the negro abodes be thus divided, number one will make some fifteen per cent of the total number of houses, number two about thirty per cent, and number three over fifty per cent. If they be classified

again according to the number of rooms, about fifteen per
cent have only one room, about fifty per cent have two
rooms, about twenty per cent have three rooms, and five or
ten per cent have more than three rooms. The proportion
of houses with more than four rooms is exceedingly small
and varies with the prosperity of the community of negro
individuals. In the larger towns and cities, exceptions are
more numerous. The average size, then, is about two
rooms, the average family consists of four persons. A considerable number of negro women live alone, occupying
ten to fifteen per cent of the total number of cottages; many
others live in small cottages with their children, there being
some ten per cent of the total number of families with a
woman at the head. The proportion of parents without
legitimate children is large, in general from fifteen to twenty
per cent of the families. On the other hand, besides the
typical family of three, four, five, and six members, many
have from seven to twelve, although relatively few are
found with more than eight or nine. Quite a number of individual instances have been noted where a family of ten,
eleven, twelve, and even fourteen, have occupied a cottage
of two and three rooms. Such a family may include the
daughter who has been deserted by her husband, or who
has deserted him, or an unmarried daughter with one or
two children. A physician reported an extreme case of
fourteen living in two rooms, and when brought to his
attention there were four cases of pneumonia, three of
which were fatal; and the case, while extreme, is far from
exceptional. It is true, however, that the average family
among the negroes is not so large as in former years.

In such crowded quarters—not infrequently in one room
—must exist the entire family with living apparatus. The
interior of the houses is not better than the exterior. With
a bedstead or two, or couch, box, tables, bureau, dresser,

tubs and basins, buckets and cooking utensils, one would scarcely expect the conditions to be conducive to comfort or health. In addition to these, accumulations of worthless articles serve to make the room more crowded. A box or corner of the room with rags, strings, pieces of ropes, boxes, papers, attractive circulars, and various trinkets together with articles kept for superstitious reasons contribute to the general trash. However, pictures may be seen on the walls. They are usually nicely framed, being bought from agents. Enlarged photographs of the members of the family, the Lord's Prayer, the Ten Commandments, and certificates of membership to fraternal and insurance societies are the most common. The negroes value their membership certificates to secret societies very highly, and often undergo hardships to get them framed. Sometimes they leave them to be framed, and do not call for them until several months afterwards. As soon as the money can be spared, however, they return and call for them. Generally the furniture is of a fairly good quality; this is usually bought on the instalment plan, when such is possible. The article is not infrequently half paid for, when the negro decides he does not want it or cannot meet the required payments, and it is then forfeited to the dealer. Likewise costly articles of no practical value, clocks, sewing-machines which are little used, organs are bought at the persuasion of the agent. In the case of the organ, it may be little used, or perhaps no one in the family can play it; but it has its attraction and answers a purpose. The Negro's question before marrying is not whether he can support a family, but whether he has anything to go in the house.

With such crowded conditions habits of uncleanness naturally grow. A glance inside the average negro cottage is most discouraging. The negroes themselves have described the picture in a number of songs. Says one of a house where he had been courting:

Clothes all dirty ain't got no broom,
Old dirty clothes all hanging in de room,

lines which exactly portray the room. Another complains
of grease and dirt, while another stanza goes:

Honey, babe, honey babe, bring me de broom,
De lices and de chinches 'bout to take my room.

It will thus be seen that even with the above-mentioned
conditions the home is not without much disorder. Add to
these the further conditions under which the negroes must
earn a livelihood. With those who do laundry work, besides the living apparatus, the soiled laundry is kept in the
house, and in stormy weather the washing and drying of
the clothes, as well as the ironing, must be done in the
house. The men come in with dirty clothes; the nature of
their work makes this necessary. There is not time, even
were the disposition present, to keep the house clean.
Throughout the day the negro home is full of haste and
disorder. The mother who cooks for a white family is up
and off early in the morning, leaving the children uncared-
for at home; the man soon leaves also for his work. The
children thus have no care and attention, nor do they always get breakfast; often they must wait for the return
of the mother, who brings something from the table of the
whites. Not infrequently this is late in the morning; so
it is with the other meals. It is often late in the evening
before she returns from her last duties, and then she wishes
to go out among her friends or to some gathering. And
too often, in spite of duties, which she does not recognize
as such, she does go. In the meantime the household is
kept together as best it may be under such circumstances.
Not only the cooking, but laundry for two or three
families is the part of the more industrious negro women,

which but adds to the duties of the day and consequent neglect of home. The children who attend school at all must be gotten ready with little care. The men who are regularly employed are at home little of the time, and those who do not work regularly are more of a hindrance than assistance. The negro woman is not unfrequently the head of the negro family. Many negro men loaf about the home, depending upon their wives and children to support them, while they work a little here and there and abuse the family. On the other hand, there are many women who refuse to do any kind of work and at the same time they completely neglect the affairs at home. The husband must return in the morning and make the fires, get the wife something to eat, besides doing many trivial things which please her fancy; and unless he does all that she requires of him, she threatens him with infidelity. Sometimes the man's patience is exhausted and he leaves her; usually he endures it and is all the more " foolish " about his wife. A negro thirty years of age lived with his wife and child, a boy of six years, in a cottage of two rooms; his place of work was within a few yards of his home. This negro would often leave his work and run over to the " house " more than a dozen times a day. This evidently had two bases, the one because he wanted to please her by showing his attention—he was very " foolish 'bout his babe," the other because he feared the constant threats of his wife, that she would let some " rounder " in. During a single week they have quarreled and separated three times; but as soon as separated they would become reconciled again. Often the wife would run out of the house screaming for help; this she did to make him do what she wanted; at other times she maintained that " her ole man " had threatened to kill her, a thing which he admitted—the threat at least was justified. And still at the close of the week or day of such an

occurrence the negro laborer cheerfully and begrudgingly
turned over his pay to her.   The wife immediately wasted
it, leaving him to get supplies for the home as best he could;
and unless he furnished what she wanted to eat and wear,
she threatened again to leave him.   It is thus that the negro
woman is proverbial for her skill in getting the " dollar "
from the man.

Since the sum of his earnings is small, and since he
spends much for unnecessary things, for church and lodge,
and whatever pleases his fancy, the negro would not be expected to keep an abundant supply of provisions in the
home.   Dietary studies show that he does not.   He buys
small quantities at a time, and there is much irregularity in
even this amount.   He is generally required to pay cash
for what he buys; this he has in small quantities only.   In
some instances the negroes are considered quite trustworthy,
but in most cases to give credit to him means not only the
loss of the amount owed, for the time being, but also the
loss of his patronage.   For he will not come back again
until he has paid what he owes.   When the negroes have
comparatively plenty of money they buy groceries of the
first quality, otherwise they buy the inferior quality, the
latter condition being the rule.   But the negro not infrequently lives from hand to mouth.   The man may get his
meals at his place of work; the woman at her place.   If
she cooks for the whites, she brings provisions from the
white man's table and pantry, which she invariably brings
in the bucket or basket carried for the purpose.   One need
not expect to hire a cook if she is not permitted to carry
her bucket along with her.   The negroes thus economize
not only in the matter of actual provisions, but also in fuel
and time.   Often the men do not go home for dinner, but
with a nickel or dime they buy from the lunch-counter a
pie or an egg, sandwich, cheese and crackers, and eat them

on the streets. They apparently eat such a dinner with relish. The same method often follows for supper; the restaurants run by the negroes supply a part of this demand. Negroes often buy fruit when it is cheap; sometimes they prefer a couple of bottles of soda-water to a meal. Negroes often go for many hours without eating anything. The negro sings longingly of the good things to eat and says dolefully,

> It's three long weeks since I have eat a meal.

It is not surprising, then, that he eats ravenously when food is set before him. One marvels to watch such negroes eat; enjoyment shines from their faces and they are at their best wits, while eating enough to seemingly kill the ordinary man. The " hand out " is proverbial. This is sometimes earned by a little odd job, sometimes it is begged. Sometimes it is furnished by the cook at the back door or yard of the white man's house. For the irregular negro it is his chief source of livelihood, and he sings,

> All I want's my strong hand-out,
> It will make me strong and stout.

They pride themselves on getting the best meals and with the least work. They sing of good things to eat, of buttermilk and " greasy greens," of chicken and meat. The handout represents the ideal in such a case. Says one:

> I wus goin' down the railroad, hungry an' wanted to eat,
> I ask white lady fer some bread an' meat,
> She giv' me bread an' coffee an' treated me mighty fine,
> If I could git them good hand-outs, I'd quit work, bum all de time.

Again, the negro tells of being invited to dine, of eating hog-eye grease, burnt bread and ashes, as well as the better things. One stanza of the song goes:

> Ask me to de table, thought I'd take a seat,
> First thing I saw wus big chunk o' meat,
> Big as my head, hard as a maul,
> I eat cake, corn bread, bran and all.

It is readily seen that the negro does not need to keep large supplies of provisions, and that he lives much to his satisfaction. It is also unfortunately true that the associations and good cheer which might come from the home and meals taken together are almost totally wanting. It is a sad picture for any people to exist from hand to mouth, now not having enough to eat, now too much, never eating quietly and with the warmth and fellowship of the family.

It will thus be seen that there is little orderly home life among the negroes. Health conditions and daily habits are no better than the arrangement of the house. Sometimes an entire family consisting of father, mother, large and small children occupy the same rooms. Nor do they ventilate, and especially when any of the inmates are sick they are loath to let in the fresh air. Many superstitions constrain them to endanger their health by foolish practices. A negro family refused to remove ashes from the fireplace for several months, fearing thus to cause the death of the sick one. Other foolish notions relating to a change of clothing prevail. Consequently there is less hope of recovery in case of serious sickness, and more opportunities for sickness to grow. In the day, at night, when sick or when well, the negroes have no conditions for inspiring love of home or for health of mind and body. Physicians testify that three or four often sleep in a bed together; they do not change clothing before going to bed in many cases, and often go for many days without a change of garments. They go through the rain constantly without umbrella or coat and remain wet all day; at night they sleep in the same clothes, but sleep soundly and peacefully enough. They do not bathe nor do they think this unusual. It is related that young negroes often sleep with their heads toward the fireplace and their feet uncovered in the opposite direction, and that children cover their heads while their feet remain cold. It has been suggested that the personal habits of the negroes are filthy; such is the case. Filth and uncleanness is everywhere predominant. One must refrain from a description of the worst phase of the negro's personal habits. Yet their own best witnesses testify that nothing seems to improve such habits, nor do the majority of negroes seem to care. Says one of their number: " Preaching the laws of health and hygiene to them in this age has about the same effect as preaching the gospel has. They hear willingly but heed slowly. Many hear but only a few will believe; a few will be saved but many will be lost." In many instances the best white physicians are unwilling to practice among the negroes. The existence of such conditions of home-life as obtain among them makes any attendance upon their sick unpleasant and repulsive, besides difficult. In addition to this, the fee is uncertain and the physician cannot afford to attend many of such patients. Indeed, one feels the pathos of the situation in its essentials when he sees a negro frantically trying to get a doctor but is unable to do so. The negroes have very few physicians of their own; the average town is without such a man. The list of applicants for license shows, however, that they are on the increase, and this indicates a better condition for the future.

Furthermore, the relations existing between the parents, and among the other members of the family are not pleasant. Little time is spent at home with the pleasures that properly belong to the home. Even the short time thus occupied is rarely conducive to pleasure or harmony. The father and mother are often against each other, and loud in their war of words, sometimes fighting. The children

are witnesses to this quarreling and fighting; sometimes
the children are hostile to either mother or father or both.
The relation between the younger and older children is not
one of harmony, nor are the general relations between the
older children and parents better. The parents in turn are
reckless and severe in their abuse and punishment of the
children. Such phrases as " I'll skin you alive," " I'll beat
the life out o' you," " I'll wear you into er frazzle," " I
sholy am gwine kill you " are every-day expressions. With
the negro such expressions of feeling seem to indicate the
natural outburst of expression signifying to some extent
the characteristic love of "bluff." Such utterances are
more common to mothers. Perhaps they do not intend
severity of any kind; it is most likely that the offending
chap will go unpunished, and a short time later he may be
heard surpassing his mother as he threatens with great
vociferousness to annihilate his playmates. Again, the parent often begins to administer corporal punishment and
never knows when to stop, and finally when tired out he
sees that he has abused the child, and his sympathy takes the
expression of " Now go on, you little brat, I didn't mean
to kill you; you sholy won't let me ketch you at that no
more." Many negroes devise ingenious methods of punishing their children, some of which are effective. For instance, a negro man always brought his boy some candy
just before punishing him. When he called George and told
him that here was some candy, George began to cry, for
he knew what it meant. The parent would insist that the
child eat the candy, and as soon as he had begun to enjoy
it the thrashing would be forthcoming. The idea with the
negro seemed to be two-fold: he would make the punishment impressive by contrasting it with the thing which the
boy liked, and he would also show him that the punishment
was not anger, but paternal love. This latter element the

negro never admitted, but it was apparently there. So others have devised equally interesting modes, but on the whole, the scolding and punishment has just the opposite effect from that which it should have. The children rarely feel kindly towards their parents. So it is that after they have grown up the family is not united in purpose, spirit, or in physical presence. The statement is a common one— and there is much to substantiate it—that the members of negro families are more separated now than in the time of slavery. Such is undoubtedly the case in many families where the children have grown up to maturity. Many examples seem pathetic, but are apparently forgotten. Instance after instance has been noted where parents, old and almost helpless, have been deserted by their children. Nor do the parents know the whereabouts of their children. Often they say that sometime ago the children were at such-and-such a place, but with a vacant look of sadness the parents say they do not know where their children are now. The one desire of the younger negroes—and it seems to be a natural one—appears to be freedom from work and parental control.

The conditions of the home are not made better by the reading of literature; for the most part the influence is entirely wanting, for good or bad. A few newspapers are read and the advertisements enjoyed. The negro newspaper is growing in its circulation and influence. The majority of those published by lodge and church are a positive influence. They generally contain much sound advice and give glimpses of negro life as they should do. The Negro is loyal to his paper, and the pride in it is an incentive to better work, when the paper is sound and conservative. A few daily papers are read by the negroes, while the mass of information regarding the negroes and popular events are easily spread from individual to individual, or from lodge meeting and church. The younger negroes are far too fond of books of vulgar stories and songs and of the dime-novel type. A favorite story among the negroes of a town was picked up. The opening words began: " Hit him ag'in, Sarp." " I shorely will, Billy." " Slap! Smack! Bump!" While a number of church papers are read by the leading church members, the influence is relatively small. What is more surprising is the fact that there are few Bibles among the negroes. One would expect that they would at least own Bibles, but a great many do not. Some confess that they do not want them, while others think they do not need the Bible; still others seem surprised to know that they are expected to have a Bible. " Naw, suh, Boss, I ain't got no Bible; ain't got time fer sich in mine; I does well to git a livin', I does;" or, " I don't need no Bible, huh." The persuasive agent has failed to make the Bible as attractive as many other things; the church societies look little to their distribution.

Growing out of this disorder, confusion, and lack of home training, two things might be expected: immorality and crime, on the one hand, and disease on the other. Such is the case. The indiscriminate mixing in the home leads to bad personal habits; the utter lack of restraint deadens any moral sensibilities that might be present. Nowhere in the home is there restraint; the contact and conduct of its members belong to the lowest classification. There is little knowledge of the sanctity of home or marital relations; consequently little regard for them. The open cohabitation of the sexes related by no ties of marriage is a very common practice; little is thought of it as it relates to the race; there is apparently no conscience in the matter. They are aware, however, that the law operates against such a practice, and just preceding court week the mode of living is abandoned, indicating that they know such relations are wrong. An illustration will indicate the exact nature of the cases. Sam, the house-boy, was, to all appearances, an ideal darkey. He was supposed to be free from the accusations of sexual immorality, if any negro in the community was. The facts of his case showed otherwise, however. He lived in one room of a two-room cottage. In the other room lived a woman with four children. This woman had a visitor from the country, and since there was no room for her, she was assigned to stay in Sam's quarters, to which he readily assented. She remained there for two months, until the other woman " got tired o' such doins in her house," although she had instituted the proceedings. She threatened to report Sam to the town authorities and frightened him by telling the white folks about it. He in turn borrowed the money and bought a license, married the woman from the country, although he had appeared never to have thought of such a procedure before. When the neighboring woman knew that they were to be married she begged the white people not to say anything about the matter, adding that it was all right, they were to marry and she did not mean what she had said. After the marriage it would, of course, be unreasonable to assert that there had been aught of wrong or disgrace. Such ethical views are significant. This wife has done nothing for Sam save to make him miserable, and she is as " ugly as the devil " besides. She makes him worthless at his work, leads him into trouble, and gives him no home. Nor is this example extreme; on the contrary, it is but a mild one, and the number of such cases is very large. Indiscriminate cohabitation of members of the family, with its train of consequences, is common enough among the negroes. Apparently nothing will restrain the negro in his present stage except the law. The negro preacher was not far from the basic need when he affirmed that the greatest need of

his people was "moar laws and streaker laws;" he wished
to give emphasis to this verdict. Too often for the good
of the race, the law overlooks the majority of such practices, taking immorality of all kinds as a necessary and natural adjunct to negro life. Religious allegiance seems
powerless to uphold and purify the lives of the many; the
law is the best expedient. Outside the home, on all occasions and continually, there are no less indiscriminate practices. Too often every home is considered a place of de-
bauchery; the negroes know full well the numerous houses
to which they are invited and to which they go. The
"creeper," the "rounder-shaker," and the "eastman" are
too well known to elicit surprise among the negroes. Every
home is liable to their criminal influence, when every man
and every woman becomes common property.

Perhaps nowhere in negro life does the problem of
immorality appear more stupendous than among the children. Innocently they reflect all that is not innocent; guilt-
less, they show the superlative of filth and indecency. The
amount of knowledge of evil and evil practices possessed
by small children is unthinkable. Their practices are no
less appalling. The unconscious depth of depravity to which
the children have already come is appalling. Their "fun"
is one continuous product of damning influence. Their
brightness of mind is turned into shame and is witnessed
in the seemingly inexhaustible fund of what they call
"funny" songs and sayings, which in reality are to the
highest degree indecent and profane. Nor is it surprising
that the children become so early in life masters of the unclean and immoral. They hear unclean words and witness
obscene deeds on every hand. They but reflect on a small
scale what their elders embody in their daily life.

There is no better and more accurate story of the immoral and unmoral life of the Negro than is told in his

songs. Yet, only the better songs may be given to the public; the great mass of vulgar and indecent songs do not admit of publication. Often such songs are in the majority, and they are generally favorites among the negroes. With the life of immorality comes its expression in story and song. With the gifted " music physicianers," " musicianers " and " songsters," a vast throng " swelling with song— instinct with life, tremulous treble and darkening bass," with the " gift of story and song," comes also the inexpressible wilderness of vulgarity and indecency. Their songs tell of every phase of immorality and filth; they represent the superlative of the repulsive. Ordinarily the imagination can picture conditions worse than they actually exist; but as in negro life deeds are beyond reason, so in these songs the pictures go far beyond the white man's conception of the real. The prevailing theme of this class of songs is that of sexual relations, and there is no restraint in its expression. In comparison with similar songs of other peoples that have been preserved, those of the Negro stand out in a class of their own. They are sung at the dance and other mixed gatherings. They are sung by groups of boys and girls, of men and women, and they are sung by individuals who revel in their suggestiveness. Here the vivid imagination of the Negro makes his constant thought a putrid bed of rottenness and intensifies his already depraved nature. Openly descriptive of the grossest immorality and susceptible of unspeakable thoughts and actions, rotten with filth, they are yet sung to the time-honored melodies. The words of the song are visualized into the deed and incorporated into the imagination—children from ten to twelve years of age knowing a hundred such songs; songs varying in all degrees of dirty suggestion and description sung in the home, not collectively, but by individuals, with no thought of impropriety — these

constitute pictures for the student of the race to con-
template. It is a marvel of the Negro's mental tendency
that he can keep together such a vast heap of moral refuse
and filth. Nor are the religious songs free from the in-
vasion; parodies as vulgar as the accumulations of indecent thought can contrive are sung to standard tunes and
stately measures. It is the saddest side of the Negro's
nature. Must he continue as the embodiment of fiendish
filth incarnated in the tabernacle of the soul? He cannot
aspire in filth nor experience longing for anything that is
good, while reveling in the evil. These songs come ill-
harmonized to the soft, stirring melodies of a folk-life; and
sadder is it to know that the song reflects his true nature.
Will the Negro not check his downward path and make
good the cheering possibilities that apparently lie dormant
in the race?

Add to this disorder and immorality extreme health conditions and prevalence of disease. The Negro rarely knows
what it is to be in good health, although he troubles little
about his condition. The fact that the great majority of
negroes rarely ever enjoy good health, a natural conse-
quence of their habits, has been transmitted from generation to generation in their well-known replies to inquiries
concerning their health. He never answers that he is well,
but only fairly so: " O, I'se doin' tolerable, I guess," " I'se
only po'ly to-day," " I ain't well no mo'," and many similar expressions. While the reply thus given has become
habitual, it is almost invariably the correct statement of a
chronic state of health. But aside from the fact of general
health conditions, it is true that the diseases most destructive to a race are increasing among the negroes. Hence
the death-rate is far greater than among the whites. There
can be no more than a reference to these diseases here.
Suffice it to say that the testimony of all the practicing

physicians among the negroes, in so far as their experience and observations go, bears out the fact that the diseases described by the specialists are prevalent and on the increase. The facilities for obtaining accurate and exhaustive information in the smaller communities, as well as in the larger cities, do not exist. But so far as the investigator is able to discover, the condition of the Negro of to-day in the communities studied does not differ from the general summary which follows. The minor points of variation and the professional opinions of practicing physicians will give added concreteness to the general statement concerning the diseases of the black man. President G. Stanley Hall, of Clark University, states the summary of medical studies upon the Negro's liability to disease as follows:

To select the single question of health, from many of the racial differences above enumerated, we find in compiling many medical studies of the blacks, that their diseases are very different from ours. Their liability to consumption is estimated at from one and a half to three and a half times greater than that of the whites. This is only partly due to their transportation from equatorial Africa, because there they are peculiarly prone to tuberculosis, and measurements show less average lung capacity than is found in the whites. Very striking is their immunity from malaria and yellow fever, which shows a different composition of the blood, and which enables them to work in so many places where the whites cannot. They have extraordinary power to survive both wounds and grave surgical operations, with less liability during convalescence to reactions of fever and other complications. There is less suppuration, better and quite different granulation and scarification. Their lymphatic glands are more developed and more effective in filtering out bacteria, so that to most infections they are more antiseptic; and the specific energy of their serum, bile, and phagocytes against toxines is different from that of whites. Cancer, especially of the worst or carcinomous kind, is very rare, as are varicocele, enlarged prostate, stone in gall and bladder, and ovarian tumor. They are far from exempt from congenital deformities, whether those due to arrest or perverted growth, so that humpback, clubfoot, harelip, spina bifida, are [not] unusual. There is more syphilis, but it less often results in tabes; more passion for alcohol and more consequent congestion of the liver, but less pure alcoholism. There is less insanity, mental defect oftener takes the form of idiocy, and all acute psychoses like mania issue sooner in imbecility. Epilepsy is far more common, and is connected with their general erethism. They are naturally cheerful, and so very rarely suffer from melancholia or commit suicide. The strange sleeping sickness, they have practically all to themselves. Tetanus is common, chorea rare. General paralysis or softening of the brain, said never to have occurred in slavery, although now sometimes found, usually lacks, when it does occur, the characteristic stages of delusions of greatness, perhaps owing to their humble position. Many eye troubles are infrequent, and various other differences have been noted. Now these distinctions involve profound diversities of constitution and diathesis. All their diseases have a different prognosis and require modifications of treatment, so that the training of physicians for the two races needs differentiation. Immune to many conditions morbific for Caucasians, they are very susceptible to others harmless for whites. In tropical Africa men and women are extremely fond of bathing, which their very active skin needs; but this disposition decreases almost exactly as clothing increases, and as the Negro goes North is often changed into exceptional aversion to the bath, which is suggestive for cooks and nurses. Of course mixture of blood with the whites brings approximation to the pathological conditions of the latter. Many of these differences are so radical that a Southern physician has said in substance, perhaps somewhat extremely, that a successful experience in treating one race impaired a physician's usefulness with the other, and made two hygienes and two regimens necessary—as different as the application of veterinary medicine for horses is from that applied to oxen.[1]

Some physicians have held views differing in particulars from some of the generally accepted facts. From the summary of the opinions of the practicing physicians consulted, the main thesis is true, however. Many factors are left out in the general consideration of the Negro's diseases. They rarely send for a physician until the disease is far spent; he calls once or twice perhaps. The majority of cases are never known and the combined complexities are not considered. It remains to conclude that the three most potent factors in their diseases and vitality are tuberculosis, venereal diseases, and the general state of physical and moral habits. Further insight into their lives is well given in the following statement of a physician who has had years of extensive practice among the negroes of smaller communities and on the plantations. He says:

The greatest factor in the mortality rate of the negroes just now is tuberculosis. Their disposition to move from one place to another, or from one house to another, is respnsible to a great extent for its rapid spread, few of them being landowners, they seem to have a natural tendency to want to move at the close of the year, and a family free from tuberculosis will move right into a house just vacated by a family that is infected, without a thought of danger. The only wonder is, that it does not spread more rapidly. I do not believe that they are as readily infected as the white race and I am sure they are more amenable to treatment. The tendency of the planters to build them good, close houses at present will be a factor in increasing the spread, as well as the mortality. I have little difficulty in treating tubercular infections among

[1] "The Negro in Africa and America," an address at the University of Virginia, July, 1905, p. 10 *seq.*

them if seen in time, and if I can gain their confidence and co-operation. They are also more resistent to sepsis than the whites and are better surgical subjects. Pneumonia, colds, lagrippe, and similar diseases go hard with them and are difficult to treat among them. Venereal diseases and gynecological affections are very common, and I see few of the women that are perfectly free from them. Abortions are common among them and are becoming more so. Few of them have a physician at the time of confinement and suffer the effects of negligence and ignorant and meddlesome midwifery. Virtue is rare among them if not altogether unknown. I do not believe I have ever examined a negro girl sixteen years old that did not show evidence of sexual congress.

Another glimpse into the home life of the Negro reveals the extremely immoral phases of his life. While the following opinion would seem to be extreme, it is nevertheless noteworthy, and is not inconsistent with the results obtained from other physicians and from thorough investigations. He says:

In his home life the Negro is filthy, careless and indecent. He is as destitute of morals as any of the lower animals. He does not know even the meaning of the word. Three things are wholly unknown to the Negro—virtue, honesty and truth. We have few exceptions to the above rules. Syphilis and tuberculosis are his worst enemies. To the latter disease he very easily succumbs, due to the close and filthy manner of living. They will pen up four to ten in a small room at night, hence very little oxygen. This is my observation from twenty years of professional work in a section where the population is largely negroes.

The testimony of another who has made a specialty of negro practice may be selected from many others of similar nature. Concerning the Negro at home, he says:

Few know what home is and have little desire for it. He has no morals. None are virtuous, not even the better class. Many girls under twelve years of age seen by me cohabit with men and are frequently found with venereal troubles. The leading preachers are frequently treated by me for syphilis and gonorrhea.

The conditions among the negroes seem to be worse as the majority of the population is negro. There are few exceptions to these conditions, and no physician has been found who would testify to the contrary; a few have expressed a hope for better possibilities. None of the communities studied differ materially in this respect.

The responsibility and extent of the situation begin to dawn on the student of social welfare. For those primarily interested in the negro race or in the white race or in both, the facts are equally important. The fact is undeniable that venereal and pulmonary diseases are the worst that afflict mankind; they are everywhere on the increase among the negroes to an alarming extent. Those who are in a position to know hold that such afflictions are dangerous, not only to the negroes, but menacing to those among whom they dwell. And it is a deplorable fact that if the course of these diseases is not stopped, it may come to pass that many who deserve to be free from all impurity will not escape these afflictions. This one thing itself ought to cause the officers of the law no longer to countenance the gross carelessness and immorality existing among the negroes. The realization of these facts ought to stimulate those who are in a position to do most to direct and to execute positive measures along the proper lines. It is earnestly hoped that the mass of people will become informed concerning existing conditions; it is of vital importance not only to the Negro, but to those who would assist him,

and those who would promote the purity of the white race.
The small town might be supposed to be free from the
maladies, at least to have a minimum affection, but in reality they show an alarming percentage of diseases. The
habit of using cocaine has constantly grown, and among
the better classes, with its evil results. Its extensive use in
the cities brings the inevitable influence to the smaller communities. The present tendency in most Southern cities
makes its sale difficult by statutory ˙regulations, and
few druggists in the smaller towns care to run the risk of
selling it. Thus when one views the situation of the Negro
in its entirety, and remembers that they have inadequate
medical attention and moral direction, and that they are
extremely careless in treating their maladies, it will be seen
that the specialists are not alarmists.

The conclusions as to the moral conditions of the Negro
do not rest simply on white testimony; they are confirmed
by many of the current views of leading negroes of their
communities. They are admitted and deplored by their
most earnest workers; they are verified in almost every
phase of negro life. Conservative opinions from representative negroes are noteworthy. A principal of the colored
school in one of the towns thus sums up the condition of
his people:

The neglect of our parental duties has filled our children with
lies and cursings, theft and immorality, gambling and drunkenness, envy and covetousness—well I tell you it runs on from
petty fault to absolute crime. A very sad picture and sadly
have I pictured it. But thank God, these defects do not apply
to all the race; no not by all means, for (even here) we are
not united together. But wherever this neglect has gone, it
has broken the peace and destroyed order between the races.
It first exists in those families where home life and training

has been neglected—father and mother against the children and children against both. I tremble when I hear it said that such individuals are viewed as a type of the race. This may be a type of all the race sometimes; it may be the type of some of it all the time, but I am pleased to say that it is not the type of *all* of it *all* the time.

This statement is worthy of a careful consideration; unwittingly, perhaps, it is a wonderfully accurate judgment of the Negro race.

There is a brighter side to the picture of negro home life in the form of exceptional negro families. But it is extremely difficult to see the better side of negro home life and environment, and the worse so predominates as almost to overshadow the better. Not all homes are equally disorderly; there are to be found many homes which show marked pride and do credit to the occupants. The house is well kept, the yards clean and orderly, pots of flowers may be seen arranged with taste, and flower-beds indicate the pride felt in the home environment. The interior of such homes is well furnished and with good taste; pride expected of an educated people seems to be the dominant factor. Many of the best influences of the home are represented. The mothers appear to take a proper pride in the training and helping of their children. They are given appropriate amusements and furnished with necessary commodities. They are the children at school whose appearance reflects a true home training, and whose lessons and enthusiasm are well worth emulating. Their mothers wish them to be " somebody," " no cheap folks," or " just good, honest folks." But here again the seriousness of the situation is revealed. There is little permanent environment which is conducive to the growth of character and worth. The student and well-wisher stands back again in sorrow for the struggle that such children must needs make in their growing lives. Amidst the circumstances which surround the negro home, is it surprising that it is almost impossible for these children to grow up into men and women of stability? Even in those cases where the negroes own modest homes and keep them clean, and whose children give promise to grow up virtuous, the idleness which is at times prevalent among them, together with negro environment in general, and their inherited tendencies, make it impossible for them to develop into that which they gave promise to become. The truth of this profound situation is well illustrated by the following incident; it is but one of many that come to the attention of those who have tried to uplift the negroes in their life and practices: A lady had chidden a negro girl for her immorality, and then in kindly words urged her to change her ways, saying all the while that such conduct as she practiced was wrong and disgraceful. To which the negro girl responded: " It's no use talkin' to us colored girls like we wus white. A white girl is better thought of if she has never gone astray, but a colored girl that keeps herself pure ain't liked socially. We just think she has had no chance." Is it possible that a people who do not frown on such a code of morality would clamor for social recognition? Many of their leaders need to be reminded, carefully, but firmly enough, that there is not, nor can there ever be, any hope for their race in any line of permanent achievement until their moral status is changed. And so, without detracting one bit from the credit due those homes which reflect honor upon the race, it must still be said that the bright side of negro home life lies only in the probable possibilities.

If the second and third generations of negroes are worse than the first, the condition may be attributed largely to the lack of home order and training. In the home, which is the unit of social measurement and the gauge of social progress, the negroes appear to be void of conscience. If the home, which Ribot has called the atom of the social structure, is bad, it needs no logic to see that the total organism is bad. Individuals have no training school in which they may develop worth and self-respect. And while it is true that they have many difficulties in the way, which are not given enough consideration as a rule, it is also true that the great majority of negroes care little for bettering such conditions. The Negro's conception of home is little more than a place to stay; when in trouble or in want he longs for such a place; otherwise he thinks little of it. And home would be complete if there were complete rest and opportunity to do as he pleases. Just as many negroes have no homes, neither in the sense of a house, nor a home town, so the conception of the true requisites of the home are only vaguely conceived, if they exist at all. Where he has the " moest friends " is the best home for the wandering type of negro; and such a class of negroes exert all too great an influence upon the home in general. He says:

> Now a good lookin' man can git a home anywhere he go;
> Reason why: de wimmins tell me so.

In cases where persons have hoped to educate a few negroes up to a better standard, and to this end have kindly insisted that a part of their wages go to the improvement of the home and to supplying it with necessaries, the negroes have nearly always refused to work. Free time and money, actual " change," represents to the negro his greatest want; it is his dire necessity to have them; they are above health and gentility and self-respect. His vanity and eagerness in the strife of vain competition in his superficial life leave him far behind in powers of improvement.

The charge will be made, however, that the white man

does not exert himself to bring about better conditions in the negro home, and that many of the superior race even take part in its defilement. And this charge undoubtedly has much to substantiate it. On the one hand the whites bestow little or no attention to ascertaining the welfare of the negroes at home. Nor do they know of the details, although they are conscious of the lack of morals in general, so that it is a matter-of-fact necessary evil. The Church and organized society do not exert the influence and interest in behalf of the Negro that becomes their privileges. It is hopeful to note a change for the better and a growing interest and determination to see that the Negro gives an account of himself, and to uplift him as far as possible. On the other hand, the defilement of both whites and blacks continues to considerable degree among low-down whites, by which is meant not a class, but individuals, contemptible and despicable in their disgraceful conduct; they are often prominent in business and professional circles. But they are invariably from the number whose influence is felt less and less. If the facts were more generally known our people would hang their heads in shame. And these men of the negative-character type are unworthy of any place in the social organism of either whites or blacks. Their forgetfulness and degradation have led them to the lowest depths of criminal relations, and they are a disgrace to Christian civilization and a stain upon the community's record of decency. And it is encouraging to find that the true verdict is being rendered by the white people of the South and that such a crime is reaping its reward in the punishment and ostracizing of the individual. Many whites are exerting their best efforts to make the decrease in the amount of illicit intercourse far greater than it is, and to reduce the intercourse between the races to its lowest possible proportions. There is being crystallized a sentiment among the whites which will trifle with this thing no longer. Although it is an unpleasant task, many of the leading men in the South are determined to leave no stone unturned in their efforts to eliminate this crime. And to this end steps are being taken to punish all offenders without compromise. In full justice to the situation facts must be fairly stated. In Article 3, in *Things Fundamental in the Adjustment of the Problems of the Races*, Ex-Governor Northen of Georgia says:

As we are the superior race, superior in intelligence, in wealth, in authority, in shaping of governmental control and in a longer and older civilization, can we not easily afford to protect the rights of the weaker race, and defend, not only their property, but their homes against brutal assaults made by corrupt men of our own race? Is it not true that the negroes are, practically, helpless against such moral uncleanness as has been perpetrated upon them by very many impure and lecherous bad white men? Is it fair to sit idly by when we alone have power to punish, and see the home of the negro destroyed, his family dishonored and disgraced by unclean men of the stronger race? Surely our statesmen, philanthropists, preachers and teachers can devise some way of punishing bad white men who destroy the homes of negroes and become the fathers of a mongrel people whom nobody will own. If we will wipe this shame from the record of our own race and purify our own people, we will then have better reason to expect better things of the negroes.

Such words are indeed worthy to be pondered and acted upon. Governor Northen has done a most efficient service preaching law and order throughout the State, to many of the best citizens of county and state. He has received much co-operation from both whites and blacks. And the fact must be recognized that the sooner a beginning is made the better will the end be accomplished.

It remains to be seen what the Negro, with the co-operation of the whites, can and will do for the up-building of
his race.   Not all the shortcomings of the negroes have
been mentioned; not all the good.   Their leaders are proclaiming, perhaps more than ever before, the law that the
home must be purified and made better.   But they are not
proclaiming it universally and with sufficient zeal.   Their
words are not expected to count; their examples are not of
sufficient strength nor their purposes clearly pure.   And,
on the whole, they do not appear to grasp the first essentials of the true situation.   They should study and work
in their own homes rather than with abstractions and personal gratifications.   The portrayal of the negro home
shows an utter lack of restraint there, and a most complex
situation.   Without Bibles and family fireside, in a land
of Bibles and in a Christian country, a Christian people
among a Christian people, a veritable catagory of para-
doxes—what movements are the negroes making, not theoretical teachings by their " big men," but everywhere,
movements which go to the bottom with the individual, in
which rests their only hope—what movements are the negroes making upward in the practical ethics of living?
However, it is but fair that members of the race should
speak for themselves.   With reference to family control and
parental responsibility, a teacher says:

A parent having children must ever consider his duties and
responsibilities toward them.   He must make laws and regulations for their guidance.   He must see to it that these laws
and rules are just and reasonable.   He must enforce them in
a just and firm manner.   He must exercise a just and explicit
judgment upon the children's obedience or violation of these
laws.   He must provide his children with shelter and food,
education and clothing.   Education in the broad sense of the

word embraces the child mentally, morally, physically and spiritually. I have thus given what in my judgment are the duties of all parents—*the Negro* in particular.

Thus is given a formal compilation of doctrine strong and good; but there is little realization of it in practical application. Whenever the leaders who utter such truths, as well as the people at large, come to consider such a course seriously as a code of conduct, then in the next generation marked improvements will begin to be visible; scarcely sooner.

The lack of scriptural influence and the reading of Bibles in the home has been noted; as a practical factor they should exert the most powerful influence. Such is not the case, and any steps toward a better condition will increase the possibilities of the race. Again, it is but fair to quote negroes who have given utterance to sound advice to their people. A minister says:

We must teach the Bible by good deeds and proper living, in the home first, in the school, in the church and in the community. By all means teach the boys and girls by our example first, by words afterwards, not to steal, not to commit vicious crimes. Have family prayers and family talks. Teach morning and evening. So many wait till the Sabbath to teach the young and then we teach more creed than Christ-life. . . . Let us teach what our Savior would have our children do rather than what we would have them believe. In short, buy Bibles for the home instead of bottles for the riot. Read the Bible and let them know that it means for them to live by it. Keep children at home and off the streets. Teach boys that if they violate the law they will be punished in this and the other world. Teach them what a disgrace it is to wear stripes and appear at the mayor's court.

And yet such doctrine as that just quoted is absolutely beyond the comprehension, not to say execution, of the mass of negroes. The theory is there but it does not ring with the true sincerity of one who knows the field and is willing to devote his life to it. Perhaps the criticism is harsh; but do these teachers and preachers earnestly mean what they say? Are they not able and willing to demonstrate by example and substantial efforts the possibility of overcoming the weaknesses against which the race must fight?

Such are the partial glimpses into negro home life, with its resultant morals and diseases, with the facts and forces now at work for good and evil. Much might be added. It remains for those who are interested to note carefully the conclusions which these facts bring out. It is necessary for the Negro to consider all that has been said, and in the true spirit, if he would approach substantial happiness and prosperity. Pessimism will accomplish nothing. The study of world-wide problems by the negroes will help little. The sooner a beginning is made at the proper place the better it will be for all concerned. For the whites the necessity is a proper study of conditions, in which the fundamentals are magnified, and a willingness to meet the situation fairly; truth must be respected. For the negroes the first duty is to work upon a platform of definite significance, to recognize their own intricate problems in their simplest elements. Earnestness and fidelity, the despising of sham superficialities, a willingness to work and meet the situation, hard as it is, with daily precision—these will bring results.

CHAPTER V

The Negro Offender

WHILE little attention has been given by students of the Negro problems to the home life of the negroes, much has been said and written in a general way concerning their vices and crimes. The so-called criminal tendency has been emphasized without proper analysis. Fragmentary statistics have been gathered wherever available and generalizations have been drawn from them. Exhaustive and extensive data on the subject are almost entirely wanting in so far as they have been collected and tabulated. Popular estimates and opinions have been verified apparently by observation. The results thus gained have not been without value nor have they lacked a measure of accuracy. But searching inquiries such as would enable the student to find important results concerning the most essential phases of the subject seem to have been neglected. What is most needed at the present time is a true insight into the life and environment of the negro criminal, information dealing exactly with the nature and extent of the crimes committed, their source and principal causes, probable tendencies and propensities, with their total effect upon race character, and some inquiry into possible remedies.

There can be no doubt that crime and vice among the negroes in Southern communities have assumed alarming proportions. That they are not decreasing can scarcely be doubted by those who know the situation best. On the other hand, it is generally believed that the extent of criminal offences among the negroes is growing and that the nature of the most common crimes and the prevalence of vice is growing more serious. Education and contact with the white man under conditions that have existed since the war have failed to make conditions essentially better. Nor is there a more important phase of the entire negro question, both in its relation to race development and to the attitude of the races toward each other, than that involved in the present criminal status of the Negro. It will be the purpose of this chapter to inquire into the underlying conditions which are back of the criminal record of the mass of negroes and to note something of the essential quality of the offences shown in records that are thoroughly representative. To this end the effort is made to find the answers to certain inquiries that appear to be fundamental, the results obtained from inquiry into public and private opinion will be given, and records of smaller and larger communities will be studied. The way will then be open for the discussion of the more general aspect and of possible means of ameliorating present conditions. The conclusions reached can at best be accepted as only tentative and the chapter, to a great extent suggestive in its method, should be considered the beginning of a much more extensive work on the negro criminal.

The conditions obtaining in the negro homes and the standard of sexual morality reveal much of the nature of the soil from which the vices commonly practiced among negroes arise. The Negro's state of being and his attitude toward the community at large constitute an important source from which his aggressive actions spring. To know what the negro's criminal propensities are it is necessary to understand much, not only of his environment, but of his chief traits of character and disposition. A comparison of the traits manifested by the negro slave with those of the present-day negro may give some insight into possible tendencies at the same time that it will indicate something of the factors involved in the total situation.

The ante-bellum negroes were noted for their cheerfulness and gaiety. Their good nature and amiability, their good sense of humor and lack of resentment made their conduct especially agreeable to those with whom they were constantly associated. Almost constant song and pleasing musings while they were kept constantly at work were factors in the Negro's life that kept him for the most part within the bounds of a reasonable standard of rectitude. The Negro of to-day is fast losing his cheerfulness and is far less disposed to manifest the spirit of gaiety either among his own people or among the whites. The negroes sing far less while they work than formerly, many of them showing an attitude of sullenness. " Happy as a nigger " is much a truth of the past. Again, politeness and courtesy were among the most noteworthy traits of the older negroes; especially was this true in their attitude toward white women. To-day the spontaneous politeness is far less observable, while in its place are found either rudeness and inconsideration for the welfare of others, or the assumed politeness of the valet. Respect and reverence toward the aged were marked characteristics of the old Negro, while this attitude is now very rare and perhaps almost gone. Kindness and attention to the sick and the care of children were especially marked characteristics of the slavery negroes both old and young. Faithfulness to master or the family of the master constituted the fundamental principle of conduct. To-day untrustworthiness seems to be an almost differentiating trait of the Negro. Again, the older negroes could be entrusted with missions of importance, and with safety. Rarely did they steal things of value, even when there was every opportunity to do so. They were always noted for their petty thieving, considering that they were entitled to a share of the things with which they came in contact. The marked contrast manifested by the negro criminal of to-day is seen in his tendency toward robbery, bold burglaries and purse-snatching.

At the same time the negroes of slavery days were equally noted for certain negative tendencies which have become magnified in the negro of to-day. The proverbial laziness of the Negro in freedom has developed into shiftlessness and vagrancy to a large degree. The general carelessness with which the negroes unrestrained performed their tasks is now manifest in a lack of efficiency in the negro laborer. The improvidence of the slavery negro is further revealed in his lack of managing ability and financial aptitude. The old negroes were skilful in inventing " tricks " by which they could deceive their masters, either in order to obtain a desirable end or to evade unpleasant tasks. It was an habitual practice, wherever practical for them, to feign sickness, lameness, stupidity or fear in order to be relieved of an unpleasant task. Their ability to conceal and evade was almost an art, and it was their policy, when more than one person was involved, " never to tell." This trait may be observed much developed in the present-day Negro's tendency to conceal stolen goods and criminals, as well as in the effective and rapid methods of communication in matters of racial importance. The oversight of the white man in slavery days kept the home of the Negro in a more organized state, and the quarreling and fighting of man and wife were almost unknown. Likewise the open lewdness of their women was not known in the proportions of the present-day Negro. The more serious crime of rape was almost unknown.

The traits already suggested reflect the extent to which the common traits of the African Negro had developed under the influence of slavery and the new environment. The tendencies of the present-day Negro, his restlessness, his vagrancy and loafing, his love of excitement and sensuality, his bumptiousness, the child and savage elements in his nature, still reflect forcibly the prevalent traits of the Negro in Africa. It is thus expedient to take into consideration the fact that the Negro inherits these chief traits and inherent tendencies through many generations. The successive stages of his development and the growing tendencies may then be studied more satisfactorily and his present status better understood.

In seeking a final estimate of the criminal negro certain important questions suggest themselves at the same time that they are recognized as essentially those inquiries which should begin the proper study of the subject. First, what is the most marked criminal tendency of the present-day negro, and as compared with the whites, what essential difference, if any, is there in the nature and number of offences committed by the negroes? Second, are the crimes committed by the negro against his own people of the same inherent nature as those committed against the whites? Third, what circumstances, on the one hand, and what traits of the negro on the other, seem to be most responsible for his present criminality? Fourth, in particular, what are the effects of vagrancy upon negro crime, and what are the chief factors leading to vagrancy? Is vagrancy in general increasing? Fifth, what is the effect of the Negro's home life and morals upon his criminal acts? Sixth, what part does disease and ill-health play in actions of the criminal negroes? What proportion of negro criminals are " half-witted " or affected by some form of insanity? Is insanity increasing among the negroes? Seventh, what effect do charitable aid and reformatory measures have upon negro offenders as compared with the whites? Eighth, what is the best method of treating negro offenders and what is the most effective method of checking the criminal nature, if it be such? Can the Negro be saved from a tendency which his present status seems to indicate.

The consensus of opinion held by the general students of the Negro may be given very briefly. Many careful students believe that there is no marked tendency toward criminality in the negroes distinct from the whites except that of rape, while some do not think this to be a distinct tendency. Others hold that stealing and adultery are the primarily criminal tendencies, while still others add gambling in its adapted form and brutal jealousies with their consequences. Again, there are many observant men in the South who believe vagrancy is the one characteristic trait growing out of a shiftless nature, and that all offences against persons and property grow out of this. Drunkenness is considered one of the chief causes of the direct aggressive criminal acts and may almost be said to be a special tendency of the negroes of the present generation. Except in the specific crimes mentioned, it is not believed that the Negro is essentially worse than a corresponding class of whites with similar lack of religious and social restraints. The number of offences far outnumbers those of the whites and the rate per capita is very much higher than among the whites, due largely to ignorance emotions and passions, traits considered instinctive by many who have had large dealings with negroes. The negro would prefer to steal from the whites but does not hesitate to steal from members of his own race. Among the chief circumstances which are believed to lead directly to the criminality of the Negro are idleness and the use of intoxicating drinks and general ignorance. Education as it is understood by the average negro is also considered a prime factor in the vagrancy habit. Perhaps, too, the Negro has not become thoroughly adjusted to new industrial conditions. The willingness of negro women to support negro men in idleness is an important factor. The chief traits which lead to the committing of offences are thought to be the emotional nature of the negro with his sensual proclivities. For the most part vagrancy is thought to be on the increase to a marked degree, although there are those who do not believe that it is increasing at all. Home life and good morals are as essential to good negro citizens as for white men. Nurtured with some hatred toward the whites, taught no morals, with a fanatical religion, itself leading to erratic actions, with little regard for common decency, and bred in filth and adultery, the negro is considered peculiarly liable to crime. The reformed negro criminal is rarely seen, and it is well known that the negro offender is not cured by the ordinary punishments. A general feeling of hopelessness is predominant when the subject of the negro offender is to be discussed. Prevention and segregation with industrial education are suggested. These opinions while not drawn from conclusions made from accurate data, nevertheless are important in the consideration of the general aspect of the subject. They represent much careful observation extending over many years. There are many exceptions to the current beliefs both conservative and radical in their directions. Further answer to these inquiries must be gained from the study of records.

While the records of negro crime in the larger cities constitute important evidence, the Negro at large should not be judged by these alone. For the negroes in the cities constitute a special case in which conditions make them more liable to the ordinary offences and arrests. The average negro is found in the smaller towns throughout the Southern States; he is neither so industrious and diligent as the country darkey nor so shiftless and reckless as the city negro. His environment, too, represents the average conditions of the mass of negroes in the Southern States. First, then, will be given results obtained from the study of the criminal dockets in the smaller communities investigated, showing both the general and the specific nature of the offences.

Although the negro population of the communities studied averages only a little more than forty per cent of the total, the negroes commit, nevertheless, eighty per cent of the total number of offences recorded on the criminal dockets. The offence most commonly recorded, regardless of sex, is disorderly conduct, by which is meant general misconduct in public places; drunkenness is the second most common offence, and fighting is the third in numerical proportion. If the offences of the males be considered alone, disorderly conduct is most frequent; if the offences of the females be taken alone, fighting is the most common. The most common offences of the males are further, drunkenness, fighting, assault and battery, gaming, retailing liquor, and vagrancy. The list of crimes most commonly committed by negro women includes drunkenness, lewdness, profanity, promiscuity, quarreling and fighting, disorderly conduct, assault, the keeping of bad houses, gaming, retailing whiskey, and vagrancy, especially at night.

A prominent fact is observed in the lack of white women convicted and the large number of negro women. As a rule there are few cases recorded against white women in the towns having a population from two to fifteen thousand inhabitants. Exceptions are comparatively rare. The percentage of negro women is apparently increasing, and reference to the list of common offences given above indicates the serious nature of their crimes. In a number of towns the chief offence is drunkenness; in others prostitu-

tion seems to have been established so firmly that it is difficult to diminish it. In a town where one hundred and sixty-
three women were convicted during the year, fifty-five were
prostitutes, fifty were convicted for fighting, twenty-eight
for drunkenness, twenty for bad language, eight for petit
larceny, one for selling cocaine and one for discharging fire-
arms. Similar details may be noted in the tables that follow.
Some of the women have been convicted for as many as
five different crimes or offences during a single year, and
for the same offence a number of times. And not only do
the negro women play a prominent part in the criminal
records themselves, but they encourage the men in various
ways to commit offences against the persons of others.
Jealousy of an insane sort is often the ruling passion. There
are, as a rule, in each community a number of notorious
characters in this respect. They quarrel and fight in their
own section of the town or when they come in contact in
other parts of the community. Knives and razors are not
infrequently prominent weapons. But the special characteristic of these quarrels is the vile abuse and profanity that is
exchanged with reckless proficiency. Nor do they spare
the officers who arrest them. A case has been noted in
which such a negro woman cursed the judge of the local
court more excitedly at each successive sentence until the
sixth fine had been placed upon her for this offence. Nothing seems to have a restraining effect upon these women,
who appear as raving, angry maniacs. As a factor in the
race life this feature is coming to be a very serious problem.

The criminal records from one town of each general
class studied may illustrate further the exact nature and
proportions of the offences committed by blacks and whites;
these records do not differ essentially from the majority
of other towns studied. The first table represents Oxford,

Mississippi, with a population of 1650 whites and 525 negroes. (1906).

Name of Offence	Whites	Blacks	
	Males	Males	Females
Disturbing family	2	2	1
Disorderly conduct	7	3	1
Drunkenness	22	10	
Petit larceny	2	5	3
Cursing	2	6	5
Gaming	7	27	
Carrying concealed weapons	1	1	
Trespass		3	1
Malicious mischief	2		1
Assault	4		2
Assault and battery	6	13	4
Lewdness			1
Vagrancy		1	
Jumping on train		1	
Riding on sidewalk		1	
Refusing to heed curfew		2	
Retailing liquor	4	8	1
Disturbing public peace	1	3	1
Operating without license		1	
Reckless driving		1	
Discharging firearms	2		
Violating city ordinance	1	1	
Total	65	89	21

The next table represents the total record for the same year of Covington, Georgia, in which disorderly conduct includes various minor offences not recorded separately. There are in the town no less than 1950 whites and 800 negroes.

Name of Offence	Whites	Blacks	
	Males	Males	Females
Disorderly conduct	33	79	11
Drunkenness	13	18	1
Retailing liquor	3	6	3
Violating city ordinance	2	2	....
Disturbing the peace	....	2	....
Vagrancy	....	1	....
Gaming	1	3	....
Lewdness	....	....	3
Drunk and disorderly	7	7	2
Drunk and retailing liquor	....	....	1
Keeping bad house	....	....	2
Total	59	117	24

Biloxi, Mississippi, a larger town, presents some exceptions, especially in the proportion of white women convicted of offences. The records are kept much more in detail and are for the year 1908. A study of this table will indicate the relative proportions and kinds of offences committed by the whites and blacks. A little more than twenty-five per cent of the population is colored.

Name of Offence Committed	Whites		Blacks	
	Males	Females	Males	Females
Affray	10	5	10	6
Larceny from the house........	1	....	4	5
Simple larceny	6	1	11	9
Larceny after trust	....	....	1	....
Trespassing	2	....	....	....
Burglary....................	1	....	2	....
Forgery	2	....	....	....
Drunk	51	12	73	24
Disorderly conduct	19	14	9	34
Assault and battery	6	....	7	1
Wife-beating	1	....	....	....
Neglect of children	....	....	2	1
Non-support	1	....	2	....
Adultery and fornication......	2	....	4	4
Lewdness	....	29	....	31
Keeping bad house	....	2	....	4
Criminal assault	....	....	2	....
Rape	....	....	1	....
Stabbing	1	....	2	....
Shooting at another	....	....	1	....
Discharging firearms	2	....	....	....
Carrying concealed weapons...	4	....	2	....
Retailing liquor	2	....	3	....
Gaming	30	....	37	....
Vagrancy...................	....	1	2	4
Misdemeanor................	14	....	16	14
Lunacy.....................	....	1	1	....
Concealing criminal	....	....	1	....
Contempt	....	....	1	....
Bestiality	....	....	3	....
Disturbing public worship	2	....	19	....
Disturbing the peace	7	....	11	5
Total	164	65	215	142

This record is much larger than the average and is given by the chief of police. For 1907 there were 703 arrests, for 1906, 421, and for 1905, 411, while the first six months of 1909 is much less than half of the preceding year, with only five per cent of drunks, owing to the prohibition laws. One negro youth was lynched in November, 1908, for assault upon a young white girl of fifteen.

Before giving records showing the Negro's criminal acts in the cities, one other table, representing a still larger town, will be given. Columbus, Georgia, combines industrial conditions with considerable manufacturing interests and agriculture. It will be seen that disorderly conduct includes a majority of the misdemeanors.

Name of Offence Committed	Whites		Blacks	
	Males	Females	Males	Females
Larceny from the house.......	10	....	30	8
Simple larceny..............	5	....	18	4
Larceny after trust	....	....	2	....
Burglary.....................	....	....	3	....
Forgery	3	....	12	....
Drunk	201	36	350	60
Disorderly conduct...........	604	181	750	300
Assault and battery...........	3	....	4	....
Keeping bad house	....	10	....	6
Murder......................	....	....	2	....
Shooting at another	....	....	1	....
Discharging firearms	12	....	8	....
Carrying concealed weapons. ..	11	....	14	....
Retailing liquor..............	13	....	6	....
Gaming	5	....	11	....
Failed to appear.	51	....	62	....
Total.................	919	227	1283	378

The inconsistencies and inaccuracies of all such records are apparent when a searching investigation is made into the conditions existing in the smaller towns and those having a population of less than thirty thousand. The records are carelessly kept and cases are recorded with little accuracy; further, it is difficult to separate the whites from the black, since they are not usually distinguished on the records, and the memory of the court must suffice or that of some officer. Again, many offences occur that are not taken into account

by the authorities. Trivial offences cause many arrests.
Local conditions have much to do with the strictness of
municipal regulations and their enforcement. Some offences
quite common in one community may be almost wanting
entirely in another, due apparently to suggestion or past
occurrences. Vagrancy is one of the chief sources of the
Negro's unfavorable record, yet comparatively few cases
are found against him. The negro cares little for conviction. Even in the smaller communities many are convicted
during a single year from three to five times, especially is
this true of selling whiskey; nor do the fines, aggregating
from one to five hundred dollars, deter them in every case.
Many negroes convicted of offences in 1905 were convicted
of the same in 1906 and 1907; many are found on the
dockets for several successive years. Punishment thus
seems to be no adequate restraint, and even less than the
law, other influences affect him. A negro had assaulted
another with an iron bar; as he was led away by the officer,
although he knew his victim was probably fatally injured,
he laughed, joked and sang, nor was he under the influence
of drink. Many similar cases are recorded. Another negro
who was sentenced to the gallows, played a " coon song "
on his guitar while a jail comrade was being executed a
few yards away. Few of the capital crimes are found on
the records studied; many of these occur in the rural districts at public gatherings and entertainments given by the
negroes, hence do not come under the town's jurisdiction.
Little can be learned as to the ages of the offenders from
the records, although the average opinion represents the
average age to be about twenty-three years. Nor are the
numbers sufficiently large to enable one to draw conclusion
as to the months in which the negroes are most commonly
arrested. But further generalizations must be given in the
conclusions which follow at the end of the chapter.

Keeping in mind the total proportions and apparent tendencies of negro offenders as given above, and also the relative kinds of misdemeanors as they are represented in the detailed tables, it will be well to compare similar reports from the larger cities of the South, giving, first, the general figures, then the more detailed. The records are for the year 1908.

	Whites			Colored		
	Males	Females	Total	Males	Females	Total
Atlanta, Ga..........	5,014	507	5,521	8,211	2,340	10,551
Memphis, Tenn.	2,816	192	3,008	2,638	521	3,159
Nashville, Tenn.	5,322	596	5,918	4,132	1,896	6,028
New Orleans, La. ...	....	....	19,131	....	....	11,082
Birmingham, Ala. ..	2,138	243	2,381	2,454	794	3,248
Galveston, Tex.	1,440	113	1,553	523	276	799
Savannah, Ga.......	2,883	159	3,042	3,665	1,363	5,082
Macon, Ga.	859	58	917	1,411	380	1,791
Charleston, S. C.....	1,266	55	1,321	2,094	516	2,610
Columbia, S. C.	1,552	139	1,690	2,700	662	3,362

While the colored population of the cities just cited is a little less than one-third, the negroes are held for more than fifty per cent of the crimes. Atlanta, with a colored population of about one-third, has nearly twice as many negroes on the criminal records as the whites. Noteworthy also is the large number of negro women, as also at Savannah and Nashville. For the year previous (1907) Atlanta's record showed a total of 24,882, or 8,810 more than in 1908, the decrease due largely to prohibition; in 1907 there were 12,-455 cases of disorderly conduct and 6,508 drunks, as opposed to 8,890 disorderly conducts and 2,650 drunks for 1908. The decrease was thus large in these causes. In 1907 15,207 of the total number were negroes and 9,675 were white. In 1906 there were in all 21,702 cases, or 3,180 less than in 1907. To see the enormity of the criminal record of the city in 1907 one but has to contrast it with that of Memphis, Tennessee, which had a total of only 5,122, although Memphis has some twenty-five thousand more inhabitants than Atlanta. The climax in Atlanta was reached in September in the riot. Since that time the arrests have been fewer, although they are the largest of any city in the South except New Orleans. A part of this, however, is due to the fact that minor offences are all included; 1,463 were arrested on " suspicion." A further study of the situation in Atlanta may be found in the following table, which shows the relative ages of persons arrested, arranged by race and sex:

Age of Persons Arrested	Whites		Colored	
	Males	Females	Males	Females
Under 12 years	66	6	243	21
Between 12 and 15 years..............	235	7	604	60
Between 15 and 20 years..............	575	65	1566	554
Between 20 and 30 years..............	1941	274	3705	1096
Between 30 and 40 years..............	1303	105	1354	407
Between 40 and 50 years..............	609	37	502	154
Over 50 years	285	13	237	48

From this table it will be seen that out of the 16,072 arrests, 3,992 were under twenty years of age and 1,242 were under fifteen years. The average of whites is higher than for the negroes. Only about one-fourth of the negroes are

above thirty years of age, while nearly half of the whites
are more than thirty. Nearly one-third of the negro males
are under twenty years, while only a little more than one-
sixth of the whites are less than twenty. In the record of
Memphis for the same year only one person was arrested
under ten years and only 899 under twenty; this takes a
total of three thousand from the record of Atlanta made on
the same basis. A similar table showing the ages of persons arrested in Nashville may be compared:

Age of Persons Arrested	Whites		Colored	
	Males	Females	Males	Females
Between 10 and 20 years................	938	177	1200	757
Between 20 and 30 years...............	1897	222	1821	853
Between 30 and 40 years...............	1087	113	605	197
Between 40 and 50 years...............	960	55	264	60
Over 50 years	440	29	242	29

From this table the same general tendency is indicated. Of
the negro males less than one-fourth are above thirty years,
as compared with nearly one-half of the whites; of the
negro females a little less than one-sixth are over thirty
years of age, as compared with one-third of the whites.
Again, of the negro males nearly one-third are under twenty
years of age as compared with a little more than one-fifth
of the whites. A striking feature of Nashville's record is
found in the fact that the excess of negroes over whites is
due to the large number of negro women; the white males
exceed the colored.

From the general reports it would seem that the months of July and August furnish the greatest amount of arrests; this is usually explained as being the result of the extreme hot weather. Other causes, however, enter into the consideration. The following tables will show the relative numbers for the months as reported in some of the cities:

Nashville, Tenn	Whites		Colored	
	Males	Females	Males	Females
January	469	44	263	73
February	436	58	306	103
March.	507	53	365	176
April.	514	47	301	193
May	386	62	379	209
June	359	44	332	203
July.	413	60	384	201
August	458	64	445	223
September	480	54	366	134
October	395	42	343	147
November	439	31	318	123
December.	466	37	330	111

For the colored, both male and female, the greatest number of arrests was in August. With the total whites, March, April and September each exceeds August. A marked falling off of the negro females in September is observable, while there is little variation in any of the months in the case of white women. With the negro males, July, the next highest, still falls considerably below August. March and April for the white males are considerably in excess of the other months. Compare these relative numbers with those of other cities.

Memphis, Tenn	Whites		Colored	
	Males	Females	Males	Females
January	220	12	331	38
February	333	6	176	28
March.	252	5	250	42
April.	158	14	188	46
May	209	25	226	54
June	167	9	239	48
July	222	31	210	70
August	251	8	190	35
September	247	27	190	61
October	222	7	147	26
November	262	34	270	38
December	268	14	216	35

This table does not agree with the apparent tendencies shown in the foregoing one. For the negroes, August reports fewer arrests than any of the several months, January, March, May, June, July, November and December. Especially is the number of negro women small in August. For the negro males January furnishes the most arrest and for the females July. For the whites February is first for the males and July for the females, although nothing can be gained from the differences shown. Again, compare these tables with a similar one representing Macon, Georgia.

| | Whites | | Colored | |
Macon, Georgia	Males	Females	Males	Females
January	35	6	105	18
February	86	....	149	29
March..............................	60	8	113	25
April	88	2	89	53
May	42	7	102	33
June...............................	69	3	119	47
July	73	8	155	34
August	69	11	104	39
September	65	2	78	42
October	73	1	89	44
November	72	5	84	10
December	27	1	43	6

For the colored males July has the largest number and for the females June, while February and April are next. For the whites April and February are largest. September, October, November and December appear noticeably less than the four months preceding, in the case of negro males. Savannah, Georgia, reports July to exceed all other months by a very marked margin, more for the negroes than for the whites. For the whites August is second and for the negroes December. Columbus reports the same relative figures. Other towns report December and January as the leading months. It will thus appear that the curve is far from regular and that little can be gained from the reports of so limited a number of criminals. The records do not always bear out the conclusions given by the police and other officers.

The detailed examination of the records of the largest cities gives a qualitative study of the relative offences committed by the negroes and whites in larger numbers, and may be compared with those of the smaller towns studied. These reports, however, are very difficult to obtain and rep-

resent much labor. Charleston, S. C., makes its report thus
fully:

Name of Offence Committed	Whites		Colored	
	Males	Females	Males	Females
Assault	26	....	38	9
Assault aggravated	14	....	33	11
Assault on police	3	....	12	....
Applied for lodgings..................	39	....	3	....
Allowing chimneys to blaze	....	1	8	5
Allowing dogs to run at large........ ..	4	....	1	1
Arson	3	....	1	1
Breach of peace	33	1	89	51
Breach of trust and larceny...........	....	....	2	....
Burglary	....	....	4	....
Burglary and larceny	2	....	6	....
Carrying concealed weapons	19	1	58	....
Cruelty to animals	1	....	8	....
Careless driving......................	....	....	8	....
Disorderly conduct	80	5	288	97
Disorderly persons	66	4	369	137
Drunk................................	42	2	56	15
Drunk and disorderly	132	15	166	47
Disturbing public worship	....	....	2	....
Embezzlement	1	....	....	....
Forgery	5	....	....	....
Firing pistols........................	1	....	6	....
Firing crackers on street	....	....	5	....
Fast driving	4	....	1	....
Gambling	2	....	174	....
Housebreaking	....	....	2	....
Housebreaking and larceny	2	....	14	1
Highway robbery	7	....	10	2
Handling contraband liquor	3	1	6	....
Homicide	5	....	3	....
Insane	3	3	13	6
Interfering with officer...............	2	....	5	2
Indecent conduct	2	....	....	....
Jumping on cars in motion	....	....	2	....
Keeping gambling houses	72	....	....	....
Petty larceny	15	....	112	29
Grand larceny	8	....	28	14
Larceny of livestock..................	....	....	3	....
Larceny from the field	....	....	1	....
Larceny from the person	....	....	....	2
Lodged for safe-keeping	53	1	9	2
Lodged on warrant...................	11	....	22	4
Mayhem	....	....	....	2
Obtaining money by false pretense	1	....	2	....

Name of Offence Committed	Whites		Colored	
	Males	Females	Males	Females
Obstructing streets	....	....	2	....
Obstructing sidewalks	....	....	4	....
Obstructing officer in discharge of duty..	....	....	1	....
Passing counterfeit money	....	....	1	....
Peddling without license	1	....	1	....
Rape	....	....	2	....
Attempted rape........................	1	....	1	....
Running vehicles without license	95	....	48	....
Running automobile without light......	1	....	....	....
Rolling wheelbarrow on sidewalk	....	....	3	....
Riding bicycle on sidewalk	....	....	11	....
Riding bicycle without light	....	....	3	....
Selling lottery tickets	....	....	190	....
Selling cocaine	1	....	1	....
Selling vegetables without license	....	....	3	....
Swindling.............................	3	....	....	....
Trespass	5	....	12	....
Using stolen license	....	....	1	....
Suicide	3	....	....	....
Using unstamped measures	....	....	5	1
Violating dispensary ordinance	381	2	5	....
Violating health ordinance	5	....	2	....

In addition to these offences a number were detained for
witnesses, eighty-five negroes were " found sick " and
sixty-four whites, one hundred and ten negroes were "found
wounded " and fourteen whites, fifty-three negroes were
" found injured " and thirty-two whites, and eleven negroes and two whites were found dead. Besides these there
were a few others, including some minor offences, than
those recorded and a number of accidental deaths. From
the above table it will be seen that the negroes exceed the
whites, in a large degree, in disorderly conduct, disorderly
persons, drunk and disorderly, gambling, larceny, selling
lottery tickets and breach of peace. But the proportion of
whites " drunk " is large, as also with " drunk and disorderly." The whites exceed in homicides, and one at-

tempted rape is recorded against the whites, against one attempted and two committed by the negroes. The population of Charleston is approximately equally divided between the two races; Birmingham, Alabama, has less than one-third of its total population colored. The following table shows the relative proportions and natures of the offences in that city. The report transcribed from the original record is for the year 1908.

Name of Offence Committed	Whites		Colored	
	Males	Females	Males	Females
Affray.	314	37	263	93
Burglary and grand larceny.............	32	....	79	4
Simple larceny..........................	93	15	450	71
Larceny after trust	6	2	15	3
Trespassing	76	7	221	7
Forgery	24	....	4	1
Drunk....................................	537	29	156	207
Disorderly conduct.	327	70	338	207
Wife beating............................	26	....	48	....
Adultery and fornication.	25	3	17	16
Seduction.	1	....	....	....
Criminal assault.......................	3	....	3	....
Rape....................................	....	....	1	....
Murder.	5	2	14	6
Arson	....	....	....	....
Shooting at another	14	3	31	10
Discharging firearms...................	13	....	17	1
Carrying concealed weapons.	38	1	79	7
Violating prohibition law..............	290	8	181	29
Gaming	210	1	286	1
Vagrancy	52	63	169	112
Lunacy..................................	7	....	4	5
Concealing stolen goods	21	....	46	13
Concealing criminal	....	....	....	1
Contempt.	1	1	....	....
Bestiality	21	1	27	....
Perjury.	1	....	2	....

This table is more nearly representative of the average gained from the whole study than any other; noticeable,

however, is the excess of whites who were arrested as
" drunk," explained in part to the number of laboring
whites in Birmingham.   A striking feature of the total
record is the large number of negro women and the nature
of their offences.   Note especially the number of drunks
and vagrants and those charged with disorderly conduct.
Shooting and carrying concealed weapons are included, besides six murders.   The cases of larceny by the negroes
are much in excess of the whites.   Compare this table
with the record of the Fulton County prison or the " tower "
of Atlanta, Ga.   This number represents in a large measure the prisoners who are brought over from the city court
and those from the county at large, of which there is only
a small number.   The report, made from the private records, includes 2,952 cases, of which 1,882 are negroes and
1,068 are white.   This is the total number entered for the
year 1908.

Name of Offence Committed	Whites		Colored	
	Males	Females	Males	Females
Larceny	150	6	282	38
Misdemeanor	158	11	310	43
Vagrancy	48	8	64	19
Assault.	47	5	80	14
Forgery	18	....	13	1
Murder.	8	....	18	5
Burglary.	119	....	138	22
Carrying concealed weapons.	35	....	81	20
Drunk on public highway	53	....	78	1
Bail trover	8	2	6	1
Cheating and swindling.	35	2	35	....
Stabbing	10	....	25	4
Selling liquor	81	6	63	7
Sodomy	4	....	9	
Fornication	11	1	8	6
Adultery.	10	8	85	20
Felony	15	....	18	8
Seduction.	11	....	5	....
Robbery.	9	....	14	....
Abandonment	9	....	7	....
Bastardy	2	....	3	....
Arson	....	1	5	....
Bigamy	2	1	3	....
Affray.	....	....	3	....
Embezzlement	3	....	1	....
Rape	2	....	6	....
Kidnapping.	3	....	2	....
Gaming	164	1	294	6
Perjury.	1	....	7	....
Riot	1	....	2	....

A careful study of the foregoing tables will show that it is difficult to fix the exact criminal status of the Negro; the same difficulty is found in the further study of criminal records and in private research. Contradictions and exceptions are numerous, so that it is doubtful if the exact relations can be determined at the present stage of our knowledge. Certain general facts, however, seem to warrant a number of apparent conclusions. The total criminality of the Negro is undoubtedly greater than that of the whites.

The negro exceeds most in general disorderly conduct, larceny, and offences which, in themselves, are minor. The negroes exceed in homicide and commit the majority of rapes. In the cities the sexual immoralities are revealed in the records. The large proportion of negro women convicted and the flagrant nature of their offences is noteworthy. The average age of the negro offender is considerably less than that of the whites. The summer months apparently furnish the greatest number of arrests.

Judging from the records alone, it will be seen that if the great number of offences for which the Negro is apprehended which rank as minor offences be taken away, his criminal record will not appear nearly so bad. Indeed, in many of the records, if statistics be used to their full extent, it is possible to make out a worse case against the whites than against the blacks. The wife-beating so commonly spoken of as peculiar to the negroes does not appear to a large degree. The whites, in consideration of the total proportion of white criminals to the black, have a large percentage of drunks; thus the negroes may not easily be said to be essentially predisposed to drink, when all the factors are considered. The fact may be possible, but it is not proved that, other things being equal, it is so. Gambling is not the Negro's offence alone. And when his social status is considered, it is not surprising that the Negro commits so large a number of crimes. Again, the negroes are often arrested for very trivial offences and brought to trial indiscriminately. The negroes often complain that " if a nigger had a done that, he sho' would a been 'rested," and with some reason. For many times undue severity is manifested, and the white man is often too careless in sentencing him in both small and larger crimes. He is too often not given a fair trial; he is rushed through court in many instances as a matter of fact, with very little due consideration. In every community it is the lowest stratum of society that produces the most crime, and why should the Negro be an exception? There are those who complain that the whole conduct of the Negro is in the hands of the white man and he has no sort of chance to escape. And summing up these views there are those who maintain that the criminal propensities of the Negro do not constitute an essentially unique phase of the problem.

But there are other considerations. Careful research and a thorough insight into conditions reveal many other features. The results are not pleasing, but they are nevertheless important in the total consideration and must be faced impartially. A comparison of the records with the actual conditions, gained from exhaustive inquiry, shows that many offences which would be considered criminal if committed by the whites are excused entirely to the negroes. Theft and sex immorality are the two most flagrant vices of the negro; and yet comparatively few cases are brought against the negroes for these offences, especially in the average smaller communities. The Negro is often abused by the white man and " let go " for his petit larceny, so accustomed is he to it; the negroes themselves in their lodges and churches make sometimes a formal reprimand but they do not always report to the law. The white race assumes that sexual immorality among the negroes is a necessary evil and few are subjected to the law. Vagrancy, too, is the source of many offences, and the negroes offend markedly in this respect, but comparatively few cases are made against them for vagrancy compared with the total number. The laws are becoming more stringent, and the sooner the idle hordes of negroes, who endanger their own race by making the white man's home seem insecure, are put to work, the better it will be for the two races. The idleness which leads to minor offences is a serious phase of the situation. It will thus be seen that the arrests for minor offences not only seems justifiable, but desirable in order that the more serious crimes may be checked and that the growing tendency may not increase. When the number of offences which the negroes commit and which are unrecorded in sexual immorality and petit larceny, together with flagrant vagrancy, are considered, and when it is considered that these vices are the most pregnant of evil for the race, the statement is true that the vices for which the Negro is punished are not so great as those of which little note is taken.

Again, it is well to note that many of the petty trials and arrests are instigated by negroes against members of their own race. The negroes ordinarily shield the criminal in general, and especially if his crime was perpetrated against the whites. They do not always do so, however, and when the offence is against private interests or person, involving jealousy and envy, they almost infrequently report the offence to the officers and demand immediate punishment, declaring that the more severe the punishment the better they will be pleased. This, it will be understood, is the action of individual against individual and not the group action. And negroes often impose severe punishments when the feeling of authority and power is given full sway. His judgments are both careless and without compassion when they are once directed against a subordinate. There is extreme doubt whether the negroes would fare better at the hands of their own judges, in those cases where personal prejudice and feelings were permitted to enter. But in all consideration, it should be remembered that the Negro has extreme and overwhelming odds with which to battle and he deserves the sympathy and justice due him. The situation itself should be impartially studied, and it should be remembered, too, that, so far as the white race is concerned with them, the majority of negroes are good, law-abiding citizens.

It is easier to suggest general opinions than to fix exact
conclusions; remedies may be easily suggested, more rarely
applied. Weakness should be distinguished from aggressive crime and vice. On the whole, a careful review of the
Negro's home life reveals the source of much of his weaknesses; while at the same time his undeveloped condition
accounts for his lack of home order and ideals. The youth-
fulness of many offenders and the low age-average suggests the simple gratifying of animal passions with little
restraint. The nature of the crimes committed is entirely
consistent with this view. Again, the bumptiousness of the
negro is co-existent with his criminal proclivities. His
prison songs and slang are full of the typical attitude of the
reckless " I don't give a damn," " Nobody's bizness but
my own," " Goin' to kill a kid," " Goin' to raise hell," and
many other such expressions. The hero-worship of the
" bad-man " and the prisoner is apparently a logical outcome of the bumptious spirit which characterizes the low
order of character commonly exhibited by the negroes of
the worst type. The professional ethics of vagrancy in
which the loafer develops from the " hobo," the " rounder,"
the " creeper," and the " bum " into the " bad man " and
criminal is significant in indicating the essential qualities
that make for criminality. This phase is further studied in
the following chapter. The failure of ordinary measures of
reform apply equally as much to other phases of his life,
the industrial, educational and social, in a general way.
The entire tendency seems to unite in a greater lack of restraint and a more appalling lack of application to enduring
activities.

Reverting again to the original inquiries, it will be seen
that they are only very partially answered and that the results show general and tentative conclusions. It is doubtful
if the Negro can accurately be said to have a distinct crim-

inal tendency apart from the physical propensities consistent with his development and the mental traits consistent with his training. His vices among the members of his own race are more frequent than his crimes against the whites, and with the exception of rape (and all forms of sexual vices) are not essentially different from those of the whites. In addition to the factors mentioned above, drunkenness has much to do with the immediate committing of many offences. Larceny and common theft have developed in many cases into bold and carefully planned robbery. No sufficient data are at hand to enable an opinion of the part disease plays in the criminal record. The negro lunatic is not dangerous; he is more of an imbecile. No adequate records are found to tell whether lunacy is increasing or not. The Fulton County records show an increase of 1906 over 1905 and a decrease in 1907 with a slight increase again in 1908. Other records are equally unsatisfactory, though no exhaustive study has been made of the larger communities. Lunacy in the smaller communities is not perceptibly on the increase. The remedies for immediate relief seem lacking. Enforced restraint and application to some kind of life that would lead to stability are essential. To prevent the criminal propensities the work must be applied to the very young negroes in the home and school, with some such methods as are suggested in the chapter on Education. The ultimate remedy is one of complex eugenics and environment. Work with regular and constant employment would be a most practical means of developing the Negro. The active interest of negro leaders would go far toward a beginning.

There is, however, another phase of the entire situation which cannot be expressed in records and averages. Whether the Negro has a special tendency or not; whether such a tendency is the committing of one offence or another, the facts nevertheless remain that his total record is unchanged and that it works very much to his hurt. The foregoing pages attempt only a qualitative and suggestive view of the underlying actions of the so-called criminal negroes. But all the while the impression is deeply rooted in the South that the Negro is becoming dangerous and a menace to civilization. Fear and unrest caused by the negroes by their past record is astonishing. The white man's home in the rural places and the suburbs of the cities is not considered safe. The thieving of the negroes in many places is a constant menace. The relations between the races become more strained in some kind of periodic rhythm, governed by the existence of irritating offences. In this chapter no attempt is made to study the more serious crimes of murder and rape; they have been unduly emphasized in proportion to their importance in fixing a probable future tendency. What is desired now is to reveal the condition of affairs and the qualities of the Negro which make his present and future welfare hazardous, and the relations between the races unduly strained. It may as well be admitted that practical thinking in regard to the present situation is important, and that all interpretations of records and impressions should be sane and broad.

CHAPTER VI

THE SOCIAL STATUS OF THE NEGRO

FROM the foregoing studies something may be learned of the Negro's general position in the community and also of his life among his own people. The facts brought out in the study of the Negro's schools and school life, his church and church life, the lodge and its social and benevolent activities, his home life and morals and the criminal acts of the mass of negro offenders will indicate the general status of the negro race under present conditions in Southern communities. It now remains to consider briefly the part which the Negro plays in the community as a laborer and as a property owner, and to note further characteristic habits of social activity and methods of entertainment which the negroes employ. For the total status of the Negro must be determined both by his relation to the entire community of whites and blacks and by the kind of life that is common among the negroes themselves. With this fact in mind the Negro's part in the community as a laborer and property owner may now better be understood and the facts presented in this chapter may be correlated with the studies of his private and social activities as set forth in the foregoing chapters.

Occupations among the negroes are not well defined. It is therefore difficult to classify the negro laborers according to their occupations, except in a very general way. The majority of them may be said to work at any specified labor, rather than to follow it as a fixed occupation. The Negro changes his work often, hence his occupation, and when he has reached middle age he has been employed in many capacities.   He is thus for the most part a general laborer. Such laborers fall into two general divisions: Those who work for the blacks and those who work for the whites. Each of these divisions in turn may be divided into two classes.   The first class, which is very small owing to the fact that few negroes own business property or are pro-ducers, is composed of (1) those who perform the actual labor for the blacks; and (2) those whose work is for the most part done for whites but under black supervision. Among the black workers for blacks may be mentioned the merchants, boarding-house keepers (for blacks), painters, editors, teachers and preachers.   Among the laborers of the second subdivision of the first general class may be mentioned barbers, draymen, keepers of restaurants, con-tractors, painters, blacksmiths, butchers, shoemakers and repairers.   The employees of these, where the business is large enough to require assistance, come under the first division.   The total number of either kind of workers for blacks is small, nor are all the classes mentioned represented in every community.   Few towns have a negro printing-office; in other towns the barber shops for whites, as well as the restaurants, are operated by whites.   The whites do not work in the employ of negroes.

The great majority of negro laborers belong to the gen-eral division of workers for whites, which may again be divided into two classes: those who work for the whites under black management, and the great body of negro laborers solely under white management.   The first of these classes has already been mentioned (2) under the first general division of laborers.   In the second general division of laborers, the second class includes bricklayers, carpenters, blacksmiths, barbers, butchers, hack-drivers, firemen, farm hands, room-cleaners, house-boys, waiting-servants, janitors, messengers, plasterers, painters, porters, railroad employees, drivers of teams, bootblacks, clothes-pressers, and the great majority of other general laborers and workers at " odd jobs ".   This class also includes the large number of women workers, cooks, laundry women, or both, nurses, house-girls and general farm laborers.   A strict classification would require another division, namely that of men and that of women workers.   The former have been classified more fully.   The women help clean houses, do little odd jobs of a domestic nature for the whites in addition to cooking and washing.   However, the woman laborer is most characteristic as the cook.   The whites, who do not do their own cooking, depend almost entirely upon the negroes for their assistance.   They come to prepare breakfast, go home and return for the mid-day meal, return again in the afternoon, and come again to prepare the even-ing meal; or they come early in the morning and remain until after dinner.   Many live on the premises and are able to be at home and attend the whites as well.   What the whites would do without them is difficult to conjecture, yet they are coming to be less satisfactory each year.   Should one be up early in the morning in the average town, one of the first scenes that meets the eye is that of negro women going to and fro on the streets to their work.   There are many of them, and for the most part they go silently. What they are thinking of, if indeed they go beyond child-like musings, would be difficult to ascertain.   Sometimes they see their male friends and acquaintances as they, too, are going to work and speak to them.   Sometimes they ask in passing of each other's " folks " or stop to speak concern-ing something of common interest.   More generally the women simply greet each other.   " Who you wukkin' fer, now?"   " Oh, I'se cookin' fer de Smiths, didn't you know dat?" "I thought you wus cookin' over to Miss Thompson's." "Naw, I don't wuk fer no white folks dat long." And they pass on. The domestic problem grows more serious. The nurses and house-girls, too, are less efficient and faithful than formerly. The washer-women are more satisfactory and often do good work, although less faithful than formerly.

A further subdivision of negro laborers in general is that of skilled laborers and unskilled laborers, the former class being small. There are few skilled laborers in the average community of negroes; the negro artisan, generally speaking, is not found to any extent. While studies into the progress of the Negro show that on the whole, and as a race, the Negro has advanced considerably in skilled labor, it is difficult to verify these conclusions in the smaller communities and among the general mass of negroes. The Atlanta studies and reports of Washington's students indicate that there are a great many successful and persistent skilled laborers among the negroes. Nor is one disposed to doubt the general conclusion. The present investigations, however, reveal the fact that many who have set out as skilled laborers have dropped back into general labor, for various reasons. Here again it is difficult to permanently classify the workman. There are, however, many communities which have negro skilled laborers who are efficient and industrious, ranking high among workmen of any class. On the other hand, it is worthy of note that in many places skilled labor among the negroes is on the decrease. This may be due to the fact that in many towns the total population of negroes has decreased, while the whites have increased, thus bringing about a new order of things and crowding out the negroes, or taking places for which they were not prepared. Again, such a condition may be due partly to the fact that the negroes seem to care less, in many instances, for skilled labor; few prepare themselves for it, not because they object to it, but because of the general inactivity and lack of application among the great mass of negroes. Perhaps the negroes have been displaced most commonly by white barbers and blacksmiths, carpenters, plasterers and painters, within the last decade. Among the professional workers, the preachers and teachers are numerous. There are few negro lawyers and physicians, but they are increasing, and many of them show a marked degree of adaptability.

The question of the efficiency of negro labor is the critical question of the hour; alongside it stands the question of the proportion of those laboring to those who are idle or unemployed. In any discussion of the economic situation this is an important consideration. A portion of the negroes wander about and seek to get a living as best they can without working for it; they must necessarily live at the expense of the other negroes and the whites. The number of vagrants in every community is surprisingly large. They are naturally divided into several groups: those who never work but wander from place to place, never fixed and without a home, stealing, begging, and obtaining a living from any source possible. Such men never work except when forced to do so in little jobs or on the streets or in the chain-gang. Besides these, there is a large number who work for several months, until they have accumulated a little money or until they have grown tired of labor at one place; they are then " off " for another locality, loafing and causing trouble in many ways. Then there is a large class of negro men who work only a small portion of their time, but remain generally in their home community. They are willing to work a day or two to meet actual necessities; they are often willing to work for longer periods if good inducements are offered, but their chief business is loafing.

The majority of negroes belong at some stage in their lives to this class of vagrants. Again, there are a considerable number of negro women who neither look to the welfare of the home nor perform any work; they not only do not make for the welfare of the community in any sense, but do much harm. They figure prominently in the police records and make large contributions to the immorality of the community. Such classes of loafers and worthless negroes easily make the situation more difficult for the better negroes, and the whites are coming to recognize this fact in making better provisions for their future.

The situation existing in a community with many such negroes is a difficult one. Sometimes they enter a compact not to work until a certain time or for certain terms. They are heard to boast that they can live with the least amount of work possible; the one who can exceed the usual limit is the best of the crowd. Their means of sustenance has been described in an earlier chapter. Besides the hand-outs and the supplies given them by the negro women who work for the whites, such negroes depend upon any methods possible, stealing and borrowing, visiting and begging. They thus remain idle as long as they can, consenting to work only when forced to do so by necessity. They may work one, two, three or four days in the week, and be idle the rest of the week. As a result of such conditions, it is often difficult to obtain satisfactory labor. When such negroes work at all, they demand their wages at the end of each day, nor will they work under other circumstances. They overdraw their pay whenever their employers are willing to pay them anything in advance; it is thus common for them to fail to report to work on a morning, and leave each place owing a small amount. This they will pay if driven to work again for the same employer, who in turn is glad to have any kind of labor. And indeed such negroes make the best of laborers when they are willing; often they work industriously for a few days, then become tired and lag, then stop completely. Again, labor can not be obtained at all on many occasions when most needed, although numbers of idle negroes may be seen on the streets or may be found sleeping in the houses or yards. At other times unreasonable inducements must be offered. Take an example for further illustration: An aged white minister whose spotless character and charitable deeds make him conspicuous to both whites and blacks, goes to a group of no less than ten strong, burly negro men and boys, desirous to have one or two of them work out his garden, for which he offers them a liberal wage. He almost begs them to work even a short time, yet they all refuse to go. Standing there at first in silence, each looking at the others, with expressions varying between a smile and a sneer, one finally says he believes he does not want to go; the others assent. This thing happens, not once nor twice, but many times. Another recourse of this exasperating class of negroes, especially if they are younger fellows, is to inquire into the nature of the work and the pay offered, and then as if they are offended that they should be expected to do this particular kind of thing, they calmly answer that they don't want to work. When the white man who has often befriended such negroes, thus in need of help for which he offers good rates, knowing that these are the negroes who make his home unsafe and add to the criminality of the negro race itself, and knowing that they begin to abuse him as soon as he is gone, when such a man comes to analyze his feelings, it is little surprising that his patience is gone. Again, such negroes often promise to be on hand for the desired work but never appear or send excuse. The younger negroes are coming more and more to shun unpleasant labor, and are thus becoming more unstable.

Indeed, the Negro has developed an independent ethics of vagrancy wherein he states his principles of loving idleness and shunning work. Carelessness and idleness are principles and he is not ashamed of them. This is brought out in his manners, in his boasts and conversation, in his songs and in his actions. He sees two dirty "hoboes" coming down the railroad track with grip-sacks on their backs and wittily sings that one " looks like my brother, the other my brother-in-law ". He sings and boasts his own freedom from work and complete independence to do as he pleases. Says he, "I'm goin' where water drinks like wine", " where rounders and women do as they please ", " where money grows on trees ", " where chilly win' don't never blow," " where sun don't never shine ", " where it ain't goin' to rain no mo' ' ", " where watermelon smilin' on de vine ". The Negro is becoming less efficient as a workman, not because of lack of ability, but because of his indisposition toward work and his persistency in idleness. So he sings as a typical character:

> Well dey calls me a eastman if I leaves de town,
> Dey calls me a eastman if I walk around,
> I got it writ on de tail o' my shirt,
> I'm a natch'el bohn eastman, don't have to work.
>
> When you kill a chicken save me the whang,
> When you think I'm workin' I ain't doin' a thing.
> When you kill a chicken save me the feet,
> When you think I'm workin' I'm walkin' de street.
>
> Ain't no use me workin' so,
> Cause I ain't goin' to work no mo'.
>
> Satisfied, tickled to death,
> Bottle o' whiskey on my shelf.
>
> Wake up ole rounder, time to go,
> Money-makin' man done pass yo' do'.

In addition to the fact that the growing tendency on the

part of the younger negroes to do as little work as possible
is making the situation more acute, it is easily seen that the
criminal ranks are increasing rather than decreasing because of these worthless negroes. From idleness to recklessness and theft, the negro easily develops from the va-
grant, the bum, the hobo, the bully boy, the eastman, the
rounder, the creeper, to the "bad man" and the criminal.
Whiskey, beer, pistols, knives and guns taken with idleness
make the final combination. Thus the morals of the negro
laborer vary as the efficiency of his work. The social status
of the Negro is interdependent with his application as a
workman of industry. With the Negro's present stage of
development his salvation can be worked out through no
better medium than that based on good, honest toil.

The rate of wages paid the ordinary laborer has increased
to a marked degree within the last few years. The crying
need for industrious laborers and efficient labor has caused
a steady demand for the better workers at unusually good
wages. A decade ago the unskilled laborer received from
fifty to seventy-five cents per day where to-day he is paid
from seventy-five cents to a dollar and a half. The monthly
laborer received from six to nine dollars per month where
he now gets from twelve to fifteen dollars; many, indeed, receive from eighteen to twenty-five dollars a month. While
the demand for negro skilled labor is less felt than for the
unskilled, they are paid from one to four dollars per day.
The industrious negro woman makes from two to six dollars
a week with her laundry and cooking. It is not possible
to ascertain the exact income of the average negro. His
wages vary; his income is neither fixed nor regular. A close
study of the negro's social habits will show the various
sources of his instalments of money. His living expenses
cost him scarcely more than a third of his total income from
all sources. If the Negro would work regularly and spend

his money judiciously, he would have a reasonable amount of prosperity. It has been observed that he does not do the former; neither does he spend his earnings wisely. A comparatively small amount, it has been observed, goes for provisions and home improvement. He spends the greater part of the money away from those who pay him; perhaps the greater part goes for the satisfaction of the Negro's own peculiar social wants, lodge, church, entertainment, and whatever pleases his fancy. He pays a great deal for fines, to the city treasury. A town having from five to ten hundred negro inhabitants receives annually from five to twelve hundred dollars in the payment of fines placed upon negroes who have been convicted in court. Many of these fines are paid by whites, while the negroes in turn work out the time. A general estimate of the Negro's conception of expenditures may be given. For the common mass the importance given the relative items indicates what the ideal state of conditions would be. While house rent and food are often so imperative as to exclude other items for the time being, still they are secondary in the social concept. The order may be stated: For the case of the organized family, expenditures are considered (1) churches and lodges, including the varied social functions and demands; (2) clothing; (3) " unnecessaries," including luxuries, trinkets, etc.; (4) house rent; (5) food, and (6) fuel. In the case of the " high-quality " idlers and " rounders " the order is (1) clothing, (2) lodges and social expenses, (3) unnecessaries and (4) food. They can easily find a place to " stay ". With the lowest class of loafers and itinerant laborers the care is for (1) unnecessaries, (2) a place to sleep, (3) something to eat. The better class of laborers fall into the first general type.

As a property owner, the Negro does not play so important a part in the community. Comparisons between the real and personal properties of the negroes with that of the whites show a marked contrast. The amount of personal property assessed per capita among the negroes averages from four to ten dollars; the amount of real property per capita varies from fifteen to thirty dollars, making the total amount of property among the negroes from twenty to forty dollars per capita. With the whites of the same communities the average per capita of personal property varies from three hundred to six hundred dollars; and of real property from three hundred to five hundred dollars, or a total or from six hundred to eleven hundred dollars per capita. Among the negroes the personal property is distributed among some twenty-five per cent and the real property is owned by some forty per cent of the negro population. It is true, however, that records of personal property are very inaccurate and further investigations indicate that the negroes own considerably more personal property than is assessed to them, consisting of small articles. In a careful study the omission of articles of small value is much more noticeable among the negroes owing to the fact that the negroes own less belongings. Of the real property not less than fifty per cent is reported to the authorities assessing in the name of women or those not required to pay poll tax. This is done in order to prevent the confiscation of property for debts and taxes. Few negroes pay the poll tax, and the laws relating to the enforcement of its payment are rarely carried out. The Negro cannot or does not care to vote and he sees no necessity for paying the tax. If the officers are questioned in regard to the non-payment of this tax, they simply reply that few negroes ever pay it and the failure to pay it elicits no surprise; further than such a general comment, little is thought of it. Houses and lots constitute a large part of the property recorded to negroes. Many of these are mortgaged to the whites, others are nearly paid for, while still others are free from debt. In addition to the taxable property usually assessed, the negroes own a good many hogs, cows, chickens and turkeys; the dog should not be left out of the consideration, though the town negroes do not own so many as the country negroes. According to the tax books, the negroes own no fire arms, or practically none. As a matter of fact, however, they own many pistols. The younger negroes take great pride in keeping a " gun " at hand for all occasions. It would seem that the negroes own a relatively larger number of pistols than the whites, though few guns of other kinds are found. So the hardware dealers report that the negroes buy many cartridges. On the whole the substantial property of the Negro is not increasing to any marked degree, if at all. Taking into consideration the corresponding conditions of the whites and the improved opportunities for gaining property, the Negro appears to be going backwards. A study of his expenditures and the social life of church and lodge will indicate much of the explanation for this state of affairs. Perhaps conditions in the fraternal organizations give the best estimate of the negro's economic tendencies. There are, however, a few negroes who seem to be able to save their money; those who have property are thus gaining, in many cases, while the great masses accumulate nothing. The average negro seems to be moved neither by a desire to accumulate property nor to prepare for a day of need. It is little surprising, then, to find poverty the ruling condition. Just as ignorance, negligence, shiftlessness, vice, intemperance and weakness in the home were shown to lead to disease and to intensify each, so they are also the causes for continued poverty among the negroes. The fraternal orders are attempting to own property in the form of banks, schools, cotton-oil mills, and the like, for which they assess members freely. But they retard the growth of individual property all the while; so, too, much money is wasted in quickly-gotten-up stock companies which rarely materialize. And after all, the Negro's capacity as a property gainer and owner must be measured by that of individuals rather than by that of a few organizations.

In spite of the unfavorable conditions already mentioned as being correlated with negro life and work, the Negro nevertheless has a most distinctive and interesting society of his own. To understand all its phases one must take into consideration the facts recited in the entire story of the Negro's activities. Certain characteristic features of his social life may indicate, however, the main qualities of his social intercourse. With the Negro society is the means of satisfying other wants besides the simple craving for food. It is more important for satisfying various immediate wants than it is for the production of industry. The Negro is essentially gregarious and loves companionship. He very naturally seeks companionship, whether it be of similar tastes and natures or not. This gregarious feeling is manifested naturally and continually. It has its special qualities to be sought and its apparent prerequisites to be fulfilled. It is seen in his every-day life, in his church and lodge, and in various other social gatherings. A great part of what the average negro conceives to be real life is found in that common hilariousness which marks all occasions of festivity and freedom from duties.

Sunday is a " big day " for the Negro. He rushes through his morning's work, if he is employed, and is off. He clothes himself with the best that he has; he calls. He goes to church and Sunday-school. He joins small groups at a friend's house or gate, on the street or at church. Such groups may be seen on the streets at many times during the day, especially among the younger negroes, who include many well-dressed " sports ". He enjoys conversation that is lively and characteristic; he feels important. His hat is on the side or back of his head. Sunday is also his big driving day and those who are fortunate enough to obtain turnouts enjoy this distinction. Many also ride on the trains on Sunday, taking advantage of special rates and free time. Few negroes are willing to work on Sunday afternoon. Large numbers gather at the depot Sunday afternoon to see the train and meet any acquaintances. This crowd is perhaps as characteristic as any to be found. Here are gathering large numbers, first in small groups, then in larger ones. If any were strangers, they are not strangers long. Most white people waiting for a train sit aside or walk the platform. The Negro in most cases does just the opposite; apparently he sees little, while he talks and laughs, at the same time jesting and mingling freely with his fellows. Here the negroes will be found in their lighter vein. They talk freely about everything imaginable. They are dressed in their most gorgeous apparel; green and red, with as many other colors as can be had, mark the dress of those who are specially " stylish ". Many are dressed neatly and in good taste, though one may find a young fellow wearing no collar, but displaying a red tie, nicely tied, about his neck. A description of the finery of the women is scarcely possible. While the observer watches with interest a group here and another there, a negro will be seen to approach a group, and with an air of great importance will say to one of the number : " Let me see you a minute ". With equal dignity the other responds and they go aside; with gestures and expressions of apparent great concern they appear to be discussing matters of great import. Presently they return and enter into the conversation of the group. Now the cry is made that the train is coming; the climax is reached; the negroes rush to the cars in which are the colored passengers. Those inside scarcely wait for the cars to stop before their heads are out of the windows. There is great noise of many voices; time is short for the stop; the train pulls out amid shouts, laughter, and good-byes. Then in groups the negroes stroll to other places; they call again. They gather in groups before the evening church service. Some go to church and remain there until a late hour; others seek resorts of a very different kind; in either case they do not return home until a late hour. Even those who have attended church instead of going directly home must remain together, for some time; Monday is an off day.[1]

During the week the negroes gather in groups whenever, and wherever opportunity presents. They meet at night in small groups and larger ones, at home or at an agreed meeting place, at church or lodge or at the social gathering. They love to attend all picnics and all-day services; they especially like the larger gatherings and "big days", it matters little what may be the object of the meetings, they are proverbial for their good attendance. They not infrequently get into serious trouble at these gatherings, where personal difficulties often arise.[2] In addition to such gath-

[1] The negroes often fail to appear for work on Monday morning; many make it a rule not to work on Saturday afternoon or Monday morning. The most provoking feature, however, is the fact that the negroes get to work at a late hour on Monday; this makes the domestic situation somewhat more difficult.

[2] Three special exercises were to be observed at a negro church just outside a town; these were to extend through the greater part of the day—being on the third Sunday of May, June, and July respectively. On the day of the first two men became involved in a fight with the result that one of them was badly cut with a knife; on the second occasion three men became involved in a difficulty (the trouble being a dispute about a woman) two of whom were shot, but not seriously injured; on the third Sunday one negro was killed and another shot. Every negro on the grounds fled and the body of the dead man was left to be taken up by others; the occurrence caused great excitement in the town among the negroes. This is but typical wherever negroes meet.

erings the negroes "have somewhere to go" practically
every night; it is generally accepted that young negroes are
seldom at home in the evening except there be visitors.[1]

The social gatherings and entertainments fall into two
general divisions: those which are held under the auspices
of the church, and those which are not. In the first class
are the numerous "socials" held for church benefits and
charitable purposes. Among these may be mentioned box
suppers, open-door suppers, banquets, feasts, torch-light processions and receptions. The methods of entertainment and
collecting of fees do not differ materially. A short description of some of their church entertainments will suffice.

The torch-light procession and supper is more elaborate
than the average social: A starting place is fixed; a bon-
fire is built and each person secures a torch of some kind
which is lighted before the procession starts. There is some
delay around the bon-fire and much fun indulged in. When
all is in readiness the torches are lighted and the procession
moves toward the church where the supper is to be had.
While they advance in line some sing, others talk, and those
who have brought their stringed instruments, render music.
Such a procession presents an interesting spectacle. When
the church is reached the torches are put aside and all who
come forward with the admission fee prepare to enter; such
a fee is usually fifteen and twenty-five cents. Inside the
church are baskets of food prepared by the women; further
charges are not made. While eating these provisions, the

---

[1] Frequently young negroes do not return home at night nor do their
parents have any idea as to their whereabouts. This is not confined
however, to the younger fellows; the husband often goes off to a
frolic and does not return for some time. On one occasion when
a negro man had failed to report to his work, the "white lady" who
employed him, sent down to his cottage to know if he was sick. The
wife of the negro responded: " Huh, I don't know where he is; I can't
keep up wid my ole man; I guess he ain't dead."

negroes entertain themselves in various ways; they talk and laugh, ask and answer conundrums and riddles, have various jokes and amusements, together with music, and sometimes the graphophone. The supper lasts until eleven or twelve o'clock. The " banquet " is very similar to the torch-light supper except that the procession is omitted; so with the " box supper ". The " feast " is conducted on a slightly different plan: The women prepare baskets as before; in this case there is no charge for admission. Each woman selects a man who is to buy her basket; for this he pays twenty-five or fifty cents.[1] Those who do not buy are called " beggars " and are served promiscuously. On such occasions the church is supposed to be decorated; it is after social intercourse that the refreshments are brought out. In each community there are many such socials during the year, each church, as a rule, holding from five to twelve.[2]

Besides the church entertainments others are given by individuals. Concerts, banquets, " at home " parties, moonlight picnics, dances, and various socials are frequent. At the home parties, they " joke, laugh, stroll, return, sing and dance " until late in the night. The description of one of these dances would be repulsive. The negroes have " good

---

[1] Among the negroes " the ladies " are nowhere more important than in the church work; the men take pride in the work done by them. On such occasions as have been described these women preside with much grace and pleasing manner, as they are seen by the " gentlemen." The men and boys make special efforts to attend the suppers and buy from the women. The youngsters feel that they are in desperate straits if the time for the social finds them without the necessary money. " Please, Mister John, jes' let me have a quarter, jes' dis one time an' I sho' will work jes' long as you wants me; I jes got to have it; my woman's over to de church an' I ain't got nothin to buy a box."

[2] Several churches reported from twelve to eighteen church socials of various kinds during the year.

times " on such occasions and will go a long distance to attend.   The whole trend of the dance is toward physical excitation; they are without order and the influence is totally bad.[1]   Many home parties are arranged by individuals (mostly men) who expect to make a profit selling ice cream, lunches or lemonade among their friends whom they have called in.   The negroes appear to enjoy all such entertainments, and the manager is looked upon as a kind of a hero. It is true, however, that such a social may end in a free-for-all fight, caused by some fellow stealing a dainty, or by other trifling matters.   In such cases the manager not only loses, but is held responsible for the entire disturbance. Not infrequently he sells whiskey on such an occasion. Many of the capital crimes committed by the negroes among themselves are committed at these gatherings.   The town negro loves to go to the " country " to the dance or picnic, where he again almost invariably gets into some mischief in conflict with his rural brother.

Beside the above-mentioned ways of social enjoyment, the Negro has various means of satisfying his social wants. The church services, the funeral services, lodge meetings and women's societies, conventions and other phases of church and lodge life play an important part.   The Negro

[1] The dance among the present-day negroes lacks the decorum and decency of the old time dances given by the darkies; whatever of decency might belong to it is taken away by its coarseness. Further, young boys often say that they have learned the most vulgar songs at a dance and " they sho' wus havin' a good time."

[2] The town negro enjoys going to the country for several reasons. He has somewhere to go and receives special gratification in having gone to something away from his home; he believes that " they have good times in the country "; he is shown much deference by the " womens " in the country. He thus feels himself distinguished and consequently is overbearing in his manner; this offends the country negro who often calls him to account.   Town negroes also fight among themselves at the country entertainment.

appears never to tire of music and where concerts or min-
strels appear they love to attend and will make determined
efforts to obtain money for this purpose. Similar efforts
are made to go on railroad excursions. Great numbers of
negroes take advantage of special excursions and few occasions are looked forward to with more general anticipation.
On these trips the Negro gets some of his knowledge of
persons and things; and much of his grace and affability.
Here, too, there is much of strife and disorder, perhaps nowhere more so. No one can completely appreciate the Negro
until he has seen him on such a trip. The Negro enjoys
most games; perhaps " marbles " is the favorite with the
young fellows; in base-ball season they play this game when
there is no conflict with other plans. The well-known and
proverbial " shootin' craps " seems to appeal irresistibly to
the average negro, and he seeks every occasion to enjoy this
pastime, though it leads to many arrests. In all these gatherings, whether it be at home with a small number of friends,
picking the guitar, or " shootin' craps ", or at church, or
at a grand " literary social ", the Negro is seemingly ob-
livious of fatigue, and prolongs his pleasures to undue hours
of the night, heedless of the weather or health conditions, or
the duties of the morrow.

While the Negro is losing much of his cheerfulness his
song, nevertheless, reveals much of the real negro self in
his freer moods. Perhaps he is very much less disposed to
sing while at work; he is more inclined to silence and moroseness. The Negro, notwithstanding, has more songs of
the secular kind than he had in former days. The love of
song and music is still characteristic. His songs are of a
different kind, and since they are more representative of his
life, they are thus sung more within the race and at social
gatherings. The Negro has a song for every occasion; yet
the song is adapted to all groups. It may well be said that

the Negro sings on all occasions; it is but natural that the
song should become the Negro's song, and that he should
sing it in as many ways and on as many occasions as there
are different scenes in his life. Wherever the negro is seen
he may be heard singing, chanting, humming, or whistling
a tune at some stage of his activity. In the morning the
first sound that one hears along with the birds is the clear
tone of the negro's tune. The laborers sing and whistle as
they go to their work and when they return from it. The
children sometimes sing continuously for hours, the matter
of song being an unconscious accompaniment to their mo-
tions. Loafers and vagrants sing as they wander from place
to place or while they tarry for a while in each locality.
Women sing while working at home or while tending the
children; they sing while they wash and iron or cook for the
whites. There is satisfaction in song and it harmonizes the
surroundings. " Comrades " in rags and dirty overalls
grin and sing their arguments to prove that they are " musical coons ". The deliberation of a puzzled moment is often
relieved by the singing of a simple song, and mischief, mean-
ness, or impulse becomes an enacted fact. The dusky group
of boys vie with each other in knowing and singing the
" moest " songs; " 'cause I'm a nigger don't cut no figger ",
sings one to the accompaniment of his feet, then turns with
brag to " Who's a nigger? I knows all de new song, my-
self." Pleasant circumstances evoke the best environment
for song; sensuous pleasures prepare the feeling for response. One need not mention the scenes of the half-drunk
negroes with their unlimited supply of songs and their
equally persistent efforts to render them over and over again.
The Negro is often at his best while eating a good meal set
out before him with plenty of time and no restraint; he sings
" grace " to his dinner with consumate skill. The crowd
of darkies treated to all the watermelons that they can eat

are jolly good " songsters " after they have indulged freely
in a face-washing and rine battle.   " Music physicianers ",
" musicianers " and " songsters " add much to the total
of negro gayety and satisfaction.   From the crap game
of the youngsters to that of the idlers and profes-
sionals; from the rounders and loafers to the roust-
abouts at play and at work; from the negro cabin to the
docks, the song of the Negro may be heard in its characteristic measures.   Thanksgiving and Christmas, dance
and frolic, corn-shucking and log-rolling, with the various
other activities of work bring forth songs of all kinds.
Uncle and auntie, Dinky and Titsy, Fess and Cornelius, and
the sundry horde of happy darkies swell the total of song
and chorus.[1]

It will thus be seen that the Negro is very much occupied
in a social way.   But to point out a social standard by which
he is governed is a difficult thing to do.   Certainly there
is great need of social conventions by which they shall gov-
ern their conduct.   Little accurate information is to be had
in reference to the number of divorces among any large
number of negroes; so far as has been ascertained, there
are comparatively few formal divorces.   There are many
cases of separation of husband and wife, sometimes permanent, generally only for the time being.   The negroes in
their social life are, for the most part, careless in action and
boisterous in their conversation.   They are coarse and sensual in their association.   The average young negro does
not know what it is to think seriously about better things,

---

[1] Such a reference to the Negro's songs only suggests the part which
song plays in his pleasures.   For further reference, see the songs and
interpretations in the volume on *Negro Folk Song and Folk-Thought*
to which reference has been made in the preface.   See also " Religious Folk-Songs of the Southern Negroes " in *The American
Journal of Religious Psychology and Education*, vol. iii, pp. 265-365.

and the average group never discusses for any length of time at their chance meetings anything of serious import. Their lives are spent in emptiness. There is in the negro community life little of the spirit of self-sacrifice for another's good or for the establishment of a better unit of society. So, too, the social affections, benevolence, conscientiousness, and ambition appear to be almost wholly lacking in the Negro in the present society of the negroes in the South.

It remains to note further the attitude of youth to old age, and to call attention to the Negro's ideas of caste. The attitude of their young people toward the older ones is a good test for the possibilities of any people. The degrees of respect for women, children and age is a standard measure of the better social nature. Much has been observed concerning the lack of these qualities in many of the negroes. Perhaps their carelessness, thoughtlessness and ignorance have never reached the stage of a lack of respect for women and children; but in the case of the young men, there is much positive haughtiness and scorn of advice from the older generation. It may be well to quote one of their number, a teacher of thirty, who knows conditions well, and states them impartially and conservatively:

I said that the relation between the old men and the young men was not always pleasing. For there exists a rivalry among them for supremacy, and in nine cases out of ten if the young man is rated as an educated man, he succeeds. Our young men do not put much stress on the experience of the older men. The old men must use what the young men call "good English." Failing in this, he brings reproach upon his head. He is criticised in his words and gestures, and his words are looked after so carefully that whatever he might say is lost and he falls into the pit prepared for him by the younger men. There does not exist between the fathers and sons of the negro race that paternal relation which should exist. The son is a terror to the family. He wears finery and his clothes are of the latest style. He takes in all the gatherings, and sleeps while the father feeds the stock or attends to other work. This ought not so to be. However, there are some young men of color who are beneficial to the race and loyal to their family, and a blessing to the community in which they live, dispensing lasting good wherever they go. It is enough to say that open rupture and race riots have often been averted by the conservatism of the old men of the Anglo-Saxon, and Afro-American races.

Woman occupies an important place among the negroes. Among the better class of negroes many flattering things are said of their women. In general, it must be said that the Negro holds woman in high esteem, according to his own standards. Negro men give of their money freely to the support of their women; negro women are recognized good workers and providers. It is true, however, that the negro woman does not have exacting requirements to meet in her standards of living. The attitude toward woman seems to be a matter of fact one governed by the general principles and conditions already described. " Woman ", " sweetheart ", " honey ", " honey-babe ", " babe ", " girl " are all more or less synonomous with the object of physical affection. The worst comment of the negroes upon their women is the fact that they are not expected always to be faithful and that they are often considered unclean. Still they are more unmoral than immoral, and the general status of negro women and their place in the total of negro life are not inconsistent with the whole situation of negro environment and character.[1]

Among the negroes there are many petty jealousies and rivalries. Envy runs riot when there is opportunity for ex-

[1] See *op. cit.,* Chapters III, IV, for ideas of negro women.

citement. Such jealousy manifests itself in the love affairs between man and woman. It is strong in both sexes and among the men it causes many fights and much crime, while among the women, it is more marked and leads to many quarrels and personal encounters. It is further manifest in the attitude of the less prosperous and less fortunate toward those who are more successful. It shows itself in church and school and hinders permanent results to a marked degree. It is manifested in a slightly different way by those who laud their superior advantages and attractiveness over those whom they believe to be their inferiors. This last type of rivalry when developed to a greater degree becomes social prejudice. Many people may be surprised to know that even in some small communities social prejudice exists among the negroes. Many negroes think the whites guilty of a great wrong because they do not consider the negro a social equal; yet they themselves pretend to be very much offended if they are asked to associate with certain negroes who are pure blacks.[1] However, when opportunity is offered for association, individual with individual, they accept it without hesitation, not to raise up the lower, but to degrade both classes. In the smaller communities individuals do not hesitate to associate with individuals, but they do not wish to be considered in the same class. One of the leading negro preachers recently said at a conference held in the interest of better homes and home life, after he had urged his hearers to visit one another: " To this some will put in objection: Will not these people presume upon our social reserve? Will not the higher class be dragged down by the lower? To the first of these I would say that there is not the least danger of the plainest people mistaking our kindly

---

[1] The basis of such distinctions seems to be ideas of caste rather than prejudice.

interest for an invitation to our private social functions."
Such feelings of social superiority are often pronounced
and are manifested in many amusing ways. Along with the
consideration of this phase of negro life, it will be well for
the negro leaders to consider a more important duty. Unless they are willing to struggle upward; unless they are
willing to recognize purity of family life and race pride, and
unless they are willing to put off much of the superfluous
and superficial notions of their social life and practices, the
results may well be considered doubtful. For what service
does a negro who feels no pride in his race render in the
economic bettering of his society, or in the development of
those permanent and lasting qualities which are useful to
a race? It is refreshing to hear many leading negroes at
recent church, fraternal, and business associations, speak out
for race pride and a determination to strive for the upbuild-
ing of their race. They should begin with present advantages and continue to the utmost; such men will establish
worth and recognition along the proper lines.

CHAPTER VII

The Emotions of the Negro and their Relation to Conduct [1]

It has been assumed generally that the Negro in America is of a highly emotional nature. Before and since the war he has been represented as the exponent of certain kinds of feelings and of the emotional nature. Many writers have emphasized various forms of his emotions and have described the feelings of the black folks with no little skill. The sadder strains have been emphasized and undue emphasis has been placed upon the expression of the emotions as a psychical influence. Likewise it had been generally assumed that such emotions were the results of a condition of slavery and of habits of life common to the negroes in America. Little thought has been given to the Negro's inheritance and to the study of his physiological and psychological qualities, as such. Scientific students, too, have assumed that the Negro was differentiated by a distinctive

---

[1] This chapter is offered only as a general suggestive outline of a study of the Negro's emotions in which the evidences taken from the Negro's private and social life were given to illustrate the conclusion here summarized. The greater part of this concrete and specific evidence it has been necessary to omit in order to bring the chapter within the scope of this work. Besides, the statements here made are only tentative pending the final results of experimental studies. However, the facts herein presented may be correlated with the foregoing chapters and with the final chapter and in this way much of the Negro's general status and conduct may be better understood.

emotional development. It thus becomes necessary to enquire into the exact nature of the Negro's emotions and their causal relation to his society. Is it true that material for the study of the primitive emotions is abundant in the feeling processes of the negroes? Is it possible to deny that in the Negro's emotional states may be found intermediate stages of development, the understanding of which will be most valuable in the study of individual and social conduct?

The question which has been raised may be emphasized further by the statement that the primitive emotions predominate to a marked degree among the negroes. Furthermore, they are largely physiological with little objective content. The Negro reveals himself a mass of physiological reactions and reflexes. His whole being is volatile, without continuous or stable form, easily disturbed, as easily quieted. With all this there is yet a persistency and intensity developed by the constant flow of emotional currents along the tracts of least resistance. With the passing of the immediate stimulus, therefore, the emotion is likely to cease; likewise the feeling lasts only while the process of immediate stimulation and reaction is going on. A strong physical organism with powerful sensuous capacity thus gives the Negro a rich emotional nature, which together with habituation and facility, with little inhibition save that of conflicting emotions, renders him pre-eminently subject to the feeling states. Add to this the fact that the Negro is unable to attend intellectualy to other things when the feelings are aroused and the result may be understood.

In order to develop this viewpoint it is necessary to examine the primitive emotions most prevalent among the negroes. The way will then be open for a statement of general conclusions, the nature of which, for brevity and clearness, has already been indicated in the preceding paragraph. First, the characteristics of fear may be noted.

Among the negroes forms of fear are less definitely marked, less concrete and specific than among the whites, so far as the general manifestations and expressions go. Fear is most common as a feeling apart from individual experience. A fear-impulse apparently influences and determines to a large degree all forms of fear, so that there is a continuous sub-feeling of fear among the common mass of negroes. It thus happens that fear is easily excited and the Negro is ready to run at any surprising or suspicious turn of affairs. He feels a latent expectation that something may disturb his easy-going life so that what appears to be a feeling of guilt is quickly aroused into a feeling of fear, which in turn intensifies the former feeling. In everyday life this has developed in the Negro into a feeling that he *may* at least be guilty of *something* either now, in the past or in the future. This feeling, too, often reveals the secret doings of the negroes who would not otherwise be suspected. It is manifest in many ways and on many occasions both by individuals and by crowds of negroes in times of excitement. Such a state of fear leads the negroes to do many unnecessary and ridiculous things. In a number of experiments made by superintendents of farm and camp labor it has been found most expedient to first insure the negroes against all forms of fear from officers and from professional negro gamblers.

The Negro is afraid of all officers of the law to a ridiculous extent. It is a proverbial fear, a matter for fun and ribaldry when no danger is near, a matter of extreme excitement when there is immediate possibility of a visit from such officers. This has given rise to a common habit among many negroes of continuous migration from one locality to another. In such experiences the negro makes a good fugitive. The records of officers and private observers is full of rich illustrations. Likewise the Negro feels fear toward those persons to whom he has failed to keep a promise, from whom he has stolen small things or to whom he owes something. His attitude toward such persons is one of adept slyness until he is brought face to face with the object of fear, when he is seized with what, for the moment, approaches terror. While fear is thus present the negro is active in the doing of what he believes is demanded. Again, the average negro is afraid of all suspicious persons, of strangers, of negroes who have reputations of notoriety. His doors are barricaded at night and many precautions are taken as a result of immediate suggestion. When no cause for fear is evident he goes to the other extreme. When in excitement from fear the Negro is without control, he sees all sorts of images and hears all sorts of sounds.

Much of the Negro's fear may be explained by heredity, through habituation and superstition. He fears superstitious objects, conjurers and magic workers. He fears thunder and lightning, changes of the weather, eclipses, explosions and such experiences as indicate the mysterious, to a marked degree. A similar feeling of fear is manifested toward God, the devil, heaven, hell, which assumes various forms. Morbid fears are common and sometimes continuous, such as the fear of death and the dead, the fear of not being buried and various imaginary fears.

The second stage of fear, that based upon individual experience and emotional memory, is less marked than the first. Perhaps the Negro's vivid-vague imagination accounts for much of the fear-state in general. It also apparently accounts for the intensity of the more concrete forms of fear that are immediate. The Negro is very much afraid of death, yet he has little fear of incurring death by the riding of rods, climbing to dangerous heights and other feats of daring, unless he is reminded that such an outcome is likely.   That is, the Negro may become fearless when the self-feeling gives him joy in doing the dangerous.   Again, the Negro does not fear ill-health until it has brought him to the contemplation of death.   It is thus difficult to state clearly special forms of fear as they may be seen among the negroes.   The Negro is afraid of certain animals; he fears the dog, the black cat, bulls, wild animals to an extreme degree.   Negroes are much afraid of pistols, knives and weapons in general when in the possession of others.   The Negro shows little courage in trying circumstances.   The fear manifested in the crowd, the panic or riot is not unlike that of the individual much intensified.   It appears without bounds.

The manifestations of fear and its physical signs are several according to the intensity of the fear.   With fear of the first stage the attitude is one of restlessness, uneasiness, and in the case of more intense fright, terror, while a sneakish, roguish expression is characteristic of the less intense fear of being detected by someone.   The furtive shifting of the eye constitutes the most noticeable expression.   When the fear of the second stage is only moderate the muscles are tense, eyes roll with much of the whites showing, and a general state of restlessness and uneasiness, shows him ready to run.   When such a fear becomes intense there is greater tension of the muscles, the white of the eye shows more, with eye apparently almost protruding, excitement and terror, begging, pleading, dancing, hiding, running, striking wildly follow.

Like fear, anger is easily excited in the negro, revealing a powerful impulse which but needs to be set off by the proper stimulus.   When once excited it is generally uncontrollable but is easily forgotten when once it has passed. The great majority of examples where anger has been observed belong in the one class of animal passion, momentarily excited. Righteous anger and indignation caused by a series of long-standing events, is seldom noticed. In those instances where anger of longer standing has been found, it is often the outward expression of a perverted notion, which has for its end personal satisfaction in the gratification of the animal impulse. The fundamental causes of anger in the negro seem to arise from inherited impulses and the accidental causes which give direction to outbursts of anger are good indications of the state of character development to which the individuals have come. Anger in its epileptic form is coming to assume a more complete state in the form of dementia. It is seen in its simplest form in the case of negro women fighting and quarreling. It rarely takes the form of suicide, the nearest approach being the infliction of bodily pain or threats of violence because a personal whim is not granted. Perhaps anger never approaches acute mania, though the manifestations in quarrels and fights appear to be of such a nature.

Anger is found in its most violent form among negro women in their quarrels and fights, if appearances are to be relied upon. These negroes show absolutely no restraint. No adequate description of them can be given. At once ridiculous and pathetic, they stand in a class of their own. Torrents of the most violent abuse imaginable, words coined and used for the occasion, cursings and every form of profanity—these are the prelude. Threats are more common than actions and the usual conviction can be only for disturbing the peace or for assault and battery. However, knives and razors are not infrequently brought into play and slight wounds are often the outcome; sometimes more serious ones are inflicted. During excitement of this kind such negroes are raving. amazons, as it were, apparently beyond control, growing madder and madder each moment, eyes rolling, lips protruding, feet stamping, pawing, gesticulating with the usual accompaniments of anger. This frenzied madness, containing also a large degree of pleasurable feeling, seems beyond control to all powers of the negro community. While the positive knowledge of a fine and imprisonment has little or no restraining power, it has been learned that the fury can quickly be checked by eliminating the pleasurable element.[1] With the men the manifestations are less violent and are more easily subjected to control, inasmuch as they are more open to restraining influences. Their anger, however, results in more harmful results, and homicides are very frequent. Anger in the Negro seems to summon a wild and inexpressible desire and a blind instinct to destroy, and if the conditions are favorable, the destruction follows. The great majority of capital crimes committed by the negroes occur in this way. In many cases the desperate character suddenly becomes a wild and frantic maniac killing every one within his power. While such a condition is doubtless much dependent upon former broodings and plans to injure others, the coming of a posse unexpectedly, for instance, turns the full force of the negro's passion loose, and undoubtedly the ruling passion is anger. A number of instances have been noted in which the angered negro has bitten off an ear or finger and even the nose of his victim.

[1] One who had almost despaired of having peace and effective work among his laborers, because of the constant quarreling and fighting of some of the negro women on the place, decided to try a new plan. To each of two negro women whom he had tried in vain to quiet even to a reasonable degree, when it looked as if they would tear each other to pieces the very next moment, he gave a large butcher knife and pistol (which was empty), after the negroes had been tied together with a cord so that they could not separate more than a few feet. He then told them to "go for each other" and settle the matter and do it quickly. And there was immediate peace.

The Negro, however, sometimes plans to injure those who are the object of his anger, and if he has all the advantage on his side, he will provoke occasion to give vent to his feelings. But such a feeling is of short duration. Sometimes the Negro is very determined in his purpose to wreak vengeance, and for a time goes quietly about his plans, but he rarely persists; rather his fury is abated and soon forgotten. Such is the general quality of the anger commonly found among the negroes. There is observed too a milder form of anger caused by wounded feelings or disappointment. This is rarely expressed in action, more generally in the everyday language of abuse so common among the negroes. Threats made against the offending party to others and made in a bragging monologue, appear to give great satisfaction. Some negroes, however, are willing to back up their words by deeds. When thoroughly angry the Negro is irresponsible and apparently void of human feelings or sympathy. In the crowd it not infrequently happens that the individual will work himself into a frenzy, beginning with simple boasts and threats, reinforced by a weapon and what he feels is admiration from the crowd. Intoxicants have such an effect upon the Negro's conduct. Such a tendency and facility for violent explosions renders the group of negroes peculiarly liable to crime and their society unsocial.

The accidental causes which arouse the Negro's anger are found in circumstances such as have been indicated and in sudden physical stimuli. The Negro is easily angered by those whom he thinks his inferiors. He is easily angered by members of his own race and is easily provoked when no other emotion is felt to conflict or when fear or jealousy combine. Many young negroes manifest an ugly attitude toward white children and apparently show anger toward them. But the Negro more rarely becomes angry at the white man's abuse; he rather submits, and his matter-of-fact yielding takes away the possibility of a momentary excitement of anger, while his spirit of sullenness afterwards hardly goes so far as anger. He is characterized by the lack of vindictiveness so far as thought or feeling take the form of action. There is, then, in the typical negro little of the intellectual anger intermingled with the emotional, as compared with other forms of anger and with the same emotion among the whites.

A further analysis of the negro's anger indicates that a very great part has its origin in jealousy over persons. This is not only true of the women, who fight and quarrel because of jealousy and envy, but it is also true of the men, and it would appear that at least eighty per cent of the fights and personal encounters among the negroes are ordinarily caused by the woman in the case. And just as jealousy leads to intensity of the animal passion peculiarly in the case of the negroes, so with this emotion go laughter, shrieking, singing and various expressions of wanton recklessness and morbid pleasure in the pouring-out of the animal passion. The vocabulary used to give expression to feelings, the probable reflex origin of his anger, possibilities of restraint in training, in reflection, in the presence of witnesses, and what the treatment should be, will furnish interesting phases of the subject in connection with the general interpretation of the Negro's status.

Again, in the case of sympathy and the tender emotion, the nature of the feelings indicates that they are more hereditary than intellectual development. Or perhaps such emotions have developed only incompletely, and the more intellectual as well as the spontaneous expressions of real sympathy are governed much by *feeling in general* or by the special forms of sensations. Fear and self-feeling appear to completely overshadow what might otherwise develop into real sympathy. But where there is no restraint, and the sympathy conflicts with no personal interest or unpleasant effort, the physiological form of the emotion is clearly seen. Such is spontaneous sympathy of the negroes for each other and for an occasion in their public meetings. At church they are in sympathy with every word and motion of the preacher, and they are in sympathy with each other's movements. They sanction what the preacher has to say, whether they understand it or not, and their exclamations of assent include many regular forms of " amens." They nod, bow, their bodies sway to and fro according to the stage of the sermon, until yielding to the impulse there is a perfect harmony of bodily rhythm and a perfect rhythm of sympathetic feeling. So too, when the white man speaks to the negroes, they assume from the beginning the attitude of approval and there is a distinct evidence of sympathy. So it is in most of the meetings if no personal interest is challenged, and many negroes have been seen to nod their assent weakly to everything a whiteman was saying, though his total utterance was the abuse of the Negro in his political aspirings. Under the influence of music and dancing the Negro has little control over his body and feet, and when one foot has begun to " pat " and beat time, it would indeed be an interesting problem to prevent others from joining in. An unconscious and sympathetic movement corresponds to each wave of rhythm in the music and to the movement of the fiddler. And one has yet to see the negro " music physicianer " picking his banjo with his feet still. Again the Negro easily adapts himself to various circumstances and a part of his imitation may be explained by noting the original element of sympathy that exists. The Negro often seems ill at ease unless he is able to conduct himself as those about him, and in a way feels ill-adjusted unless he can perform an action exactly as he knows it should be done; on the other hand thoughts of himself and sympathy for his own hard time, not infrequently transcend the former feeling. Negroes are usually in sympathy with those for whom they work, if they work in harmony, and commonly speak of the work and property as " ours ", and laud the superiority of their boss's methods to any other, thus showing a bit of sympathy along with the self-feeling.

The sympathy may be one of fears. Negroes when panic-stricken, are easily thrown into tumult, and all are very likely to follow the prevailing opinion of the leader, or the first impression most generally becomes current. Excitement spreads more rapidly among them than among the whites. A report of a crime, death, or sensational thing, and especially if it is of racial interest, appears to travel almost twice as fast as among the whites. The negroes form a medium unsurpassed for the transmission of news, and the lack of resistance is due partly to the sympathy feeling. So in superstitions, a single report with little foundation soon becomes a common belief. And the fear or belief thus quickly and easily fixed in the Negro's mind, can be removed only with the greatest difficulty. The sympathetic emotion is nowhere more prominent than in the tendency of the negroes to protect their criminals and furnish information to those who are fugitives. Race feeling against the white man, whether in the negative sense or the positive aspect, is partly one of fellow-sympathy. Out of this grows the society or clannish spirit of the more recent negro, and the secretive nature of the Negro is explained to a large degree by the same principle. The sum of it all may be seen in the various societies, unions, and orders and whatever appeals to the gregarious instinct, and out of these grows the increased race agitation. With them comes much that will build up the race within itself, and also many perverted notions and much wasted energy. Nowhere could the sympathetic feeling be analyzed better than in this phase. Again the Negro sympathizes much with his own poor, down-trodden self and often broods into sullenness and gloom over seeming injustices. Such is a racial sympathy. It is not observed the one toward the other. For in their societies they quarrel and dispute over the majority of measures that come before them, and personal prominence in the management of such affairs plays an important part; envy and strife are everywhere. The criminal records and the testimony of many lawyers, indicate that a very large per cent of the negroes convicted for smaller crimes have been reported by other negroes who wish thereby to repay a grudge of short standing. It has been a common criticism of the negroes that they will not work together in harmony long enough to accomplish a work of lasting worth, and there is much to substantiate the statement. Again it is the overshadowing self-feeling and interest that takes away the probability of sympathy.

Some evidences of the higher forms of sympathy may be seen in the working of the fraternal societies in ministering to the sick, the widows and the orphans, and in paying off benefits. While the obligation of the society upon its members seems in every case to be the direct cause of the service, sympathy often grows out of the deed, and the members of such societies grow enthusiastic in their advocacy of the cause, giving these deeds of service as evidence. So it happens that the leaders of the various societies have come to feel, in addition to the personal gratification of succeeding in rivalry, an eager interest in their work. Much of the formal sympathy among the negroes may be observed in their prayers, for the preacher, the " sisters " and the " brethren ", the " sinner " and the " dancers ". The prayer is uttered with apparent feeling and it may be that a resultant state of sympathy is produced. Again, there is apparent

sympathy among the negroes for whites whom they have
known for some time, or for those who have befriended
them. In a somewhat listless way they show sympathy for
their suffering; they come and inquire about those who are
sick, and when one dies they ask to be permitted to go to the
funeral and to look upon the face of the dead. This is the
case with the older darkies for their masters or the family
of former masters, and it is often so with the children of the
old slaves who have remained near the children of the former
slave owner. It is indeed an impressive scene to see these
negroes with bared heads following the procession of the
funeral of a white friend, and after the burial walking
around listlessly; or if a white friend is ill, to see them
coming and going at intervals or standing around the
premises in silence. It is a scene which Southern whites
are loath to give up, a sympathy which they love. Negroes
often manifest marked sympathy for children in their plans
and play, and miss them when sick. The older negroes
show their sympathy by efforts to administer to the comfort of their little friends. The younger negroes with less
experience seem utterly at a loss. As a people they are very
sympathetic, governed much of course by their treatment,
since their feelings are easily played upon. A number of
men of broad experience have insisted that in case of sickness a servant comparatively new will be most careful and
all-attentive, whereas in a healthy state she might be careless. Many instances have been noted on the contrary where
they have taken advantage of adverse conditions to demand
more pay and if not granted they have stopped working.
There are, however, many cases of sympathy and fidelity
that may not be questioned. The negro also apparently
manifests a kind of sympathy at all funerals and burial services among his own people, both for the ceremony and for
those who are called upon to bury the dead. But in all cases

where the negro shows sympathy there is little outward expression. His face is set, and his eyes have the look of appeal, awe and wonderment.

Much remains to be known about the tender emotion of the Negro. The scenes just mentioned seem to indicate a feeling or sometimes real affection, blind and vague it may be, but having the qualities of the tender emotion. The old love of the slave and his master, the former love of boy comrades, and the faithfulness of the slave and his children to the master and his family, will scarcely be surpassed in the records of many peoples. But if this affection has passed so quickly, what must have been its nature? Was it the affection of servitude and had it only in it the negative self-feeling? Among the negroes of the present generation there is little of this spirit of affection seen and it becomes necessary to inquire into the nature of the tender emotion as it is found most generally among the negroes of to-day. While it is doubtful if there is enough evidence to warrant a full statement concerning the affections of the negroes, it is apparently based on the gregarious impulse and upon a passive sympathy rather than upon individual emotions intellectually developed. The emotion is rarely of long duration. The protective instinct, too, seems to have an important place in the make-up of the tender emotion, and may be seen in the attitude of the parent in protecting the child from abuse. The mother will sing to the child in her arm for an hour or more, and perhaps the very next moment will abuse it unmercifully, but she will not permit it to be abused by another. Jealousy resembles affection in its surface manifestations. On the other hand, filial affection seems to pass away with the coming of youth, and most negro youngsters apparently have no love or care for their parents. They wish rather to be free from parental control and work. Perhaps the majority leave home, many do not return for a long time, many never return, nor do these negroes inform their parents of their whereabouts. Many of the negro parents were asked if they knew where their children were. Few could tell exactly, many had an idea that they were at such and such a place, still others affirmed that they were at a certain place some time ago, while many knew nothing of them. With sometimes a vacant look of sadness in their eyes, with sometimes a careless manner, they declared that they did not know where they were. And while one can not affirm that appearances are true, such a state of affairs seems to carry with it no special sorrow. The negro mother rarely mourns for her wandering child, or sits up at night waiting for his return or thinking of him. The father shows little care except that of losing a laborer from his work. They have often been known to attempt to enter suit against the husband of the daughter in an effort to get her back for no other reason than for her work. The nature of the affection of the child for the parents seems to be purely that of dependence, and when he has outgrown this feeling the relation between child and parents has changed. Often when without food or shelter, the negro wanderer longs for his childhood days with the parents and appeals for pity as a " po' boy 'long way from home ", " got no whar to lay my weary head ", or " ain't got a frien' in dis worl ". But when his physical wants have been satisfied, he no longer thinks of home or parents in general. The Negro has no loved ones. Numbers were asked for the names of those whom they considered friends or whom they loved or those who loved them. The question was put in various ways with different subjects, but the returns were the same. They often seemed surprised at the question and answered, sometimes at once, sometimes after reflection, that there was no one, nor did they seem to feel the sadness of the situation. A few thought that a number of white people were their friends. But as a rule the Negro is without friendship among his own people. Pathetic would seem the life that is lived in loneliness, nor looks to aught of love for the lightening of a peculiar labor, nor ever lingers by the light of a lasting affection. Full many a negro has served faithfully his day, has come to old age, neglected and forgotten by his race, destitute. Is it surprising that in his own emotional way he is thankful that his " time ain't long " or that he longs to pass over " de ribber " ? So they say, thus they sing, how shall their feeling be analyzed?

The negro's infatuation for his sweetheart is yet to be mentioned, for the lover's life constitutes the greater joy and consumes the greater part of the young negro's thought. One could never doubt this after perusing hundreds of their crude lyrics and love ditties. The nature of this love is discussed fully elsewhere. There is need to mention here the element of jealousy which, with the quality of physical attraction and sex-feeling, make up the complete affection. Negro courtship would indeed be a dull and monotonous matter were it not for the quarrels and fights, the infidelity and changeableness of parties on both sides. The negro lover is often unwilling to be out of the sight of her with whom he is infatuated, but such is invariably of short duration. The Negro is not constant, and is happy because he " has woman an' sweetheart, too. If woman don't love me sweetheart do ". Jealousy is the principle means of attaining desired personal ends.

Self-feeling or the sense of self is strong in the Negro, and is peculiarly characterized by both its positive form and its negative form, each in a distinctly marked degree. The sense of self in its positive form is expressed in the feeling of importance and manifests itself on various occasions and in many ways. Perhaps nowhere is it more marked than in the negro preacher, who stands lord of all that comes within his domain. In the pulpit, while preaching and administering the affairs of church, he assumes and feels that the destiny of the hour lies in his own importance and his ability to make his followers feel the same attitude. When visiting another church or a conference he appears to feel even more of such a dignity. In the home his lordly airs and condescending grace and manners approach the perfect art. He is irresistible, his self-feeling is superb. His efforts to evoke admiration are not in vain and he is a universal favorite among the " sisters ". His whole attitude is one that would have his word the final law and it would be difficult to find his parallel. So important is he that he is beyond sin and his self-feeling gives him free and unquestioned license to do whatever he wishes. Likewise he expects special favors from the white man and assumes that the assertion that he is a preacher will identify him on all occasions. It is indeed a rare spectacle to see a hundred or more of these preachers at their conferences and conventions. Dressed in their long coats, and sometimes tall hats, they vie with each other to look the biggest man. Some there are who have traveled in " furrein lands " and can " speak in seven languages ". They are indeed kings and lords. The fact cannot be denied that they are a distinguished-looking set and their looks are only surpassed by their utterances. The same general principle is true of other negro leaders, officers of the various churches and societies, and the young " educated " negroes, the latter having slightly the advantage in the feeling. So with the youngsters who delight in being the " sports " of the town. Watch one of them! With his " Sunday clothes on ", his hat tossed on the back or side of his head, a cigar or cigarette in his mouth, language is entirely inadequate for his expression and he stalks there the perfect image of human nothingness. So, too, the " rounders ", the " eastmans ", and the "creepers" go from place to place, the favorites of the women, the envy of the men in general, and the terror of the country negro. Swaggering and sweeping all before them, such negroes feel a sense of self that is not measured within the bounds of wanton recklessness.

The self-feeling is very much in evidence in the love of dress as such. Both men and women often value fine clothes above all else. They sacrifice the actual necessities in the effort to "dress up". The boys model after the latest fashions; the women strive to outshine each other in new dresses and brilliant colors. Dress and adornment are the horizon of their vision on a Sunday. Negroes often work and save their earnings for weeks and months to have the satisfaction of walking up the aisle in church to contribute five to twenty-five cents, though it takes as many trips to the table as there are coins to be put in. Each thinks she is the envy of every other one in the congregation. Love of dress, love of show, and anything which is conducive to self-centered feelings, anything to give the impression of being above the others, and thus gain attention —these experiences rank among the first of those which give the Negro the highest pleasure and enjoyment. The effort to eliminate the kinks of the hair and other racial features represent another evidence of the self-feeling and skilful advertisers have learned this well enough to make a profitable business from the manufacture of various remedies.

In children, the self-feeling may be seen in two general phases. The first is that of proud feeling similar to that already mentioned. The same markings are in evidence: boasting and bragging, the abuse of smaller children, sex-superiority, at home, in school, on the streets, with defiance for all ordinary conventions. The small boy can whistle a better tune and much louder than the average white man and his path is the path of conquest, his face wreathed in the simplicity of impudence. The small negro girl can make faces at her playmates and assume attitudes of superiority equal to the task of a comic slave. The small boy's look of innocence and unconcern while executing or planning to execute the most intricate plots of mischief would rival a sleeping Mercury. His commanding presence is good. His composure and positiveness on most occasions are remarkable. The second form of self-feeling in negro children is that which they feel when first they recognize that they are negroes, and are limited to certain bounds. This has been discussed in Chapter I.

The effort to make felt the self-feeling is seen in numerous other ways: the letter-heads and stationery of negro leaders, teachers and preachers, with sometimes their photograph and titles of a half-dozen offices inscribed thereon, the inserting of photographs in all reports where possible. Witness a single report from a conference which has no less than seven hundred and sixty-eight individual photographs, besides others in groups. Their love of committees and honors, their eagerness to get into print, and the extravagance of their self-commendation and commendation of one another is typical. Their list of adjectives is quite extraordinary. The self-feeling is seen in the wounded pride of such negroes when asked to do some little menial task, and in the insolence of laborers of the sorrier class. It is expressed in a phrase now common among the negroes: " I'm jes good as any white woman " and many others. It is seen in their love of big words and their efforts to use eloquent language on all occasions.

The outward markings and physical manifestations of the positive self-feeling have been indicated: Holding the head high, stepping high, throwing back the head and shoulders, strutting, or on the other hand, walking in a wanton, reckless swagger, and general bumptiousness; gesticulating, being puffed up with conceit, attempt to attract attention—bluff in all of its forms. The description must be left to the master cartoonist. It would seem that some of the negroes actually look bigger after having made a journey or having held an " important " position. This same spirit and satisfaction in self-feeling is manifested in a larger degree in the rituals, regalia and ceremonies of the secret societies and in the titles given the leading officers. Such is indeed a gay procession and few things are enjoyed more than these processions of celebration or funerals. The evidence of the positive self-feeling is seen in an almost universal tendency among the negroes to abuse the weak, neglect the aged, and to form superficial conceptions of all social ideals.

It will thus be seen that examples of the positive self-feeling are to be found almost wholly among the negroes in their relations with one another, and that this peculiar sense of self is a significant characteristic. The negative self-feeling has been most commonly depicted among the negroes. They have been known as easily a subject-people, proverbial for humility and submission. The Negro is still marked by these traits in his relations to the white man. This feeling may be seen in his humility and in his mock humility. He is easily intimidated and submissive, manifests the spirit of weakness and inferiority. Deference and needless giving way to the white man, walking on the outside of the street, tipping the hat and various acts of deference are typical representations. It is also evident in stealth, sneakishness, cowardice and the lack of some of the better qualities. These well-known facts need only to be mentioned. The degree to which they are being overcome will constitute an interesting phase of his development. The saying has been a common one, and the belief a general one among certain

people that the man never lived who could manage and work
negroes successfully without the assistance of profanity.
There is much in the statement, for the negroes are easily
influenced by overbearing and positive conduct. But the
negroes submit almost as easily to injustices done them by
members of their own race who have attained or appear to
have attained some superiority. The unreasonable demands
and actions of the preacher are absurd; the negroes look
upon their so-called learned men with awe and respect. They
yield readily to demands made by negro property-owners,
though unreasonable. They are preyed upon by quack-
doctors and tricksters who assume the part of magicians and
conjurers.

Many careful students of the Negro have asserted that
the only striving which the average negro has is a desire
for social equality with the whites. Many others have
maintained that such a desire is not common. Testimony
from both negroes and white men conflicts. It is not
possible to make an accurate statement concerning such
aspirations. Likewise it is difficult to describe the spiritual and philosophical strivings of the Negro. His ideas
are simple and vague, seeking the place of least resistance
and of most pleasure to be expressed. So far as is expressed
there is little of definiteness to the Negro's thoughts, but
more of the loose physiological processes, feelings and reactions. There is little of the pure ego or self-consciousness
in the spiritual sense, so-called. Likewise the Negro's ideas
of God, of the devil, of heaven, of hell, reveal a general
attitude of doubt and fear but with little particular questioning. The Negro sympathizes much with himself as
being one of a down-trodden people; there is apathetic moroseness but little effort for individual striving. The Negro
loves to talk to himself, to sing to himself and to muse on
many themes. The dramatic feeling is strong and the sense

of impersonation is developed to a marked degree. Negroes impersonate with skill and show a marked descriptive power. Impressions are easily made upon the Negro and many are permanently retained. The feeling of not being like others leads to imitation, where it would otherwise be neglected, and this itself is largely a self-feeling more than a desire for approval as such. Adaptation as it is commonly found among the negroes is the self-feeling in its negative form and positive intent. The strivings of the group are chiefly for emotional satisfaction and for a recognition by the world at large.

It has generally been assumed that the Negro is differentiated by a distinct sexual development. It is affirmed that the sex development crowds out the mental growth. It is affirmed that the period of puberty in boys and girls is marked by special manifestations of wildness and uncontrol. It is true, too, that the practices of the negroes leave little energy for moral and mental regeneration. Their lives are filled with that which is most carnal; their thoughts are most filthy and their morals are generally beyond description. Again, physical developments from childhood are precocious and the sex life begins at a ridiculously early period. But granting these truths it is doubtful if there is sufficient evidence to warrant such a conclusion. The Negro reveals a strong physical nature; the sex impulse is naturally predominant. But its manifestations are probably no more violent and powerful than are the expressions of other feelings already suggested. The Negro's sensuous enjoyment of eating and drinking and sleeping, relatively speaking, are no less marked than his sexual propensities. Likewise lack of control and extreme manifestations characterize the discharge of other impulses. It is true, again, that the part played by sexual life among the negroes is large for a people; but to state that the Negro is inherently differentiated and hindered by a sexual development out of proportion to other physical qualities is quite a different proposition. But whether the question here raised is answered in the affirmative or not, it still remains that in the practical life of the Negro his better impulses are warped and hindered by his unreasonable abuse of sexual license. And it is safe to suggest that the Negro need hope for little development of his best qualities until he has learned to regulate and control his animal impulses.

The continuous expression of various emotions has given rise to many morbid feelings among the negroes. Such feelings are expressed in both morbid pleasures and pains. It is seen in the appetite for various filthy things to eat, in the extreme gratification of impulse and in many kinds of perversion. In his anger the Negro often finds great pleasure in laughing, jeering, striking madly about him. Such is the common boast over a stricken body, the desire to look upon dead bodies, to attend funerals. Again, the bragging, handling of knives and pistols, boasting, singing, love of criminal notoriety, abuse of the weak, hoodlumism, and extreme feelings of megalomania are touches of the morbid pleasure. It is seen again in the expression of sullenness and moroseness and the new melancholia which is clearly an affective state of little sudden or positive development. Morbid pain is less recognized among the negroes; many extreme manifestations of emotion are pain experiences unrecognized. The pleasure-pain impulse is everywhere predominant from the lowest pleasure to the gratification of religious sentiment.

The two general characteristics, then, of the Negro's emotional nature are the lack of restraint and the consequent extreme expression of the feelings. The Negro's emotions, then, are little more than impulses. The tendency is, in all manifestations, for the emotion to run its course with little inhibition, thus giving rise to many violent forms of expression. It thus happens that those feelings which require less of the physical stimuli are little developed among the negroes.

The emotional worship of the negroes and their social group-feelings have been noted in Chapters II and III. Mention has also been made of the Negro's social self-feeling as manifested in his love of display, praise and notoriety. All of the Negro's emotional states are highly intensified by the crowd; the sympathetic like-response is powerful to sway the many as one individual. While the Negro is very much of a social being his social self has not yet revealed clear and distinct qualities of development. His attention to circumstances is passive and sensuous; his social self has not developed the love of home and family nor the desire to accumulate property. Withal, the Negro has two distinct social selves, the one he reveals to his own people, the other he assumes among the whites, the assumption itself having become natural.

CHAPTER VIII

THE NEGRO PROBLEM: AN ESTIMATE OF THE NEGRO

THE story of the Negro, even since he has come to denote the " Negro Problem," has been an intricate and complicated story. His own record, including his privations, experiences and achievements, is one of more than ordinary adventure, while the records of controversies, legislations and discussions concerning the best policies to be adopted for his welfare present a remarkable series of inconsistencies. The Negro has contributed much to the industry of the South at the same time that he has constituted its chief problem. He has contributed much of its happiness and prosperity and much of its poverty and crime. His story has been one of happiness and humor and it has been one of pathos and sorrows. It has had its comedy and farce and it has produced its tragedy. At times exciting and tense, involving the passions of both whites and blacks, of the North and of the South, and seeming to offer little encouragement for a happy ending, his story has yet never lacked the quality of hopefulness to those who have seen the deeper significance of its setting. However, the Negro's story presents a problem for modern civilization at once complex, compound, and momentous, and leaves it for the present, if not unsolved, at least continuous.

Speculations, theories and methods of solutions for the problem have been offered without intermission. It would be difficult to find a problem which has been the subject of more conflicting opinions, opposite extremes and incon-

sistencies, and for which so many solutions have been offered. Not only have private individuals, editors, authors
and politicians offered their solutions, but distinguished
educators, statesmen and judges have contributed. Sincere thinkers biased by prejudice, earnest philanthropists
lacking in judgment, individuals seeking notoriety and reputation, politicians and theorists, together with sane, conservative thinkers and efficient workers have alike contributed to the ridiculous number of solutions proposed.
Policies have been outlined, in the adoption of which lay the
only salvation of the South and the Negro, the rejection of
which would mean the utter desolation of the land or the
annihilation of the Negro. Prophecies and conclusions have
been given with consummate confidence and satisfaction.
Estimates have been based on " conclusive evidence " where
no evidence existed. To realize the full extent of unrea-
son involved in the proposed solutions and measures it is
only necessary to read the history of the discussions in general, the discussions of the problems involved in the migratory movements of the negroes, the discussions concerning negro enfranchisement and disfranchisement, negro
education and the political and constitutional history of the
United States from 1840 through the reconstruction period.
Many of the documents setting forth such measures and
policies already appear as curious and entertaining data.
It is true, however, that the Negro has survived them all
with a good degree of vigor and a hopeful future, and
that he presents a normal difficult problem of a dynamic condition of economic, political and social development.

In view of the extended discussions concerning the Negro,
it may well be doubted if anything new can be said. Not
only has the Public become so thoroughly tired of any discussion of the Negro Problem that it no longer cares for
the sensational stories, but it has ceased to give serious

thought to the consideration of the real problem. The discussions, at least, have become a national joke, and the Public responds with characteristic feeling, " It's the same old story." But on the other hand, valuable contributions have been made to the study of the situation and to the understanding of conditions. Research into the real conditions and possibilities of the negro race are yet limited and there is need of a clear understanding of the problem. And the careful student may well hope to assist in *interpreting the problem* with results that are both profitable and interesting. It should be remembered that the problem does not consist wholly of a single or even of a number of incidents to the situation, nor is it a problem of a few generations. The solution does not consist in the elimination of present unpleasant or objectionable features. It need only be suggested that the adoption of many of the policies proposed would have involved more serious difficulties than those which were eliminated. Again, it should be remembered that the conditions under which the problem is working are extremely dynamic and subject to complex forces. In such conditions the solution of the problem must begin with the most successful working of present conditions with a view to future improvements. The solution of the problem thus has two chief aspects, an ultimate solution and an immediate one. The ultimate solution can be reached only through the adoption of effective policies in dealing with actual conditions. Whatever this final solution may be, the present conditions constitute the immediate problem, and a thorough knowledge of this problem is the first essential. Such a knowledge, with its successful application and direction, must be the only solution of the immediate present.

An effective interpretation of the Negro Problem involves not simply a general knowledge of the present condition of the Negro. It involves an accurate estimate of the Negro's capacities and tendencies that go far back of his present status and reflect the history of the race. It involves an estimate of his inherent qualities that goes far beyond the present indication of what his future possibilities may be. And such an interpretation includes not only this clear exposition of what the Negro is, but also a similar estimate of the full environment in which he is to live, with its exacting conditions. And it involves a sane and liberal correlation of the sum of accurate information that is obtainable with practical thinking and with working conditions. The problem can thus be viewed relatively. It should not be assumed that because the present condition of the negroes presents a somewhat discouraging outlook, and because the " weak " tendencies seem to predominate, that there is need for pessimism. If the Negro's standard of home life and living is not high, it is also true that similar conditions exist in the slums of our cities and in other countries. If his mental ability and capacity seem lacking or undeveloped, it should be remembered that he has already advanced much beyond his racial condition in Africa. At the same time, it should be remembered that the Negro differs from the whites not only in development, but also in kind. It is a knowledge of this " kind " which is the first essential to a satisfactory discussion of the problem. If the more negative characteristics and tendencies are emphasized in the summary of negro character which follows, it is in consideration of the fact that they constitute the basic criterion of the Negro's exact condition, and that in their correction and proper adjustment lies the hopeful outlook for the race. It may be suggested that these most important traits are the ones which indicate the inherent possibilities of the Negro and that they are precisely those that are capable of being built upon. Furthermore, they are the normal outgrowth of the forces and processes that have been operating to effect the development of the Negro.

The results of careful research into the conditions of the negro race in the South show that the condition under which the negroes live are not conducive to good conduct, to the growth of strong character or to the development of a healthy social organism. The negroes live in crowded quarters and inferior houses. There is little home life among them. They move from place to place and form little home attachment. Families are much broken up and there is indiscriminate mixing in the home. Filth and unsanitary conditions prevail. Irregular habits of life, uncertain incomes and irregular food-supplies are common to the great mass of negroes. Disease and bad health are prevalent to an alarming extent Vice and immorality, excesses and lack of restraint intensify the general conditions, and take much of the Negroe's energies. He is thus incapacitated for a full degree of efficiency in the struggle for life. As a laborer the Negro is becoming unsatisfactory with the tendency increasing under present conditions. He receives higher wages but does less efficient work. The negro woman constitutes a serious feature of the situation. She fails to assist the men in a better struggle, she is inefficient and indisposed to be faithful. She is a hindrance to the successful saving of money and the industrial development of the family. The Negro is not increasing his economic prosperity nor his moral stability. He is more of an offender than he is a criminal. His weaknesses predominate over his aggressive tendencies. At the same time his offences are on the increase and are out of proportion to his numerical relation to the population. Chiefly, his crime is due to the expression of animal impulses and a lack of restraint. The majority of crimes are committed by younger negroes, and reformatory measures seem to have little corrective influence. The criminal tendency together with the various forms of vagrancy and bumptious-

ness constitute a menacing situation to both races. The fear
of the law offers the most effective check to the bad propensities of the Negro. His religion, while associating in
thought much of the moral and ethical element, has little
practical bearing upon conduct. Education, as it has been
conducted, has not made the Negro strong.

The Negro is very much of a social being. His gregarious habits satisfy his social wants. He is constantly
engaged in mingling with his fellows at large, and is less
often at home with his family. He is ingenuous in im-
provising methods of entertainment and enjoys his social
feelings. The Church, the Lodge and various other associations supplement his private functions in offering ample
opportunity for the outlet of his social energy. The quality of his entertainment is not of a high order and increases the conditions for irregular morals. Church services offer much of the better entertainment for the Negro
and occupy much of his time and energy. About equal
with the Church, the Lodge furnishes social enjoyment and
contributes to race pride. The fraternal organizations have
become an institution, sometimes rated above the home, the
church and school. They offer avenues for the discussion
and control of racial interests and for benefits and insurance
to its members. They encourage the social features of
burial and funeral ceremonies. They have had a phenomenal growth and do a large amount of business among the
negroes, thus filling an important want. The Negro shows
power for organization and for obtaining money from his
people. A remarkable enthusiasm and pride are manifested
in such societies and their undertakings. They further
encourage the founding of industries, organizations and
schools, where there is opportunity for immediate growth.
In their schools the negroes have done little; they have received little encouragement from the whites. The facilities

and conditions under which they operate are not favorable. Both whites and blacks show indifference. Their teachers are for the most part inefficient and irresponsible and the irregular attendance and application to work prevent permanent results. On the whole the conditions of the Southern Negro are far from satisfactory. Physically, mentally, morally and socially, he has serious charges to meet. It is possible to interpret the present conditions as indicating deterioration, if continued at the present rate, under the lack of restraint on the one hand and lack of constructive living on the other.

The conditions of negro life as thus briefly outlined reflect the more general attitudes and tendencies from which they grow. There is in the Negro little home consciousness, more of the general social consciousness. This has its effect upon the general standard of morals and ideals, while at the same time his low state of social consciousness and control does not lead him to develop a love of home and family. The Negro often shows much hospitality of a sort to strangers, more rarely lasting friendship and affection. Freedom from restraint and parental control are much desired by the younger negroes. There is little parental and filial affection, and little abiding solicitude for the welfare of members of the family. There is little respect and care for the aged and infirm. There are few high ideals of woman, wife and mother, and little thought of individual chastity and of the purity of the home. The Negro entertains no definite ideas of health and hygiene, nor of an individual responsibility for his own conduct. He looks upon labor as an evil necessity and is developing a professional ethics of vagrancy. He exercises little forethought and believes in an ideal condition of future material welfare much in the same way that he sings

When I git to Heaven, gwin' er ease, ease,
Me an' my God gwin'er do as we please.

He shows little desire to acquire property, and his society
satisfies his physical cravings more than it produces industry.　The negroes love notoriety and distinction; those
who do not admire their leaders and notorious characters
wonder at their powers.　Crime is not a cause for social
ostracism or condemnation.　Social prejudices and caste
ideas are entertained by the negroes of the higher class.
Jealousies and conflicts mar the harmony of social organizations and prevent effective work.　Successful display and
quantitative results are the marks of success.　Education
is valued in proportion as it makes the individual important
in the eyes of his people and as it relieves him from physical
labor.　Religion is a panacea for all sins and an emotional
belief in a future happiness to be obtained without sacrifice.
Much stress is placed upon the importance of the life after
death and much emphasis given to burial and funeral rites.
In fine, the Negro has little social pressure, concentrated
beliefs or definite conventions that control conduct in his
own society, which demand the development of homes, the
acquirement of property, the equipment for life, the faithful performance of duty or individual achievement.　Instead he quickly responds to whatever circumstances offer
the most pleasure and the least resistance.　On the other
hand, it is hopeful to compare the possibilities that lie in
the simple fidelity of a simple home and family of an industrious negro, with its patient, persistent, faithful performance of obligations and the simple thoughts of an
imaginative and emotional religion which becomes a true
reality of life.

These general attitudes and social tendencies again indicate the more specific traits, the psychological processes and

sociological tendencies of the Negro. Sensuous feelings and simple emotions reflect the predominance of the physical impulses and pleasure-pain feelings. Feeling gives rare reality to the Negro, and that which does not have such reality appeals little to his conscious or unconscious states. The Negro is strong in the expression of the primitive emotions. Fear is expressed for the most part as a feeling apart from the individual experience and involving more of the imagination. The Negro is easily aroused to a feeling of fear and this, intensified, completely incapacitates him for usefulness. He shows inability to sustain his control or convictions and is thus lacking in courage. The feeling of fear is most manifest in the fear of officers, of the law, of strangers, of the unexpected, superstitious fears of the supernatural, morbid fears of death and the dead, and in a general child-like fear of certain animals and things. Over against this feeling of fear the Negro often manifests a remarkable degree of daring and recklessness, seemingly out of the pure pleasure it gives him in the self-feeling. Anger appears as a passion easily excited, running riot, uncontrollable, insatiable, expressing itself in a blind instinct to destroy, but is quickly forgotten. Such animal passion momentarily excited takes various forms: maddened jealousy, wanton recklessness, morbid pleasure in the gratification of the feeling of superiority, and the pouring-out of animal impulse. It sometimes approaches the state of dementia in women. It is further manifest in the vile denunciation of those who are considered enemies. The Negro is easily angered by sudden physical stimuli, by jealousies, by those considered inferior to himself, and by members of his own race. Fear and deference often prevent anger in the case of superiors. The Negro does not cherish his anger for long periods of time nor is the feeling of revenge lasting. The positive self-feeling is prominent

in the Negro's feeling of importance, pride, dignity, wanton-
ness, bumptiousness, license and in his feelings of injured
dignity in relation to white children. The first person is
magnified in all thoughts and actions. The positive self-
feeling is manifest for the most part among members of
his own race. The negative self-feeling, as seen in humility, self-pity, lack of assertiveness, subjection to others,
while most commonly shown toward the whites, is equally
characteristic in the relation to negro leaders and advent-
urers. Sympathy is most characteristic in the simple physiological response to circumstances and suggestions of the
moment, and is freely expressed where no stronger emotion
conflicts. This feeling may take the form of simple unconscious rhythmical expressions of feeling, response to
the crowd, imitation, or it may be sympathy of fear or excitement. Sympathy is strong in the appeal for pity in
the child-like wail of the wanderer, in a self appeal which
enables him to arouse pity and obtain favors. Such a self-
sympathy and its objective response is the source of pleasurable feeling. The Negro manifests sympathy for the
whites in momentary circumstances. While the Negro ex-
presses a quick sympathetic feeling toward the circumstances
of the moment, he is seemingly capable of little lasting
sympathy, affection or gratitude, less so than formerly.
Hence he often appears to be void of fellow-feeling, harsh
and unrelenting in his judgment, unsympathetic, when the
positive self-feeling is uppermost in his consciousness. The
Negro shows feelings of sorrow and grief to which, by habit
and custom, he gives much form and expression, but he as
easily puts them aside and outgrows them. Love for the
most part is physical. The social emotions are little developed into strong forces, although the majority of the
Negro's emotions are expressed in the group aspect. In
abstractions of thought and moral maxims, in the satisfac-

tion of the feeling of oughtness and self-approbation, the social feelings are reflected with some definiteness. They are further seen in the love of ritual, regalia, music, love of concerted expression, love of the wonderful, and of satisfactory forms of organizations. Friendship, loyalty and recognition of worth are little apparent. The parental and filial emotions are expressions of interest and dependence. But in all cases of the expression of emotions, the Negro is especially sensitive to alternations and opposites. Exaltation and depression, gaiety and gloom, boastfulness and timidity, excitement and agitation, pleasure and pain—all these reflect the qualities and flexibilities of the Negro's emotions. The Negro may often repress his emotions, so that expectation, fear or disappointment may not be detected in his appearance. These susceptibilities to influences and the conceptions of the higher emotions in abstract ideals which are common among the negroes reveal latent possibilities, so that the emotions of the Negro may be his strongest as well as his weakest point.

By means of the careful analysis of these traits and tendencies, it is possible to summarize them into a reasonably accurate estimate of negro character-tendencies and the potentials of the race. From the more sociological tendencies, in addition to those already indicated, and in different representations, the summary shows: The Negro is *expressive* [1] in his abuse of others, hilarity, lying, exaggertion, indecent language, expression of feeling in rhythmic motion, love of music, love of display, devotion to worship and social activities, in his general emotionalism, and in his inactivity and superficiality. His *appropriativeness* is seen

---

[1] The terms *expressive, gregarious* etc. as used in this paragraph were suggested by Dr. Thomas P. Bailey in an analysis of negro character as found in some of the Negro's folk-songs.

in his love of money, covetousness, theft scheming, his imitation and adaptability and in his desultory work. He is *gregarious* in his sexual morality, sociality, conformity to law and the group, imitation and originality, his simple honesty and in his spontaneous expressiveness. *Gregariousness* and *appropriativeness* combined give vagrancy, wandering, sense of dependence, lack of restraint, provincialism, childishness and lack of moral earnestness. The Negro is *assertive* in the expression of the positive self-feeling, in agitation, and in competition with whites and blacks. The Negro is *responsive* to forceful circumstances and to the emotions. This is further seen in his imitation and interest. He is unresponsive in his lack of reverence for old age, lack of affection and friendship. From the psychological processes, the emotions predominate as already indicated. In the *intellect,* there is much imitation and adaptation, fatalism, set-mindedness, in which all the senses are turned toward the perception of one attitude, which is often misguided imagination or hypnotism by an idea, little open to reason; the Negro shows concretism, a vivid imagination, humor, lack of will-power in inertia and unsustained control, elasticity of spirit, love of euphonious words, inconsequential and incoherent thought, little reasoning power, love of the morbid and curious, but with little perceptiveness and observational power. Association plays an important part through suggestion but the association systems are meagre and there is little sustained and constructive thinking.

The Negro thus shows a remarkable combination of both negative and positive traits of mental, moral and social development. He is neither an aberrant form of other races nor a hopelessly arrested type of any race. There is unity and consistency everywhere between the forces and processes that have been working and are still working, and his present status. A spontaneous, shifting, erratic, rambling, incoherent nature seeking freedom from restraint, gratification of impulse, and the experience of sustained languor finds natural satisfaction. Its superficiality enjoys the show of apparent results without caring for the details of achievement. It avoids details and difficult tasks and recognizes no causal relation between stability and prosperity. The Negro's is an easy-going indolence seeking freedom to indulge itself and seeking to avoid all circumstances which would tend to coerce or restrain its freedom. Such character-attitude and temperament, with an inheritance of mental stupidity and moral insensibility, find their expression through a being capable of physical endurance, but improvident, extravagant, lazy rather than industrious, faithful and unfaithful in the performance of duties, easily adaptable, imitative, lacking initiative, dishonest and untruthful, with little principle of honor or conception of right and virtue, superstitious, over-religious, suspicious and incapable of a comprehension of faith in mankind.

Again, it is possible to state a compact summary of the Negro's chief characteristics in still other terms, with a view to ascertaining the proper forces which might be brought to bear upon the adjustment, co-ordination and development of the more primal traits and the stronger qualities. By these characteristics is meant a degree of tendency bordering on the extreme or approximating the complete qualities described, allowing always for the qualifications and overlappings. *First,* the Negro easily *responds to stimuli,* that is, he is *controlled by present impulses.* This results in almost complete *lack of restraint,* including both the yielding to impulses and inertia. *Second,* this free response *tends always to pleasure,* sometimes the pleasure being more or less unconscious in the simple giving way to impulse and the breaking-down of restraint or in the negative feeling of non-exertion. *The Negro is there-fore inactive.* *Third,* the Negro *tends to carry all responses to an extreme.* He loves plenty of varied stimuli. This exhausts and degenerates his vital powers. *Fourth,* the Negro has *little capacity for sustained control.* This applies to sustained efforts, conduct in general, morality, convictions and thought. He is, therefore, *weak in social-and self-control* and lacking in self-direction. *Fifth,* he does not, therefore, lend himself to the *development of deep and permanent qualities through the working out of essential processes.* *Sixth,* he is therefore *superficial and irresponsible.*

It is very necessary, however, to view such general ten-dencies of inactivity and superficiality with careful discrim-ination, and to be cautious in interpreting them as " nega-tive " tendencies. It will be observed that the positive qualities are very much in evidence but are little expressed because there is little pressure on them. The Negro shows great plasticity and much promise. His rich variety of life and the flexibility of his nature, his sympathetic adapta-bility and the plasticity of his consciousness may well be the basis for permanent ability. His love of a good time, hilariousness and boisterous nature, and the feeling for a free rhythmical expression in an unrestrained outburst of impulses should be directed into channels of positive growth. Furthermore, the feelings, emotions, the flowing conscious-ness of the Negro, his mental imagery of unusual vividness and his powerful visualization reveal a wonderful spon-taneity. Much of this is expressed at present in his artistic feelings, his gorgeous portrayals, varied versatility, his abrupt descent from the sublime to the ridiculous, the blend-ing of the homely with the awful, an enjoyment of crude humor, quick response in repartee, richness of folk-songs and thought, concreteness, vividness, clearness and directness in expression and action. Negro children show a marked degree of brightness and a reasonable measure of ability. Interest and enjoyment may grow into application and achievement. And it would be difficult to find a more picturesque life than that of the simple industrious negro, with his honest idealism and simple honesty, and his naive faith and optimism in the policies of life. There is ample evidence that it is possible for this to grow into a broader concepton of life, a consistent, steady growth in character and a substantial economic ability.

But such attainments may not be reached through sudden growth. Efficient forces must direct the processes and assist the Negro in adapting himself to his environment. The Negro must recognize his own condition and what it will require to better it. The conditions of the environment itself must be thoroughly known, and so far as possible they must be brought to his assistance. The problem then consists essentially of two parts, the developing of the Negro's ability, and the advantageous adjustment to the civilization in which he is to achieve his place. Suggestions concerning the possibilities and methods of assisting the Negro are made elsewhere.[1] It is not only essential to know the condition of the Negro but it is also necessary to understand these conditions in their relation to the environment which surrounds the Negro and with which he will have to compete. The problem of this environment is the problem of the relation between the whites and blacks. This race-relation consists of two essentially important aspects, the economic and industrial relations, and the general political and social relations which must exist in various forms and problems between the white man and the Negro. Of these two general aspects, the more important is that involved in the industrial and economic factors which will be brought to bear upon

[1] Chapter I.

the Negro in the future. The most important feature of this aspect, again, is the part which the Negro himself must play in fixing his status and in preparing for competition and progress.

And nowhere is it more important to have a thorough knowledge of the Negro's complete character than in the consideration of his present economic condition and his future possibilities. In no field of the Negro's endeavor is the causal relationship between his traits and tendencies and his present condition more clearly seen. In the sense of remedying these conditions by beginning at their source, the economic problem is the only problem facing the Negro. In the solving of this difficulty will be the solution of the entire problem for the whites and blacks so far as a progressive, dynamic problem can be solved. But there is clearly a distinct problem to be solved in thus bettering the condition of the Negro and in the economic development of the South. It is not asking too much of the whites to help the Negro toward the ideal which should apply to all laborers, namely, to do that which he is best fitted to do with the most satisfaction to himself and others, and with good pay. It is not expecting too much of the Negro to demand that he prepare himself to do his work well, and that he hold an exalted idea of labor and find wholesome satisfaction in an industrious life. For the immediate emphasis must be placed upon the industrial condition of the Negro as a laborer and his relation to the whites in this capacity, rather than his general economic condition in acquiring property. Through efficiency and successful adjustment in the former relation he will come to a substantial degree of economic prosperity in the latter. Two aspects of the situation which are interrelated throughout their development, present themselves for immediate consideration. First, the question of the efficiency of negro laborers their attitude toward labor, and the proportion of those working to those idle, and second, the opportunities for negro labor and the relations between white and colored laborers. For the results of idleness and indisposition of the negroes to work with the accompanying insolence, on the one hand, and the competition with whites in future condition, on the other, will cause more race conflicts than all other questions of social and political relations.

In the labor problem of the South there is undoubtedly a problem facing both races which did not exist even a few years ago. The chief service of an inquiry like this is to give the exact representations of conditions and to interpret the problem. In the first place, it should be remembered that the Negro is a general laborer working for and under the supervision of the whites, including agricultural laborers and women workers. There is a small percent of skilled laborers and still another small proportion working independently for themselves or for other negroes. Again, the mass of negro laborers are not united in working in industries, but for the most part each laborer works separately as a general laborer. In this general capacity, the Negro plays an important part in the industrial development of the South, in assisting to produce comforts and to satisfy the wants of the whites, and in this way he maintains his own standard of living. The Negro labor in the South is solely an unorganized and unintegrated body of negroes capable of doing a certain amount of work. There is ample work for all at reasonable wages. Within the last two decades the price of labor has almost doubled. There is a strong demand at this rate and no negro need be unemployed. In fact, the South is beginning to be handicapped by a lack of labor and for the want of efficient laborers. And still a great number of negroes remain idle much of their time, working only when compelled to do so by law or necessity. There is an increasing number of negroes who are unwilling to do manual labor of an unpleasant sort, and an increasing number who are unwilling to remain employed steadily. The influence of such negroes in the community is more exasperating that can be indicated without seeming exaggeration. They are equally injurious to the Negro in the race conflicts which they cause, the example which they set, in the vice and crime of which they are guilty, in the permanent lowering of the average of race-ability, and in the drainage which they entail for their support. Not only is this class not humiliated by such conditions, but such individuals consider their policies a point of pride and cause for congratulation. They can live without work, have a good time, and in their self-satisfaction know that they represent an ideal among many of the younger negroes. Such negroes often insolently refuse to work under any conditions and persuade others to adopt the same policies. They are thus failing to prepare themselves for any of the gainful occupations, and in this way they are increasing the difficulties for the future development of the race.

Not only is colored labor not improving in the quality or in the quantity available for practical employment, but it is doubtful if a single locality can be found in the South in which negro labor is not growing more unsatisfactory. The general grounds for complaint other than those already indicated, are chiefly the unreliability of the Negro. The employer never knows when he will be able to employ; when he has succeeded in employing, he has no assurance that the laborers will report for work, or that they will report continuously. The Negro can not be depended upon, and there is no way to bring pressure to bear upon him as in former days. The negroes themselves bring little pressure to force industry upon individuals. Again, the quality of the labor itself is often unreliable unless minutely directed.

This is due both to carelessness and irresponsibleness of the Negro and to his lack of intelligence and training. The average negro will not remain in one position for a long period of time. He must have his change, whether to work at something else, to loaf, or to visit another locality. He usually returns sooner or later where he is again employed with some satisfaction; for a time he is again a good worker. The whites employ the negro laborer in general, not on the basis of his ability or record, but on the probability of getting the work done. Only a few years ago it was very common for families to employ laborers who had remained with them for years, working regularly and faithfully year after year to their mutual satisfaction and prosperity; now it seems rarely possible to retain the same negro more than a season or a year. These particulars indicate the new proportions which the situation is assuming in its effect upon the Negro and in the special problems that make up labor conditions. The difficulty of maintaining satisfactory domestic service intensifies the " servant problem." The younger negroes are not prepared to do good work and care less for it; they are thus preparing to be forced out of their present place by white workers. Farm labor and general work that requires steady employment is beginning to suffer. Skilled labor is not increasing in quantity or efficiency. The causal relation between the negro morals and irregularities is more apparent in his work. The growing race feeling may well be expected to prevent the negro laborer from having equal competition with the whites unless his work be thoroughly efficient. He will not be allowed in the labor unions; it is thus incumbent upon him to be able to direct himself. His presence will be unwelcome, if constantly unemployed, because he can always be had for a reduced wage, thus breaking into the plans of the unions. These are some of the conditions which the Negro must willingly face and to which he must adjust himself and wake up.

On the other hand, the South prefers negro labor in general. In all domestic service, hotels, elevators and miscellaneous work the Negro is much preferred. Many employers in special industries also prefer negro laborers. There will be ample opportunity for the regular employment of the Negro if his labor is satisfactory. The rapid development of the South will demand a larger supply of labor than is now available. At present the negroes find the most satisfactory work in the municipal improvements of towns and cities, the construction of new industries, and in the work of railroads and mines. Such employment will continue to attract a large number of negroes. The labor of the farm should recall the industrious, earnest negro worker, while the small industries and promiscuous work offer a broad field. Wages are practically the same as for the whites in this general labor, and the negroes are less often abused and cheated of their time, than formerly. The Southern employer recognizes with some pride efficient, earnest, educated negro laborers, and he is not slow to reward them. The Negro is undoubtedly capable of very efficient work, both skilled and unskilled. He has much aptitude and endurance for special work. He has ingenuity and ability in some forms of inventive and mechanical labor, if he would prepare himself and apply his best energies continuously to his work. At present it must be admitted that the average negro laborer wishes to do the higher class of work without being willing to prepare for it; he has little ambition to rise through progressive efficiency. It is this lack of equipment and ambition rather than competition with the whites which is causing skilled labor to decrease in many places. In all features alike, the Negro is suffering from his weakness and the white man is not willing to save him from it. Competition in the South will not long remain so easy as it has been; the Negro may count on assistance from the whites provided he shows his ability to properly use it. Otherwise his condition will continue more unfavorable. In the reaction which followed the recent strike of firemen on the Georgia Railroad it was clear that there is a growing sentiment against negro labor in comparison with whites, where the issue is one of race. In the same reaction there was also manifest a strong feeling of justice and fairplay for the Negro. The efficient, earnest, industrious negro may count on opportunity and encouragement in the South. And the hope may reasonably be expressed that the South, needing and favoring negro labor, and seeing that idleness increases crime and inefficiency will come to take a broader view of the entire situation, so that steps will be taken to assist the Negro and insist that he shall be employed and that in this policy no field of work will be closed to the Negro. In this study of the negro laborer and in the adjustment of labor conditions through which the South must achieve its industrial development, there is a broad field for practical results in the application by Southern economists of sound interpretation and theories. The negro labor problem lacks many of the features common to the general labor conditions; it involves additional problems.

The wealth of a people must depend partly on their earning capacity, partly upon their economy, and partly upon their opportunities and resources. The Negro as a laborer has contributed much to the economic welfare of the country; he has contributed little to his own wealth. He therefore contributes to the state little in the way of property. On the one hand it is complained by the whites that the Negro contributes little to the wealth of the country. On the other hand it is maintained by the Negro that he does not cost the Nation a cent. The standards of criticism are entirely different. Again, the Negro speaks with pride of the homes, banks, churches and industries which are owned or controlled by negroes and enlarges upon the inaccurate estimates of the amount of property upon which the negroes pay taxes, while the whites assert that, whereas the negroes constitute some forty percent of the population they own only from three to five percent of the property. Such a record is neither unusual nor surprising, but the natural results which might have been expected under the conditions obtaining. It is not especially creditable, nor is it a discreditable record for a people of the Negro's qualities and experience. Comparison with the whites is a severe test. But the Negro has reached the stage when it is necessary for him to prepare himself for successful competition, to prove his ability to contribute to the wealth of the country, and to explain why his property is increasing at a relatively diminishing ratio. This explanation will be found in the traits and tendencies which have controlled his conduct rather than in the environment and the opportunities which have been at his disposal. For he has had ample opportunity to buy homes and land and to accumulate property without hindrance. If the Negro would apply himself faithfully to his work with the rate of wages which he receives, and use a reasonable amount of judgment and economy in the expenditure of his money, he could raise his standard of living and at the same time save a substantial part of his earnings. As it is the Negro spends his money as fast as he can obtain it somewhat in the importance attached to its value for church and lodge dues, for entertainments and social life under the auspices of these institutions, for clothing, for novelties and unnecessaries, for house rent and food. Much is paid for fines and a considerable amount is sacrificed in the necessity of having to seek credit for supplies.

The resulting conditions are not unlike those in other departments of his life. Ignorance, negligence, shiftlessness, vice and weakness lead to poverty as they do to unstable race-conditions. It is thus impossible for the Negro to accumulate property even if he desired to do so and if there was sentiment putting a premium on thrift and economy; it would not be possible for him to retain property if it were given him, under these conditions.

On the other hand, the Negro often proves himself capable of industry and thrift for a short period of time when he must have a certain amount of money. Many individuals have succeeded in saving year after year a part of their income and investing it in sensible ways. There are many negroes whose records show marked thrift and successful management. In every community the wealth owned by the negroes has been accumulated by a very small number of individuals who represent the more successful economic element. Again, the Negro shows capacity for organization in his fraternal organizations and benefit associations, his business leagues, and various co-operative projects. He shows a remarkable ability for advertising, for raising money through the medium of church and lodge. The negroes control quite a number of banks, stores, newspapers and other establishments. In these and in supplying provisions for members of their own race there is much economic activity and success. The Negro plans many co-operative methods of establishing successful business concerns, but they usually hinder rather than promote individual prosperity and look to an ideal prosperity. In his enthusiasm the Negro is a bad manager. Says one, " the Negro Business League is the greatest meeting along industrial lines that has ever been organized among any people," and he speaks of a state organization only. In an appeal for subscriptions to a savings institution for negroes the promoter says among other things, ". . . it behooves us, the sable sons of Ham, to fall in and keep step to the drum tap of commercialism and march onward and upward the foot-worn pedestal of success until we shall have thrown wide the doors to the vaults of the Southern Banking and Loan Company in which will be heaped the treasures of the nations." The total capital was to be fifteen thousand dollars, with shares at fifty dollars apiece, to be paid in installments of one dollar a week for fifty weeks. Such plans have been numerous indeed, and much might be done were it not all lost in the end in bad management or lack of completion. Here again the negroes contribute something to the prosperity of the whites and of a few negroes, but little to their own welfare. The problem is not so much that of wealth to the nation as it is one of helping the Negro to place himself on a stable basis. He must begin the economy of self-help and individual acquirement; he must learn discretion and judgment in the placing of his small contributions. Until he has learned more of this lesson it will be difficult for him to withstand a severe competition and not until then will he begin to add to the wealth of the State. He can best begin by adopting a policy of faithful, consistent, industrious application to his work.

While the Negro has the power of making his future prosperity in the South, it is also largely in the hands of the whites, in that he can only achieve results through the help and co-operation of the whites. Wherever negroes have succeeded in small industries and as industrious laborers. they have always had their individual or group of white friends supporting their efforts. This is an essential part of their environment. What the future attitude of the whites will be toward the Negro will depend largely on the Negro's ability to prove his worth and his assistance to the whites. Economic conditions will control the situation. So far as the present situation is concerned, this is the only important problem in the Negro's environment. The questions of social and political equality do not constitute a problem in the sense in which the industrial and economic situation does. The Negro may count upon his relation to the whites as it has been indicated in the discussion of the foregoing problems. He will achieve his place entirely as a separate race. An implicit understanding of this will facilitate his progress. Little need be said concerning social and political equality. There is no absolute race equality in any sense of the word. The races have different abilities and potentialities. Those who would assist the Negro should remember this and not exact too much of him, either in demanding his results or in offering him the completed ideals of the whites. Race prejudice will continue with an increasing intensity but the races will come to a more complete understanding. When the Negro has proved himself, the world will make way for him. So long as he is incapable of intelligently using the ballot or in assisting in the direction of, and in the understanding of public policies, he will be denied the ballot. But a broader view of the situation will be gained by both races and as the negroes become qualified they will be given the opportunity to co-operate in the political working of the South. The Negro must have legal justice and fair play, and this will be received more readily when the two races come to a definite understanding of what their relations are to be. In the characteristic feeling of the Southern whites all forms of equality suggest social equality, which is utterly inconceivable to their practical thinking.

While the question of social equality does not constitute a problem in the South, it does appear to other peoples and to the Negro as a possibility or a probability. The question is still agitated to some extent and it may be remembered

that there have been those who advocated the superiority of
the Negro to the Southern whites. This conception of
equality, with the consequent result upon the Negro, has
done more to co-operate with his undeveloped nature in
hindering his progress than any other single thing. It has
been a great injustice to the Negro as well as to the whites.
There is not a single argument in its favor; the intermixing
of the races has been judged to work detriment to both, so
far as scientific observations have been possible. As a matter of fact, however, the question of social equality is not
based on pure reason. Feeling is much more powerful than
the intellect in such a situation. It may be possible to explain the abstract situation, but a thorough comprehension
is not possible without an immediate experience of the inherent feeling-attitude which underlies it. One may persuade the intellect but not the feeling. Race-prejudice reveals the fact that the whites, while admitting the abstract
righteousness of the various forms of equality—economic,
political, religious, legal—admitting that character is not to
be judged by such external accidents as color, in practice and
feeling they refuse to grant to the Negro an actual right to
equality of treatment based on character. This has its basis
in the feeling that the Negro has not the character qualities which warrant such a treatment. But it further has its
explanation in the fact that the right of equality carries with
it a check in that the whites implicitly feel that all forms
of equality at bottom are based on at least the possibility
of social communion,[1] and that social communion holds out

[1] The explanation involved in the idea of "social communion" is
that of Dr. Thomas P. Bailey. A further discussion of the general
relations between the races will be found in his address before the
Department of Superintendence of the National Education Association
held at Indianapolis in March of this year. This valuable discussion
I am permitted to give in the appendix.

the possibility of intermarriage, which is an impossible admission. Therefore, all forms of equality are withheld from the Negro in proportion as they tend to connect themselves with " social equality." Individual negroes however excellent they might be in character, are nevertheless members of a race that cannot share the communal life of the whites, and however much they may be respected for their ability and character, they are still " outside the kin." The feeling against any forms of social equality are thus established as strong " mores " which it is impossible to overcome in any short period of time. It is stronger than religion and government. He that violates it is without religion and state. In the keeping of it is the highest culture, education, religion and conduct; it underlies purity, virtue, traditions, ideals and is also intensified in the social emotions and conduct. So long as the attitude is thus, it is needless to inquire into the advisability of the mixing of the races; such a feeling grows stronger with the developing situation. It is expedient to turn to the problem of immediate improvement of conditions as they now are, thus preparing the way for successful adjustment.

From this inquiry into the character tendencies of the Negro, his related environment and the special correspondence involved in the relations between whites and blacks, it is clear that the amelioration of the Negro's condition must come through a continued growth. Strength of moral character and mental stability with economic prosperity never yet came to a people by leaps and bounds. Such a growth can only be effected through the coming generations, by means of a training which will give a permanent character-basis upon which to build and a capacity to retain; this must be a persistent, continuous process, with efficient forces to direct. A proposed plan of beginning the Negro's education with the view to establishing the qualities of stick-to-it-iveness and development within the race has been outlined in Chapter I. But in the meantime, and in order to make way for such plans and to avert further deteriorating influences, there are certain self-evident duties for both whites and blacks. While only commonplaces in their statement, they are the very difficult essentials of any positive growth in the negro race. For the negroes, perhaps the very first essential is a complete understanding of their own condition with a clear, implicit, final feeling that the races will develop separately. There is ample opportunity for each and prosperity should be a mutual benefit. With this conception inherent, the Negro will find his unconscious strivings after the new ideals a stable basis for prosperity. Then he may stand for race purity, race pride and loyalty and race solidarity. This can only come about when he has ceased to wish to become a white man. There is and will be a large field for simple success and happiness, with progressive achievement for the successfully developed black man; there is and will not be a place for a black white man. Self-improvement should be the first result. The bettering of the immediate situation and the preparation for future growth will be most facilitated by uncompromising industrious and industrial application, and by a demand on the part of the Negro for his race of a higher standard of living. Following these, moral improvement and concerted ideals will be possible; the intellectual capacity may then have an opportunity to develop. A practical crusade for industry, economy, thrift and better home conditions is absolutely necessary if any immediate results are to be expected; each delay renders the future less favorable, unless indeed, it is the wish of the Negro to allow the process of elimination to proceed at length and then to take the remaining few for the nucleus of a new race development. It does seem that the Negro, recognizing the exact traits and tendencies and their possibilities for good or bad, would be willing to undertake the things which are absolutely necessary to his welfare. There may be conflicting opinions about the race relations in the future, about the ultimate solution, but there is no conflict in the facts already set forth; they are uncontrovertible. The Negro, then, should be willing to face the situation and work for specific, definite benefits, rather than advocate improvement on world-wide comparisons and dream of an ideal deliverance into a state of greatness and prosperity. Race agitation is more harmful to the Negro, little hurtful to the whites. *Definite* plans and means through personal strivings, beginning with ever so insignificant results and working slowly, persistently surely, outward—these will work substantial gains. The Negro must give up his superficiality, as rapidly as it is possible for him to do so, and face his problems one by one in the order of their immediate importance.

Nor should this appear to be a gloomy outlook. There is a remarkable unity in all of the Negro's weakness and stronger points. Enough of the excellent qualities of the Negro have been given expression to indicate a large possibility; to develop these capabilities should be a joyous problem for the earnest negro. Negro individuals have succeeded; negro communities have shown the power of successful self-direction. There are many sections where the negroes show a large degree of prosperity. The Negro has the capacity to enjoy life within his own race. The very satisfaction of earning honest success with honest toil, the physical comforts and the spiritual satisfaction in the present and in the outlook for the future are no little rewards. A healthy body, a wholesome thought and moral feeling, a guarantee of comforts and work in helping make a civilization, with a gradual intellectual improvement will make the Negro an increasingly important factor in the civilization in

which he lives. The problem is one of developing the possibilities of a potent race; what service could be more lofty or
more satisfying? Nothing that the Negro might achieve
inter-racially can ever compare with his services in helping
his own society. In no other way can he achieve fame so
easily or so unquestionably fixed. Such negroes will always be honored and find satisfaction in representing the interests of their people. Many recent conferences in the
South between the whites and blacks show a distinct and
healthful spirit of encouragement on both sides. The Negro
has an unlimited field before him in the higher work of
teaching, preaching and professional work among his own
people. There will be no competition there outside of his
own race, when he has once found his place. The fidelity
of the negro teacher and other workers reveals a most enthusiastic and hopeful outlook. Their wholesome enjoyment of work and the satisfaction gained from results are
most gratifying. Again, the large number of names of
negroes who have been recognized by the whites both South
and North is suggestive of the possibilities that may be attained through a devoted race struggle. The attitude of
the world in encouraging such negroes could scarcely be
more pronounced. From the viewpoint of race pride and
development, it would be difficult to find a more enviable
field for service than that of leading the negro race steadily,
safely, through the changing scenes of a growing civilization. It is easy for the white man to say to the negroes
that permanent achievement comes only through hard work
and sacrifice; that it has come in this way to every people
as well as individuals who have survived. Likewise it is
easy to say to them that such sacrifices, whatever form they
may take, are the source of unlimited spiritual satisfaction.
It is more difficult for the Negro to face the situation and
meet it squarely and unflinchingly. Still it is the best sym-

pathy and co-operation that can be offered to the Negro for the white man to join with him in meeting the situation squarely and to share with him in a practical, substantial way the hardships that must sometimes come.   It is not, then, closing the doors of opportunity and hope to ask that the best be made of a situation, in the successful outcome of which means the fate and happiness of the negro race in America.   Who would discount the life and work of Booker Washington?   There is yet a far greater work to be done.

For the whites, it is also necessary that they recognize the fact that the question of social equality is not a problem; all agitation based on the sensational fear of negro domination is quite unnecessary and harmful.   Such agitation tends to create a thought-problem where none should exist.   An implicit understanding on the part of both races is all that is necessary for the beginning of a better relation between the races.   The negroes will not want social equality; the whites will not be conscious of such a possibility.   It will more easily be recognized, then, that the development of the negro race tends to the prosperity of the whites, as does the success and prosperity of the whites make better conditions for the Negro.   With a clear understanding that the Negro is working to achieve worth and prosperity in his own field, the whites will co-operate for his betterment.   An important need for the whites is a scientific study of the Negro and his environmental conditions.   Unless we know what the Negro is, there can be little intelligent direction and assistance given him.   Whether he remain in the South or migrate to various parts of the United States, or whether he be assisted to establish a separate government and civilization, or whatever the ultimate solution might be, other than the logical development, it is vital that we know his capacities and potentialities.   In any case he must be educated intelligently, effectively, permanently.   For the sake of the whites as well as the blacks it is essential that he be given a fair chance. A thorough knowledge of the Negro will be followed by a third essential, namely broader and impartial thinking. Liberality and fair-play, legal justice and the justice of opportunity—in the sense of best fitting the Negro for his best efforts—these must be qualities of the Southern whites. Justice to the Negro and justice to society are essentials to the successful development of the future civilization of the South. Efficient laws and their enforcement will facilitate the rendering of such justice. Again, the whites may well be expected to show a greater personal interest in the life and welfare of the Negro, and a greater willingness to assist him. There can be no surer way of hindering the Negro's growth than by giving him false ideals; his path should be made plain, not necessarily smooth, and he should be intelligently assisted to make his way. In this the white man has opportunity for effective service to the Negro and the South. Such assistance can begin nowhere else than in each community by introducing among the negroes a practical, enthusiastic campaign for industry and better home life. This can be done in many ways. A negro community once enthusiastic upon the subject, coerced and assisted by the whites can do much. The whites can best start the Negro in such work and can as well continue to help him. There is room for the individual and for the church, municipality, and State to assist practically without the objections commonly suggested to such policies. To those who wish to contribute money to the problem, there is prospect of effective results if in co-operation with whites and blacks of the South. A clear understanding of all policies and a frank, sincere directness of methods should characterize all work. It is indeed a problem, which, although a difficult one and one which demands scientific knowledge and methods with judicial interpretations and sane appreciation of all the forces which operate, challenges our civilization to work wonders with it. The North can also assist much in effectively and successfully dealing with the Negro in the North—a problem more advanced in some respects. In this way the South may be able to receive much assistance in planning for the future. The Negro in the North feels his situation with more keenness than he does in the South. Again, the whites should be charitable in their judgment of the Negro. The sensuality of the Negro, while extremely developed, is but a natural inheritance. His laziness is neither surprising nor hopeless. His religion is not savage. Comparisons are suggestive. The closing of the frontal sinus of the brain may be functional and easily affected by development. The Negro has overwhelming odds in inheritance and environment with which he must compete. He deserves sympathy, encouragement, positive and firm direction, and practicaly intelligent assistance. It is now generally admitted by many students of the problem that in proportion as they come in closer contact with the situation their knowledge of the Negro seems less extensive and sure. On the other hand, there is much experience back of the common statement that " a negro is a negro and you can't make anything else out of him." But he may be assisted to be a good negro and that is the highest privilege that can be given him.

Little remains to be said. The effort has been made, first, to give an accurate estimate of the Negro, based on facts obtained by a discriminating study of conditions in Southern towns, an effort to add to our knowledge of the Negro, with the special view to his capacities and potentials. Secondly, the effort has been made to portray the conditions of the negro race in such communities as they now exist with the special correspondence between his environment and the whites, and the probable relations which will exist in the future. Thirdly, if then we know what the Negro is and what his environmental opportunities and requirements are and will be, certain self-evident duties suggest themselves to whites and blacks. It takes no prophet to add up these conditions and come to a conclusion concerning the problem. Either the present tendencies and conditions will continue at an increasing ratio with the resulting failure of the negro race in America, or they will continue at a constantly decreasing ratio until the Negro has found himself, adjusted himself to conditions, and had a chance to develop his inherent capacities with success. Nor is it difficult to see that it will take unusual efforts on the part of all concerned to achieve the fullest measure of success in the working out of the problem. The facts call for tolerance, broadmindedness and patience. They also call for a recognition of the unwisdom of attempting to treat the Negro as if he possessed the same content of mind as the whites. It would seem that if both whites and blacks knew what the conditions are, what is possible and probable, what the outcome should be, and what it will take to bring it about, that they would be willing to undertake the task. There can be no valid objection offered to the policy of helping the negroes to a healthful and healthy living. Likewise there appears no argument to favor the policy of encouraging his superficiality. Emphasis is placed on the saving and developing of the race rather than upon the economic value of the Negro to the Country, which will follow as a logical result.

It will not suffice for the critic to affirm that many of the traits of the Negro as described are found, not only among the negroes of Africa, but are common to most undeveloped peoples. This is true enough. In all cases the facts are as stated. These conditions are the potential upon which any future must be developed and it matters little what are the relative traits so long as we have in mind the development of the Negro. But a careful analysis of the traits and the quality and circumstances of their expression indicates differences of temperament in the two races which are almost indefinable but which show that the lowest whites have the defects of the whites, not of the negroes, the highest negroes have the good qualities of the negroes, not of the whites. It is not claimed that the Negroes possess such characteristics as have been described exclusively or that they are peculiar to the Negro as a race. In general it would seem that the Negro possesses the accepted characteristics of the savage mind, that is, the same kind of general manifestation of the phenomena of abstraction, inhibition and choice; he also reveals many modifications of such manifestations. But be this as it may, the Negro in the South to-day presents a problem, the particulars of which have been described in the foregoing pages. The practical application does not differ, whether the Negro possesses different laws of mental activity, whether the manifestations of his phenomena depend upon the character of individual experience that is subjected to the mental laws, or whether it is facility brought about by habitual response. That is, for the present purpose, it matters little whether the organization of the Negro's mind is different from that of the whites or whether there is only a difference of content of mind. In any case there is consistency in the policies which give the Negro opportunity to develop whatever is best in the individual and in the race, and which attempt to reveal those fundamental characteristics which at present lie at the centre of the problem. In either case the process must be essentially the same.

There is neither place nor cause for pessimism. The problem is a difficult one and it will become more difficult and complex. Likewise the problems of special labor situations, immigration and economic adjustments are difficult.

There will be conflicts just as is inevitable under race conditions and relations in a compound society. At times such conflicts will seem more intense and threatening, but they do not now constitute a serious problem and they should not be allowed to overshadow the issues involved. Likewise sensational measures and discussions both South and North should not be permitted to cloud the real issues and to throw the study of the problem into heated and senseless discussions. In any complex situation it is easy to take the extreme view, emphasize and multiply and with the aid of the imagination and probable facts, to reach a sincere conclusion as to the hopelessness of the problem. It is likewise easy to emphasize and multiply the opposite extremes and conceive impractical, utopian solutions. A civilization like that which the American people will develop ought to be able to cope with such a problem as that involved in the adjustment of the relations between different races. Pessimism can only be interpreted to mean an admission of unwillingness to face a problem at once difficult, immediate, significant and hopeful.

APPENDIX

Topic: Children Differ in Environment

Discussion: Thomas P. Bailey, Supt. of Schools, Memphis, Tenn.

My discussion shall concern itself only with the first subtopic, Southern Problems.

There is only one Southern problem, and it is one of environment. For Southern children are the truest of Americans by birth and tradition, and therefore if they are being bred in the cult of caste, nurture due to conditions and not nature due to inheritance must be responsible for their departure from the splendid type of American Democracy.

But do not suppose that even by implication I am condemning my own dear people. Public peace and the safety of the state demand that the less developed race be subordinate to the more developed, under conditions as they exist in the South today. The Caste of the Kin is the practice of the theory that blood is thicker than water; and the Sermon on the Mount can not invalidate God's own law of the Survival of the Fittest. If these widely different races can not blend their blood—and instinct and science say nay—the only real foundation for democracy, equality actual or potential, does not exist and can not be created. The principles of liberty, equality and fraternity are as abstractly true as Newton's Laws of Motion, but the real resistance of race-consciousness brings about as real a friction as does the resistance of the aid in modifying the action of bodies in motion.

603]

The all-inclusive virtue, love itself, has a biological basis, and character-values are conditioned by body-facts. Thus it happens that the Southerner's loyalty to his race comes of his love of his kind, the kind he knows and values.

But *should* such conditions exist? Must Southern children of the dominant race grow up to scorn and despise, or else condescendingly to tolerate, their less fortunate fellow-creatures? Or shall we legitimate lust and short-circuit the destiny of a Chosen People? Southerners understand the apparent cruelty imputed to the God of Israel who is represented as commanding the extermination of non-assimilable peoples. But the more refined killing of today in the South is not the occasional taking of a Negro's life but the impassive and relentless murder of a people's hopes. But better this than worse that might be. Better twenty years of Europe than a cycle of Cathay. Better praeternatural suspicion than breeding dusky broods. Sometimes we must be cruel would we be kind.

Only in the Kingdom of Heaven is there neither marriage nor giving in marriage. Now the Kingdom has not yet come in the South. Therefore, let him that would establish any kind of equality on any basis other than that of a biologically based family life, give us the recipe for life in a vacuum.

Again I ask—*Should* these things be? Must the Southern child be compelled to choose between the ideal and the real in a world where ideals must be realized in accordance with the laws of nature? Will sickly saintliness bring us salvation? Or must we seek safety in racial selfishness? God forbid the answer, " Yes," to either of these last two questions! Who shall deliver us from the body of this death!

I dare not hope to put this subject before you sharply in a hasty minute or two. But I must make an appeal in the name of the righteous God and of bewildered humanity. I ask that you leaders of education think on these things in this wise: *Let us have this Negro Question studied.* We are studying tariffs and the price of beef; we become partisans about a pole invisible and intangible; our scientific expeditions scour land and sea for specimens of fauna and flora; we discriminate nicely the uncertain tints of Mexican Indians; we explore the heavens above, the earth beneath and the waters under the earth—all these we do, and much more, without the waving of bloody shirts or the planting of party platforms.

Let us take the Negro Question out of politics, out of society, out of popular religious discussion, out of prize-fighting,—out of all wherein heat doth obtain rather than light.

Let us put the Negro Question into science, and science into the Negro Question. We have tried all else, and in vain. Parties and churches and schools, and philanthropies of all kinds, have brought us not one whit nearer a solution. The favorite prescription for a solution is education, especially industrial education. And yet there are towns where Negro artisans are not allowed to work and labor unions in plenty that Negroes may not enter. Education for *what*? Are the whites going to neglect the training of *their* children's hands? When the grandsons of the former slave-owners are dead will any one prefer Negro Labor, skilled or unskilled, to white?

Can education abolish race-consciousness and re-pattern the convolutions of the brain? Aye, education may solve the race-problem and all problems, but *when* and *where* and *how*?

Men and brethern, let us *study* the Race Problem. Let the study be national and international, for ours is not the only problem of race. Let the study be scientific and not

sentimental; co-operative and not individualistic; continuous
and not scrappy; professional and not *dilettante*; humani-
tarian and not partisan.

Let us isolate the surd and square the whole equation—
find a square deal. It is science, and science alone, star-
eyed science, truth-loving science, spiritually intellectual
science—it is the Twentieth Century's greatest power, the
scientific research of today, that can prepare us for the doing
of this Nation's greatest duty—the solution of this problem,
so as to free two unallied peoples and make the states of
this union *United States* indeed and in truth!